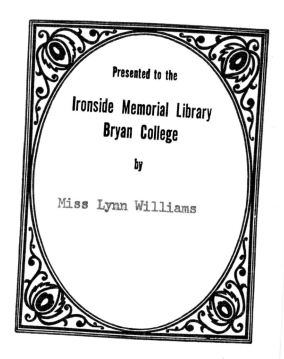

Speech Therapy
with Children

Ollie Backus
University of Alabama

Jane Beasley
Rutgers University

Houghton Mifflin Company

The Riverside Press Cambridge

This Book

IS DEDICATED WITH AFFECTION AND APPRECIATION

TO THOSE WHO HAVE COLLABORATED WITH US IN

THE LEARNING PROCESS:

THE CHILDREN IN THE CLINIC, who have needed the best we had to give and who have taught us so much;

THEIR PARENTS, who were so eager for help and who so earnestly and courageously transformed that help into a program of action at home;

THE UNIVERSITY STUDENTS IN TRAINING, who were so generous with time and effort in this experimentation both in directed teaching and later out in the field and who enabled us to test the usefulness of the procedures being evolved.

Preface

Our act of writing this book, your act of reading it, together constitute an interpersonal process. This sort of interpersonal process, characterized by a time-space separation of the persons involved, has some advantages over a face-to-face relationship. We as authors can pattern our words more carefully; you as reader can ponder those words more thoughtfully to put them into the context of your own experience. But the process has also some limitations in that we cannot interact "on-the-spot" to explain, restate, correct, enrich each other's meanings.

As one begins to function as a writer as well as a reader of books he becomes increasingly aware that the person who reads needs to index and date a book in respect to both the author and himself as reader. What we have written represents a product of our backgrounds, our special interests, our perceived goals, our experiences, recorded at a particular time in the course of our professional development. What meaning you get from the book will represent a blending of the words you read with your background, your interests, your goals, your experiences at the particular time you read it. What meaning you get will depend also in part upon the assumptions you hold about the capacities-limitations of a book as an instrument in such an interpersonal process. For this reason we want to tell you something about us in relation to this book, with the thought that it may help you in understanding yourself in relation to the book.

Both of us came to the field of speech disorders with a background of experience in classroom teaching, and with a deep interest in teaching. One of us entered the field some years ago when its body of knowledge was necessarily limited very largely to subject matter in the physical and biological sciences. Little was known or written about the treatment of persons with disordered speech. While education in the basic sciences had importance for our field then, as it does today, the facts of anatomy and physiology alone did not provide one with skills for helping clients to change speech behavior. Her sharp awareness in those early days that she, along with others, was faced

v

with a task for which few appropriate skills had been developed, together with her continuing deep interest in the process of teaching, led her to specialize in the area of therapy. And the previous scientific training made her point of view in that specialization one of research as well as one of professional practice.

It is a basic principle of science that assumptions should be subjected to verification by experiment. Thus the therapist functioning also as research worker must search out hidden assumptions which govern his behavior, test them, then modify them in the light of observed facts. To question, test out, then discard certain beliefs together with the familiar, trusted methods of treatment which implement them carried with it for some time a certain degree of threat and pain. It was so when the recognition came that breathing and tongue exercises needed to be discarded in a large number of cases. Then from the richer data that came with the experimentation in intensive group therapy some more profound doubts arose, e.g., the doubt about the assumption that each different kind of speech disorder requires a different kind of therapy. For a while the insights were mostly negative. "It isn't so — this thing we have believed and practiced." Then began the more positive task of transforming those negative assumptions into a theoretical structure for therapy which would serve as a guide for further experimentation.

It was about this time that the other author entered the field, first as student, then continuing as colleague. She had had a number of years of experience teaching in first grade and brought to the study those skills of handling young children in groups. Her professional training included both the biological sciences and the then considerable body of knowledge in the field of speech disorders which included some knowledge and skills in the area of therapy. Her interest in research in therapy came not from awareness of lack of skills but rather from the keen sense of satisfaction she derived from being able gradually to understand scientifically many of the things she had been doing intuitively as a teacher.

And so while one of us has had a certain advantage in having had personal experience with the use of the older assumptions and procedures in therapy, the other has had a certain advantage in not having had so much to "unlearn." But we share the perplexities — along with the deep satisfactions — that go with continued learning. There appears always to be a lag between recognition of problems that need to be solved and new insights into ways of solving them, between the new insights and the development of procedures for implementing them, especially in a way that can be made useful to others as well as ourselves. Time and again the perceived solutions have required that we get new knowledge from other fields and develop new skills that were not part of our past academic training. But we share with Rogers[1] the conviction that "though the scientific finding is cold and abstract, it may assist us in releasing forces that are warm, personal, and complex; — though science is slow and fumbling, it represents the best road we know to the truth, even in so delicately intricate an area as that of human relationships."

Because we have been interested in therapy from the point of view of research as well as from the points of view of professional practice ourselves and the professional training of students, we have had a particular conception of our task in writing this book. It has not been merely to supply plans for lessons as a labor-saving device for therapists, nor merely to present "something else that works"; nor has it been even to advocate "a method." We have conceived of it rather as an attempt to present a development of a theoretical structure broad enough in scope to include a large part of the accepted body of knowledge of our field but to include also a considerable body of knowledge which has not been traditionally a part of our field; also to show by illustrative lessons the kinds of modifications in basic design and procedures which can implement such a broader conception, while still permitting the use of many of the traditional techniques that a therapist may wish to employ.

In science a theoretical structure is not considered as a closed system; in this case such a structure must be considered only the barest beginning in the direction of ordering and patterning assumptions. To the best of our knowledge at this date it is consistent with the accumulated evidence in other fields specializing in the study of human behavior, as well as with that in our own. Nevertheless, it must be considered as something to revise continually in the light of new evidence.

For us the preparation of this book has served as a means of taking stock of the present situation so that we could proceed with a clearer perception of what is next to be explored, and already we have moved on with a research program involving more precisely controlled experimentation. For you we hope it can serve as both a stimulus and guide for learning.

The other night when several of us were assembled at the home of a

[1] Carl R. Rogers, *Client-Centered Therapy*, Boston, Houghton Mifflin Co., 1951, p. xi.

graduate student, an excerpt was read from "The Prophet" by Gibran[2] — the part which begins, "Then said a teacher, Speak to us of Teaching." Some years ago that passage had meant to us the process of classroom teaching. This time, as we have been absorbed in the task of finishing this book, its meaning was associated with our hopes for the book as an instrument of teaching.

"The astronomer may speak to you of his
understanding of space, but he cannot give
you his understanding."

"No man can reveal to you aught but that
which already lies half asleep in the dawning
of your knowledge."

"If he (the teacher) is indeed wise he does
not bid you enter the house of his wisdom, but
rather leads you to the threshold of your
own mind."

We have spoken of our understanding at this date of the process of therapy. Those of you with some background of experience in therapy have been moving undoubtedly in a direction which will make the ideas presented here understandable and acceptable. Those of you who find some of them strange and hence difficult will need to realize that we all must begin with what understanding we have at any given present; that one need not make a total shift all at once but can start applying those parts for which he does have some understanding; that the act of applying parts which do seem clear will bring an increasing measure of understanding for the whole. Certainly we know that understanding does not come with mere "reading about" therapy; it can come only as you yourself experiment in applying the principles. And so both for you and for us the criterion of value for this book will lie not so much in what you say about it as in what you are able to do as a consequence of having read it.

OLLIE BACKUS
JANE BEASLEY

Tuscaloosa, Alabama

[2] Kahlil Gibran, *The Prophet*, New York, Alfred A. Knopf, 1929, p. 64; London, William Heinemann, Ltd.

Contents

PART ONE

THEORETICAL STRUCTURE

PART TWO

ILLUSTRATIVE LESSONS IN GROUP THERAPY

Part One

Theoretical Structure

Chapter 1

Introduction

Speech therapy more and more is shifting away from an orientation based primarily upon devices, toward one based primarily upon therapeutic relationship.

Most speech therapists, as they used the older devices of tongue exercises, drill on word lists, and the like, produced enough positive results to make plausible a direct connection between methods used and improvement shown. Nevertheless, most therapists also had enough negative or neutral results to stimulate scientific inquiry into the process of speech therapy.

To what extent did some individuals improve for reasons other than the methods and procedures used — possibly in spite of them? To what extent might other individuals have improved if certain variables in therapy had been recognized and dealt with? Such questions first began to be investigated by research workers interested in the problem of stuttering. More recently they have been investigated in connection with therapy for persons having other kinds of speech disorders.

The material presented here is based upon research which began in 1942. We were interested in three widely recognized problems in therapy: (1) how to enable persons who presented special problems in learning to produce new speech patterns; (2) how to increase the extent of transfer of new speech behavior from use in the clinic to use outside; (3) how to bring about greater permanence in results after

3

therapy. We were interested also in a problem associated with the professional preparation of speech therapists: how to teach increasing numbers of students to do consciously what many skilled therapists have been doing intuitively over and above the procedures they are aware of using.

During the past eight years we have experimented with programs of therapy which have involved a combination of group and individual instruction, carried on for several hours each day in time units of several weeks' duration. Various kinds of speech symptoms have been represented in the membership of each group. Age groups have ranged from pre-school through adult. Programs of therapy for children have included group and individual therapy for their parents.

Gradually it became apparent that the changes in speech behavior which took place depended less upon devices for breathing, blowing, tongue exercises, "ear training," and the like, and more upon forces operating in the interpersonal relationships between child and therapist and among children as a group. Our learning in the first years was characterized chiefly by the necessity of questioning current procedures, together with the beliefs underlying them.[1]

The learning process led to extensive reading in other fields dealing with human behavior: psychiatry, psychology, sociology, anthropology, general semantics, etc. In these other fields too it had become necessary to question and modify certain older assumptions in order to make theoretical formulations consistent with modern research findings. A definite trend was evident toward formulating a scientific base which is common to all fields dealing with human behavior. This is frequently referred to as the science of man. Such exploration into the literature from other fields helped to make our own findings more meaningful: they supplied more widely accepted language forms; furnished scientific data which should be applied in our field as in others; and suggested new lines of investigation.[2]

The work to date represents only a beginning, whose scope must be

[1] Ollie Backus and Harriet Dunn, "Intensive Group Therapy in Speech Rehabilitation," *Journal of Speech Disorders*, March, 1947.

[2] Jane Beasley, "Techniques of Therapy for Preschool Children," *Journal of Speech and Hearing Disorders*, December, 1949, p. 307; Ollie Backus, "Personality Structure in Relation to Speech Therapy," *Quarterly Journal of Speech*, February, 1950, p. 51; Ollie Backus, "Collaboration Among Psychiatrists, Pediatricians, Clinical Psychologists, and Speech Therapists," *The Nervous Child*, January, 1951; Harriet Dunn, "Speech and Hearing for Children in a Rural Area," *Journal of Speech and Hearing Disorders*, June, 1949, p. 166.

enlarged by further experimental work, and whose details of structure will certainly need to be freed from limited insights and from errors yet unrecognized. Nevertheless it is our conviction that the direction in which we are moving is sound.[3]

Theory and practice necessarily go together in real life; the two words refer only to different aspects of one phenomenon. What human beings do (or practice) in any given situation they do because of the assumptions (or theories) they hold. Frequently they have little awareness of what the assumptions are that are determining the behavior. Conscious scrutiny of behavior creates the necessity for scrutinizing assumptions; this frequently leads to modifying those assumptions, which in turn results in modification of behavior. Thus as we have experimented with clinical practice, our theories about speech therapy have grown progressively broader in scope, more detailed in structure; such modifications in theory have resulted in certain marked differences in clinical practice.

Such differences may be summarized as follows:

1. Group instruction should form the core of speech therapy.
2. Group membership should be non-segregated in respect to kinds of speech symptoms.
3. The teaching situation should be structured to provide corrective "emotional" experience.
4. The teaching situation should be structured in terms of those interpersonal relationships which involve conversational speech.

In the preparation of this manual we have had the twofold task of describing procedures and of explaining the theory underlying them. Mere discussion of theory does not chart process levels specifically enough; mere presentation of procedures leaves hidden from awareness those assumptions which the therapist needs to modify if he is to use the procedures as an effective tool for changing behavior. We are presenting in Part I a theoretical structure for speech therapy, indicating at the same time how such assumptions can be applied to the solution of practical problems; in Part Two a series of illustrative lessons [4]

---

[3] We want to acknowledge in this connection the helpfulness of critics who in seeking to understand, have aided us in developing language patterns which would map process levels more accurately.

[4] The lessons presented here represent the outgrowth of a first attempt in 1945 to write down plans, undertaken as a master's thesis by Miss Beasley. Since then they have been tested and revised in many programs of therapy, both with children and with university students in directed teaching.

for meeting the needs of children with various kinds of speech disorders, indicating at the same time through notations the particular
theoretical considerations which are being applied. Thus Parts One
and Two are conceived of as together constituting a whole, with the
parts supplementary to each other.

We shall begin by trying to visualize something of a pattern in the
process of speech therapy. The layman frequently makes use of
spacial relationships in regard to behavior: e.g., "find out where I
stand"; "that man is going places"; "he's headed in the wrong
direction." Using such spacial relationships it is possible to conceive
of an individual's situation at any given present as a *region*; [5] the goal
he wishes to reach as *another region*. Changes in behavior that need
to be made can be conceived of as *paths* from the present region to
the goal region.

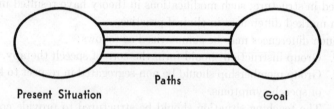

Present Situation   Paths   Goal

Procedures dealing with how the changes are to be made can be conceived of as *ways of inducing movement* or *of making progress* along
the paths. Let us investigate the structure of the goal region first.

[5] These concepts were developed in the field of psychology by Kurt Lewin.

Chapter 2

Goals in Speech Therapy

While a goal represents the region that should be reached in future time, its importance lies *in the present*. An individual's present perception of the goal region influences his behavior in the present. For instance, if he is in Chicago and views Detroit as his goal he will travel east; if he views Omaha as his goal he will travel west. If a speech therapist views the goal region as one in which a child recites practice material correctly from a phonetic point of view in a clinic class, he will organize his teaching procedures mostly in terms of drill on such material. If, on the other hand, he views the goal region as one in which a child talks freely and productively in real life situations, he will organize teaching procedures more in terms of real life situations, in which phonetic accuracy is only one aspect of speaking behavior.

It is important, therefore, for the speech therapist to be sharply aware of what constitutes his goal, both from a broad professional point of view and for a particular client at any given time. It is the purpose of this chapter to analyze the goal region from both points of view.

The Goal Region from a Professional Point of View

Speech therapy shares with other fields of human relations the goal of helping each individual to change behavior in interpersonal relationships to the extent that he can function in such relationships with greater

7

relative adequacy in terms of satisfactions and security. Such a statement of goals rests upon a number of assumptions which need to be specified, contains implications for action which need to be understood.

1. *"Speech therapy shares with other fields . . ."* The assumption is made first of all that the various fields dealing with human beings (psychiatry, other branches of medicine, psychology, education, social work, speech, etc.) share a common goal: to discover more about human potentialities and to help individuals to develop those potentialities. Each field has its own specialty, but it does not pursue that specialty as if the particular set of phenomena in which it is interested existed in isolation; it rather *focuses upon* those phenomena viewing them *in relation to the whole.* This means (1) that these fields have a common scientific base and share a common set of assumptions; (2) that in each field the particular body of knowledge and skills represent the best that a combined scientific effort is able to make available at any given time. Such a concept of shared endeavor is being expressed with increasing frequency, calling for "a better rounded and all embracing study of man-in-situation," as Beaglehole [1] puts it.

How has such an assumption about goals influenced speech therapy? First, the field of speech has had to enlarge its body of knowledge. Instead of borrowing merely from certain specialties (e.g., physics, physiology, anatomy) with the older assumptions of a separate existence of a science of glands, a science of muscles, a science of nerves, etc.,[2] it has needed to include more of the newer and more basic *science of man.* As Horney [3] in the field of psychiatry has pointed out, "It is not feasible to define the goals in medical terms. . . . The goals of therapy must be defined in terms of personality." Second, the field of speech has had to conceive of its function more and more in terms of teamwork — not merely in the sense of referral to or from another specialist, but with mutual consultation and planning. Third, and especially important, the procedures of speech therapy have needed to be modified so that they will lead toward the more broadly conceived goal region.

[1] Ernest Beaglehole, "Interpersonal Theory and Social Psychology," in Mullahy, P., *A Study of Interpersonal Relations,* New York: Hermitage, 1949, p. 78.

[2] Harry Stack Sullivan, *Conceptions of Modern Psychiatry.* Washington, D.C.: William Alanson White Psychiatric Foundation, 1947, p. 4.

[3] Karen Horney, *Our Inner Conflicts.* New York: Norton, 1945, p. 241.

An example will indicate something of the difference that results at the level of clinical practice. One boy, age five and a half, presented a severe articulatory defect. Several months of speech therapy of a type which had consisted of drill on consonant sounds had produced little if any change in his speech. The family then moved to another community, where they again consulted a speech therapist. A broader knowledge of human behavior enabled this therapist (1) to view the boy's problem as one which involved a general holding-fast to infantile behavior, of which the speech behavior was just one aspect; (2) to view the goal region for that boy as one of resolving conflicts and making the process of growing up more tolerable; (3) to structure speech therapy in terms of interpersonal relationship instead of phonetic devices. Under such treatment his speech patterns became more normal within a relatively short time. The change was brought about within the framework of speech therapy, without psychiatric referral, but done with very little actual work on particular consonant sounds.

2. "... *helping each individual to change behavior* ..." The assumption is made that the person himself has to do the changing, not have it done for him. Thus the goal must be conceived of in terms of offering help of such a nature that he *becomes able* to make the changes. This point of view is being stressed increasingly in the various fields.

Horney [4] says,

> The patient must acquire the capacity to assume responsibility for himself.

Fromm,[5] also in the field of psychiatry, says this:

> I have become increasingly impressed by the ... strength of the strivings for happiness and health, which are part of the natural equipment of man. "Curing" means removing the obstacles which prevent them from becoming effective.

Rogers,[6] in the field of counselling, speaking of a nondirective approach to therapy, says,

> This newer approach ... has a genuinely different goal. ...
> The individual and not the problem is the focus. The aim is

[4] *Ibid.*

[5] Eric Fromm, *Man for Himself.* New York: Rinehart, 1947, p. x.

[6] Carl R. Rogers, *Counseling and Psychotherapy.* Boston: Houghton Mifflin, 1942, p. 28.

not to solve one particular problem, but to assist the individual to *grow*, so that he can cope with the present problem and later problems in a better-integrated fashion. . . . Therapy is not a matter of doing something *to* the individual, or of inducing him to do something about himself. It is instead a matter of freeing him for normal growth and development, of removing obstacles so that he can again move forward.

Speech therapists are perceiving the goal more and more in terms of helping the individual get into condition for learning, so that not only will he make more progress in speech classes but will also be able to keep on learning between classes, outside of classes, after clinic instruction has ended. This trend has been apparent in respect to the use of mechanical appliances, such as posterior bulbs for persons with cleft palate and hearing aids for those with hearing loss. It has not been so apparent, however, that even in such cases the person must become able to assimilate the appliance as part of himself, must become able to change behavior in certain needed ways in order to use speech and hearing productively in real situations.

For one person it may mean modifying his perception of himself from dependence toward greater independence; for another it may mean modifying perceptions of others so that situations will not appear as threatening. Thus speech therapists need to pay more attention to aspects of therapeutic relationship: creating an atmosphere conducive to learning; helping the person become free from restrictive conditions such as feelings of dependency, fear, or resentment; aiding him in the development of positive feelings such as greater adequacy and security. This does not mean that speech therapy merely becomes equivalent to psychotherapy; it does not mean that all or even most persons should be referred for psychiatric help. It does mean that the field of speech therapy, a specialty in its own right, is learning to make more extensive use of its own tools (speech activities) for its own purposes (helping individuals to develop normal speech). Speech therapy does this with increasing effectiveness as it applies more rigorously what is now known about the dynamics of human behavior.

An example will show how such a broader perception of the goal modifies procedures in therapy. A boy age four with cerebral palsy had no speech, some hearing loss, was unable to walk. With the goal region perceived in terms of helping him get into condition for learning speech, he was enrolled in a small preschool group composed of children with various kinds of speech disorders. Specific goals for him included the development of the following needs: to relate to other children, to participate in group activity, to talk in order to do that participating. He became able to make "yes" and "no" responses within a relatively short period of time, even to the extent of an "s" sound on "yes" sometimes. This occurred without drill on sounds per se, and certainly without use of instruments to manipulate the tongue.

3. "... *behavior in interpersonal relationships* ..." The assumption is made that behavior takes place as *an interaction with environment.* Suppose that two people, say a customer and a clerk, are engaged in conversation regarding a purchase, and that one wants to understand why they both are showing signs of irritation in the transaction. Since each was observed to have behaved quite differently with another person in situations just preceding, the explanation will not be found by studying customer-in-isolation *plus* clerk-in-isolation. But if one studies customer-clerk interacting or making up an *interpersonal situation,* it might be found for instance that clerk reminds customer of uncle whom she dislikes, hence she acts rather stiffly; clerk reacts to this although he is not conscious of it at first, and while ordinarily he would not mind, today he has a headache; customer senses atmosphere and responds with irritation. The term interaction refers to a process more like multiplication than addition. Thus in order to understand behavior it is necessary to study person-in-a-situation. As Beaglehole [7] says, "The unit of study is the relations between such individuals."

Fromm [8] emphasizes the importance of whole-part relationships when he says, "If the observer isolates one aspect of the object without seeing the whole, he will not properly understand even the one aspect he is studying. — Two directions are involved: getting a whole consistent picture, and seeing what the structure of the whole requires for the parts." For the study of speech behavior an interpersonal relationship constitutes the whole; a person constitutes a part; the production of speech sounds constitutes a sub-part. Since

[7] Beaglehole, *op. cit.,* p. 60.
[8] Fromm, *op. cit.,* pp. 104–05.

the whole influences the action of the parts, analysis starts with the whole, then proceeds to parts, then to sub-parts.

A speech therapist so oriented will recognize that the act of examining a child takes place within the framework of an interpersonal situation. He will view the child's behavior in terms of an interaction with him instead of in terms of static, innate traits. For example, instead of making an inference of "uncooperativeness" on the part of the child, he would consider the possibility that he himself was representing an authority figure of which the child was afraid. He will certainly set out to examine a child instead of only a palate or a tongue. As he considers therapy he will set particular goals for that child in terms of the child himself rather than in terms of a sub-part only, say of consonant sounds. Then, later in the therapeutic situation, as he hears the child producing acceptable speech patterns in the clinical situation he will not assume therefore that the child is necessarily able to use them yet outside the clinic. The therapist will not leave "to chance" or "the person's wanting to" the problem of social pressures in various interpersonal relationships outside the clinical situation; he will structure therapy in terms of those problems right from the beginning.

Closely allied to the assumption about whole-part relationships is another assumption — that causes must be viewed from a multi-valued point of view. The older assumption of single-valued causality related present behavior to something which had happened in the past. The assumption of multi-valued causality, however, relates present behavior to conditions operating in the *present* situation. This represents a more inclusive concept. For example, a person with cerebral palsy behaves as he does now, not because of a birth injury ten years ago but because the central nervous system is *still* impaired; he *also* behaves as he does now because of a combination of circumstances in the present situation; perhaps in a given situation he has feelings of dependency, feels threatened by the presence of a person whom he perceives as "stranger," or fears that he will "do the wrong thing." One never could see in him a simple effect stemming from one lesion in the nervous system, because that one condition is embedded in different functional wholes in different situations.

An assumption of multi-valued causality still enables one to study in as much detail as he pleases any given sub-part, (e.g., muscular tension); but it also enables one to analyze relationships which exist between that part and other part-functions in an effort to account for different manifestations of the sub-part as the person interacts in different situations. This has great importance in setting up goals — the more so in conditions like cerebral palsy where the lesion itself cannot be changed but where the behavioral manifestations can be changed considerably by modifying other part-functions, which in turn modify the whole in which that lesion exists. Thus the behavior of such a person can be markedly changed in respect to intelligibility of speech, facial expression, or arm and hand movements by decreasing social pressures, increasing feelings of personal worth, or developing social skills.

4. "... *to the end that he can function in these relationships with greater relative adequacy. ...*" Several assumptions are involved. One, already mentioned, conceives of the end involved as *use* of speech in the various interpersonal relationships that go to make up living, rather than merely the ability to speak in a certain way in a certain clinical situation.

Another assumption conceives of the criterion of *relative* adequacy, on a many-valued scale rather than a two-point scale of "adequacy or not adequacy." This rules out "perfection," which does not exist really, as anyone knows, but which nevertheless frequently influences behavior both in some therapists and in many clients.

A third assumption further delineates the criterion as relative adequacy *for the person.* This rules out "statistical average" — a mythical criterion for a unique individual, and therapy is always dealing with single individuals, even in a group situation. Relative adequacy for the person takes into account *his* needs, *his* abilities, as they shift in time and in the various situations in which he participates. This puts the emphasis more upon him as a unique person, and less upon the speech symptoms by which clients used to be classified and in terms of which classification the goals for therapy used to be formulated. Furthermore, it puts less emphasis upon "a certain I. Q." or "a certain degree of adjustment." A person may not have as much intellectual capacity as many others in the clinic enrollment; yet if speech therapy can help him reach a goal of greater relative adequacy for him, such therapy will have justification.

5. "... *adequacy in terms of satisfaction and security.*" The

assumption is made that standards of value should be formulated in terms of *consequences* to the individual, rather than in terms of the personal value concepts held by the therapist. Thus "adequacy" must be related to something tangible in regard to person-in-situation. The terms "satisfaction" and "security" have been used by Sullivan [9] in the following way: an individual experiences feelings of satisfaction when basic needs are met, such as hunger, thirst, rest, belongingness; he experiences feelings of security when culturally-induced needs are met, such as social position, prestige, or occupational status. Adequacy of speech behavior in terms of satisfaction and security needs to be considered (1) in respect to specific situations: greetings, introductions, telephoning, shopping, ordering in a restaurant, small talk, or committee meetings; (2) in respect to specific persons in those situations: those of the same and opposite sex; those who are younger, older, same age; those who are considered peers, in different social positions, or in authority.

When the therapist does not distinguish between his own value concepts (many of which may be outside of awareness) and those for the client in terms of consequences, he is apt to assume that "all will go well" *after* the client achieves phonetic accuracy, or that the client *should* feel secure in various interpersonal situations because he himself does. When he views the goal region almost entirely in terms of mechanical accuracy then he is apt not even to see other problems. Too often in the past, defects of articulation have been categorized as "minor" simply because they involved but one or two recognized sound substitutions, regardless of the possibility that those differences in speech might represent a symptom of — or be associated with — seriously disturbed interpersonal relationships.

Thus in speech therapy, when the person's use of speech in interpersonal relationships helps him to feel relatively adequate in respect to belongingness, in respect to security of job, social position, and the like, he would be considered to have reached the goal region. If his speech has mechanical accuracy without such relative adequacy in use, he would not be considered to have reached the goal.

It should be possible at this point to reread with deeper meaning the original statement of goals: speech therapy shares with other fields of human relations the goal of helping each individual to change

[9] Sullivan, *op. cit.*, p. 6.

behavior in interpersonal relationships to the end that he can function in those relationships with greater relative adequacy in terms of satisfaction and security.

Goals for a Particular Client

Any statement of goals from a professional point of view must be translated, of course, into a formulation for a particular individual. While the next two chapters will contain further information to help the speech therapist do this, two points should be emphasized here.

1. *Goals for one individual should be structured differently at different stages in therapy.* Assuming that growth represents a process of progressive differentiation, a going from whole to parts, the order in which goals are structured has importance. Assuming also that the person himself must do the learning and that therapy must be concerned with helping the person achieve the best possible condition for such learning, the goals at first will deal especially with such things as reducing anxiety, building self-confidence, developing participation in conversational speech; only later will they emphasize finer details of adjustive behavior and mechanics of speech production. Too often when the order has been reversed and the goal formulated first in terms of details of speech production, the individual has not been able to progress to a point where the "eventual" goal of use of speech could be reached successfully. When, however, the goal is formulated first in terms of the individual belonging to a group, participating, using speech to the best of his ability at a given time, he is not only being helped to change in broad ways fundamental for learning but also is experiencing the very situations out of which will develop a need for more normal speech production. Goals should be formulated not merely in terms of the therapist's perception of the individual's need but in terms of needs that have importance to the person himself so that the goals can become part of his perceptions. They should be formulated too in terms of his ability at any given time to succeed in reaching them, since experiencing success makes the person more eager as well as more able to go on succeeding at harder tasks which come later.

2. *Goals should be structured differently for different persons within the same group.* Therapy must always be a highly individual matter; group therapy is never in any sense a mass production device. As

will be more evident in later chapters, it is quite possible to be helping different individuals to develop in different ways within one group. Children readily learn that different ones are aiming to achieve different goals and that evaluation of progress should be made for each person in terms of his own particular goals.

Chapter 3

Paths to the Goal

In the schema presented in Chapter 1 the region denoting present situation was connected to the goal region by *paths*. These paths represent the changes in behavior that need to be made if the individual is to move toward the goal. Thus an analysis of paths to the goal is equivalent to the attempt to answer the question, "What changes in behavior need to be made?"

It is important that questions concerned with "how" in therapy be based upon answers to questions concerning "what." Frequently it has happened in speech therapy that what appeared at first as the most direct path to a goal did not turn out to be the best one. For example, when therapists have assumed that behavior of the tongue constituted the only change to be made in persons with articulatory defects, they have centered therapeutic procedures on drill on consonant sounds, with the result that many such persons were left unable to *use* adequate speech patterns in everyday life. When they have assumed that behavior of the muscles of the larynx constituted the only change to be made in persons with defects of vocal quality, they have centered therapeutic procedures on practice on poetry, with the result that many such persons still used a "high, rasping voice" as they went about business and social life. When they have assumed that intellectual understanding constituted the only change to be made in behavior of persons with hearing loss as they began to use a hearing aid, they have limited therapeutic procedures to mere verbal

17

instructions about how to use it, with the result that many such persons did not experience satisfactory use of the aid. Usually it may be assumed that such perceptions of paths to the goal have been too limited.

Sometimes, however, such a restricted perception of paths has actually led in a direction away from the goal. It has led to drill on consonant sounds for a child who already has a tendency to compulsive, stereotyped behavior, with the result that such tendencies have been reinforced by such drill. It has led to drill on word lists for a person who stutters with the result that his desires for an easy "cure" and avoidance of facing his conflicts have been reinforced or his anxieties toward feared words have been enhanced. It has led to drill on sounds and words for a person with aphasia with the result that perseveration [1] has been increased and disorganization promoted.

It is the purpose of this chapter to investigate what changes in behavior do constitute desirable paths to the goal. Since changing behavior involves processes frequently referred to by the general term "learning," several assumptions will need to be examined first; then on the basis of these, specific possibilities for change will be explored.

Assumptions About Learning

Learning proceeds from whole to parts by a process of progressive differentiation. This specifies an opposite direction from older assumptions which conceived of learning as an additive process, i.e., starting with parts and adding them to obtain a whole. It is possible to get some understanding of this difference in orientation by viewing for a moment some process which is familiar; e.g., how one learns to recognize a person. When you first meet an individual you get a vague notion of what he looks like, perhaps not clear enough to recognize him the second time the two of you meet. Gradually a clearer perception of his features emerges; eventually you can pick out details of shape of face, eyes, hair, nose. Recognition does not come by mastering details of an eye, ear, or brow, and adding these up to get a face; rather it comes first as vague perception of the whole, then with differentiation into parts.

[1] The term *perseveration* refers to difficulty in shifting responses with resulting repetitive response.

Learning involves a process of organization. Along with the differentiation goes a restructuring, a reintegration. Such a process has taken place when after a period of trial and error a person suddenly says, "Oh —, I see what you mean," or "It came in a flash." Thus an individual does not learn simply by repeating an activity; he must perceive some over-all organization for the whole, some patterning of the parts contained. Consider, for example, the acquisition of some skill such as swimming. The person arrives at some rough approximation of the organization of behavior that is needed in order to keep afloat; then gradually he refines the behavior of the whole so that movements of parts become more precise.

It is the whole organism that does the learning even for changes in part-function. We are never dealing with merely a hand in writing, a foot in walking, an ear in hearing, a tongue in speaking. Such parts exist only in relation to the whole. If the student doubts this, let him trace, for instance, some numbers or letters with his foot or his elbow. He did not have training in school to learn to write with a foot or elbow; he used the hand, yet the whole organism learned it. Or let him recall how a part-function such as writing changed when the whole organism was changed, such as with fear, or drowsiness. Clearly both the whole and the part must be consciously considered in teaching.

Specific Possibilities for Change

In analyzing what changes in behavior need to be made for speech therapy, we must be concerned *first of all*, not with parts such as speech symptoms, facial distortions, or muscular spasms, but with the whole: the *functional organization* [2] of the person.

Functional Organization

Modern thinking in the science of man assumes in every person a very strong tendency to preserve some organization. No matter how undesirable the particular organization may be in terms of consequences to the individual, his striving is toward some sort of integration. It represents a blending of the sort of organism he was born with, together with the adjustments of that organism to the

[2] This term is roughly analogous to the term *personality structure.*

realities of his environment since birth. Cameron [3] uses the term "biosocial" to indicate the inseparable intermingling of the "inherited" with the "acquired" aspects. Because older assumptions viewed behavior so largely as coming from something called "instincts," it is especially necessary to emphasize the point that behavior has largely been learned — learned within a framework of interpersonal relationships. Our problem then is to discover those aspects of functional organization which prevent the person from growing, developing, learning; to help him achieve a pattern of functional organization which will enable him to develop his potentialities to the utmost.

Scientific knowledge about the structure of behavior is still far from adequate, but modern theories applied to speech therapy are making it increasingly possible to bring about significant changes in behavior. Since the subject is complex and this discussion limited, the material presented here must be considered as suggestive only, as a challenge for further study.

1. *Perceptions of self.* During the usual course of development in the young child there emerges gradually an awareness of something known as "me," separate from other things, other people. With this differentiation come modifications in behavior such as greater need to explore things, increasing independence, and the like. The application of this concept clinically has importance in helping the child to grow, as may be seen by some examples of children who have started clinical training with apparently little conception of self as separate entity. For example, Marilyn at first paid little attention to other children, showed little initiative. Gradually she joined in more, saying, "Me," to indicate that she wanted a turn; later saying, "Me turn," then "I want a turn," as she gained more language. Frances did not want to leave her mother at first, would dart out of the room frequently to run back to her mother yet showed very little pleasure after she reached her — mostly a sort of clinging-for-safety. Later she would run in to see her mother sometimes between activities, but after a glance at her, would run out again and rejoin the group. She too began to participate more, showed more pleasure in things and people. In such children the growth of perception of self as separate entity facilitated growth in other directions.

[3] Norman Cameron, *The Psychology of Behavior Disorders.* Boston: Houghton Mifflin, 1947.

How the child evaluates himself as a person appears to depend largely upon his perception of the evaluation that the significant adults in his environment place upon him.   If his place in the interpersonal circle at home has been characterized chiefly by weakness, helplessness, he will tend to view himself in that way.   Freddie, who had some muscular incoordination due to cerebral palsy, tended to just sit in the group; showed enjoyment at being with others and witnessing the activities, but made little effort to join in; seemed to be very much surprised when he was expected to carry his own chair to another room as the others did.   After doing this for a few days, however, and finding that he could, he showed a great deal of pleasure in so doing, even carried chairs for other children too.   Along with this growing sense of his own powers in carrying the chair, he began to show more independence in other ways: to volunteer, to produce more audible speech responses, to imitate more closely the speech patterns set.   Clearly, he became more able to learn as he showed more independence, less helplessness.

If the child's needs for love, acceptance, approval, have not been sufficiently met, he develops a vision of himself as of little worth, unattractive, unlovable.   This appears to be based not so much upon the reality of his appearance as upon his feeling of security in parental affection.   Many children who to outward appearances should consider themselves attractive have little sense of personal worth, and some children who have perhaps more outward reason for disturbed feelings of personal worth show a great deal of personal security and faith in themselves.   More often than not, however, children with cleft palate and cerebral palsy consider themselves ugly and unlovable. The presence of such perceptions can be inferred from behavior in interpersonal relationships, also from the changes which ensue when parents and teachers offer more praise and affection.   It can also be inferred from reports of older clients themselves, as they may eventually exclaim (sometimes, it would seem, out of a clear sky), "Why, I do have pretty hair, don't I?"

Since perceptions of self color to such an extent what the person observes and how he evaluates his environment, it becomes highly important for him to modify perceptions of himself in the direction of increased differentiation of self as a person, in the direction of feeling greater personal worth, greater confidence in his own ability, greater independence.

2. *Perceptions of environment.* When early experiences at home have been relatively happy ones for a child, giving him a background of security, he will tend to view new environments as potentially friendly and interesting to explore. When, on the other hand, his early experiences have included rejection, deprivation of the love that he needs, he will tend to view new environments as potentially threatening. This is frequently the case among children with speech defects both because speech may represent a symptom of disturbed interpersonal relationships and because some conditions producing speech defects, such as cleft palate, cerebral palsy, hearing loss, produce anxiety in parents as well as children, and hence greater possibility of rejection.

Such a child may fear any person whom he perceives as being in "authority." This is especially apt to occur if his early experiences with authority figures at home have been characterized in his perception as overpowering. One boy, when asked what it was about his father that made him fear him said, "He's big and I'm little." When asked if he always felt little he said, "I feel little at school, but I feel big on the playground and at the movies when they show wild west pictures." When past experiences have become highly charged for the child he tends especially to view present situations in terms of the past. Thus even though a teacher has not exerted irrational authority over him, he still fears her. Or, rather than authority figures, such a child may perceive as threatening persons of his own age, persons of different sex, persons of higher cultural status, or any situation regarded as "new."

Different individuals respond to such perceived threats in different ways. Some show fear responses, with an attempt to withdraw, i.e., to leave the scene actually or to leave by not participating. Others show aggressive behavior to fight off the threat. Such children are usually the ones who are termed "behavior problems." Others move toward the person or persons whom they fear with "ingratiating behavior," i.e., put an arm around the person or hover around the teacher. Such children are usually termed "good" and hence their problems go unrecognized.

Marked behavior along such lines, motivated more by the need to allay anxiety than to cope with the realities of the situation, interferes with the individual's ability to develop.[4] It interferes not only

[4] This is brought out clearly in the writings of Horney. See Bibliography.

with his ability to learn speech patterns in the first place, but also with his ability to use those new patterns in an increasing variety of interpersonal situations. Thus paths to the goal need to be conceived of as including efforts to change the perceptions which give rise to such behavior.

Learning in this sense has been termed by Lewin [5] as "change in cognitive structure"; by Korzybski [6] as "non-identity." It refers to the process whereby an individual becomes able to perceive a present situation as one to be examined and evaluated in terms of itself rather than be patterned in terms of past situations.

3. *Needs.* The person's needs play a decisive part in determining his pattern of functional organization. These needs, as previously pointed out, are related to satisfaction of bodily requirements — of which belongingness has most importance for our purposes in speech — and to security or culturally induced satisfactions.

We should distinguish sharply between the person's own needs and those which someone else, especially teacher or parent, thinks he ought to have. For example, a speech therapist may think that a child ought to have a need for more intelligible speech, especially if the child becomes angry when he is not understood; yet that child's own need may consist almost wholly of struggling against parental domination. This need may be so potent that certain aspects of speech training should be delayed until it has been met to some degree.

Horney [7] makes an important distinction between behavior organization which is directed toward fulfillment of needs for satisfaction and security and that which is directed rather toward safety in order to allay anxiety. For example, a child has a need for belongingness but because he views most interpersonal relationships in terms of past experiences of rejection and consequently feels anxiety in such situations, he withdraws for reasons of safety. While such behavior serves temporary purposes of safety, it leaves unfulfilled the need for belongingness. With such a pattern of behavior organization he is less well equipped to develop any sort of adequacy in interpersonal relationships — including speech — than someone else who is more free to seek those satisfactions which come from relating to others.

[5] Kurt Lewin, *Dynamic Theory of Personality.* New York: McGraw-Hill, 1935.
[6] Alfred Korzybski, *Science and Sanity.* Lancaster, Pa.: International Non-Aristotelian Library Publishing Co., 1933, p. xiv.
[7] Karen Horney, *Our Inner Conflicts.* New York: Norton, 1945, p. 13.

Hence the conditions giving rise to such needs for safety need to be modified.

A child can be helped to meet his needs in socially approved ways rather than in the ways he has been attempting to meet them. For example, a child who has a strong need for independence, showing itself by aggressive acts toward members of the group, can be helped to channel that need in a direction of assuming responsibility for certain group activities.

Needs can be induced too, so that a child whose greatest need at first may be to remain in the background can develop strong needs to gain recognition for progress. Or a child whose need seems strong at first for warding off attack before being struck, can develop a strong need to help others to succeed. The satisfactions which he gets through such behavior then become more potent than the previous need.

4. *Standards of value.* Closely allied with the person's own needs are the values that he places upon things. For example, if tripping another child serves to bolster temporarily one boy's feeling of personal worth in relation to that child, such behavior will be valued and indulged in — at least behind the teacher's back, if not permitted when she sees it. If, however, his behavior toward that child can be placed within a frame of reference of "helping each other," if the boy in question can bolster his feelings of personal worth in other ways, then very likely that original behavior will take on a negative value and not be indulged in, even in the absence of the teacher.

In some cases an individual's apparent inability to reproduce speech patterns set by the therapist may stem from the high value which he has placed upon "resisting authority" as a means of meeting a need for greater independence. If, however, such a child is in a group of children where the atmosphere is characterized by relative permissiveness and freedom from irrational authority, where the group has placed a positive value on participating and striving to produce new patterns of speech behavior, he can gradually come to place a higher value upon conforming to group standards than to battle with an authority figure.

A given value may be strongly positive or negative depending upon a child's perception of his chances of dealing with it. Take, for example, social position, about which he may have marked feelings of inferiority. He may value a certain social position highly in the sense that he moves toward persons perceived as having a higher position than he; he may pretend too that he himself has certain characteristics relating to it. On the other hand, he may give it a negative value, scorning persons of higher social position. The presence of strong value in either direction would lead one to infer conflicts centering around that, and would indicate that changes should be made in that area of behavior.

The child's level of aspiration has importance too. This term refers to the standards of achievement which he sets for himself. Excessively high or excessively low levels of aspiration can interfere with the child's ability to develop.

One child may set such high standards for himself that he experiences repeated "failure," then becomes fearful to try at all. Such a child must be helped to set more realistic standards so that he can experience feelings of "success." On the other hand, another child may have so little perception of his own worth that it does not occur to him that he could succeed. He needs to be helped to develop a higher level of aspiration so that he too can experience "success."

Learning in the sense of changing needs and values is related of course to learning in the sense of changing cognitive structure; however, it carries some implications of its own too for speech therapy. Many therapists who had been attempting to solve problems of "motivation" and "discipline" in terms of devices, have found such problems to be less acute in a program of therapy that incorporates procedures for modifying needs and values.

5. *Adjustive techniques.* The behavior which an individual uses in various interpersonal relationships is not inherited; it has been learned. The adjustive techniques he uses represent the ways he has found to be most successful in the past for meeting needs, avoiding anxiety, solving conflicts, getting satisfactions, gaining approval, avoiding punishment. Horney [8] has pointed out three directions which such adjustive behavior may take: moving "toward," "against," "away from" people. Normally human beings employ all three under various circumstances of living, but frequently it happens that an individual will use one predominantly. For example, his behavior may be characterized mostly by withdrawing from people,

[8] Horney, *op. cit.*, p. 18.

from problems, from conflicts in himself; he will use this form of adjustment even though it may not be appropriate in terms of consequences to himself. Cameron [9] points this out: "If a technique brings immediate tension-reduction, it may persist as one's habitual, characteristic solution even though in the long run it leads to far more serious and resistant conflicts."

Discovery and recognition of the child's pattern of adjustive techniques have importance to the speech therapist from several points of view.

(1) Observation of adjustive techniques enables him to make inferences about the individual's perceptions of self and others, needs and values. For instance, one child moved his arm and shoulder away each time an adult happened to touch him; an inference was made that he felt resentment against adult authority, after which steps could be taken to modify it.

(2) The adjustive techniques influence the sort of interpersonal situation which can be integrated with the individual in the teaching situation. For instance, one child employed withdrawing behavior in both individual and group classes to the extent that he did not gain the corrective experience which could come through participation; another child used temper tantrums at the first sign of difficulty in producing a response or upon hearing an adverse criticism of his performance.

(3) Adjustive techniques influence the kind of speech the individual uses in interpersonal situations. For instance, the child who responds with aggression will tend to use speech for such ends also.

(4) The adjustive techniques used influence the social pressures which the individual experiences in various interpersonal situations. These social pressures come from a combination of his own perceptions and from other people's reactions to him. Changes in his adjustive techniques can change the reactions of others and hence reduce markedly the social pressures in him. Because such pressures affect transfer and permanence of results of therapy, their reduction assumes importance in the therapeutic process.

In summary it is evident that knowledge of an individual's functional organization has the utmost importance for any kind of teaching, and especially for speech therapy where we are dealing with as

[9] Cameron, *op. cit.*, p. 152.

highly complex an aspect of behavior as speech. Because adjustive techniques are so closely bound up with our area of specialization, i.e., speech, we need to focus on them now to study them in greater detail as they have relevance for speech therapy. Such adjustive techniques will be termed social skills.

Social Skills

The behavior in any interpersonal situation should be evaluated in terms of consequences: factors which improve relations between the persons involved are considered constructive; factors which hinder such relations are considered destructive. Beaglehole [10] has pointed out that such surface manifestations as "habit," "etiquette," etc., function as integrating or constructive tendencies. Clinical experience in speech therapy has shown that the acquisition of social skills has improved the individual's ability to engage constructively in interpersonal relationships, has facilitated learning in the clinical situation as well as transfer of such learning into interpersonal situations outside the clinic. Hence changes in behavior along this line constitute paths to the goal. Let us specify certain aspects of behavior which constitute skills in interpersonal relations.

1. *Ability to follow conventional social patterns.* Many children with disordered speech have had very limited social experiences, either because they could not, were not permitted to, or did not have opportunity for such experiences. The term *conventional social patterns* refers to behavior in such situations as the following: greetings, introductions, invitations, ordering in a restaurant, shopping, dining, telephoning, small talk, and the like. When a situation appears to them as "new," when they are not sure what behavior is expected of them, they feel greater pressures, and have greater tendency to functional disorganization with attending disorganization in speech. On the other hand, as they engage in such situations right from the beginning of therapy, using the conventional behavior patterns with the appropriate speech patterns, that behavior tends to have an integrating effect even in situations outside the clinic. For example, one boy at first hung his head and refused to participate in making introductions and announcements; gradually he came to experience pleasure in participating and one day when guests were expected, he

---

[10] Beaglehole, *op. cit.*, p. 60.

even volunteered to make the introductions, and at the time of the party did it easily and well.

2. *Ability to win acceptance and support from others.* It is particularly important to the individual to be able to win acceptance and support from his peers. One boy had learned very appropriate adjustive techniques with adults, talked unusually fluently with them (despite a marked speech disorder) and was thus considered "well-adjusted" on the basis of such contacts. With a group of children his own age, however, he seemed always to be on the fringes, looking on, seeking out an adult to talk with at any opportunity. Another boy seemed very eager to relate to the other children as evidenced by his nudging them, bringing presents to different ones, etc., yet it became evident that he was not chosen, not sought out by the others. A third boy tended to alienate himself from the group by his uncontrolled outbursts of anger. As these children learned how to engage in relationships with other children — relationships which were more satisfactory in terms of the consequences of getting more support and recognition from them — they became better able to develop, to profit from group membership, to use speech more appropriately, and to use it more accurately. Such changes tend also to win more approval and support from significant adults in the child's environment; parents and teachers gain a different perception of a child as they see him better able to function with poise and enjoyment in various social situations in the clinic and outside, and they tend to modify behavior toward him on this account.

3. *Ability to share attitudes.* Ability to communicate feelings verbally has importance to the individual in several ways. As an expression of feeling it can serve to dissipate some of the force of that feeling; for example, to be able to say, "I'm afraid" can constitute a way of facing the fear. When a teen-age girl with childhood aphasia finally learned to say "mad," she achieved a degree of communication with the speech therapist which markedly decreased the severity of her frequent temper tantrums. When children with more language ability can express something of feelings there is the possibility of talking it through to arrive at more rational handling of the situation. Another value of sharing attitudes lies in being able to bring one's own private feelings more into line with those of others. An individual can discover that many "private" problems are in reality not private

but rather common human problems. He can correct distortions that otherwise might not be recognized as distortions. He can learn to understand that one may indeed have conflicting feelings; e.g., he may like and yet dislike school, may feel angry with a parent over some particular thing yet love the parent too — may have both feelings without the necessity of guilt on that account.

4. *Flexibility in role-taking.* Certain social patterns of behavior may be conceived of as "roles"; for example, a child giving a party may be said to play the role of host, a child attending a party, the role of guest. The persons involved in a business transaction at a drug store may be said to play their respective roles of customer and clerk. In the family there are the roles of father, mother, son, daughter, etc. These roles are more or less culturally prescribed, but the person plays them in accordance with his perception of what the roles should be.[11] Experience in playing different roles not only helps the child find out what is required for social purposes, but also helps him to develop an ability to shift roles more appropriately — a process which in our culture is continually going on.

Many children exhibit an amazing degree of flexibility; for example, playing the role of helpless infant with mother, that of independent resourceful individual with father, possibly that of tomboy with brother, of nurse with younger sister. Some children, however, have not developed such ability to shift roles. As a result they show a sort of rigidity in behavior, using in most situations adjustive techniques which may well be appropriate in some but not in other situations.

Cameron[12] has pointed out that practice in role-taking constitutes one way of learning to understand and predict the reactions of others, and as such, aids the person in developing useful sensitivity and adaptibility in interpersonal situations.

Changing behavior at the level of social skills constitutes a broad path to the goal: it provides a process of "doing" by which functional organization at deeper levels can be modified, serves as an instrument for the person himself to improve his interpersonal relationships, and it also furnishes a context within which the sub-part function of speech production can be effectively modified.

11 Cameron, *op. cit.*, chap. 4.
12 Cameron, *op. cit.*, p. 93.

Speech Patterns

We have followed an order of proceeding from whole to parts in analysis: first, functional organization, then social skills, then speech patterns. Within this sub-part, analysis also can proceed in such a direction.

1. *Whole responses.* The amount and kind of speech responses used are very closely related to social skills as an adjustive technique of the individual but should be noted specifically as the therapist charts changes in behavior to be made. Either extreme in amount of speech may be found: some individuals talk more per response than is considered desirable, some talk too little; some go to extremes only under certain circumstances, e.g., when fearful, angry, etc. Quality of speech responses is determined in part by perceptions of situations and adjustive techniques; for example, a child may employ as a greeting a response characterized by whining about something that has displeased him, or may attempt to relate to other children by teasing or criticizing them. Quality of speech responses is also determined in part by social experience; a child may be willing enough to use speech but not have appropriate forms in his repertoire, as when he asks, "What do you say when you want to get acquainted?" Such changes as need to be made will be charted, both for direct instruction on speech patterns themselves and for indirect treatment through modification of functional organization and social skills.

2. *Characteristics of speech production.* The following are considered as characteristics of speech — broader in structure than details of particular sounds, but part-functions in relation to whole responses just described:

> pitch
> quality
> loudness
> rate
> inflection patterns
>> (a) time
>> (b) force
>> (c) pitch (called melody)
> blending
> phrasing

Changes which need to be made in these will not be analyzed in detail here, since it is assumed that students will have studied this aspect in previous course work, or can study it from other source books. Several points will be emphasized, however.

While the terms above listed are admittedly inadequate, yet they can be used to chart what the individual *does* when he speaks. Hence they are more useful in charting changes that need to be made *in him* than the old labels which told more about what he "is" than what he does (e.g., he *is* a stutterer, a cleft palate case, etc.). When speech behavior is charted in terms of what the person does the old class boundaries are dissolved; we see that persons with cleft palate have problems in common with those with cerebral palsy and stuttering, that two persons with cleft palate may have quite different characteristics to be changed, and so on.

When specifying characteristics of speech production as changes to be made it is important to view them in relation to aspects of functional organization, not in isolation. When they are viewed in isolation then therapy — or speech education — consists only of "exercises" to improve vocal quality, or "devices" to lower pitch, or "nagging" to obtain greater loudness. When they are viewed in relation to other aspects of behavior such therapy consists of both direct and indirect approaches to the particular problem.

An ordering of these part-functions as coming *before* the sub-parts of production of specific consonant or vowel sounds has an important influence on therapeutic procedures and results achieved. For example, in persons with speech problems involving "foreign accent," to change inflection patterns before consonant sounds results in more marked and rapid improvement than when the order is reversed as has been commonly done. In persons with cerebral palsy, to stress blending and phrasing and inflection patterns *before* accurate production of consonant sounds results in more intelligible speech with less distortion. One not uncommonly sees such a person who in his attempts to make given sounds correctly distorts speech — not because he must but because he has been trained to. This occurs even more frequently probably in persons with severe hearing loss. It need not occur if therapists modify assumptions relating to order. Many of these changes can be brought about more or less incidentally in therapy if the therapist is consciously aware of the need to do so.

For example, speech patterns can be learned in blended rather than unblended form, e.g., "a truck," "thank you," "for you" as one unit instead of two.

For every individual, changes in rate in the direction of greater slowness need to be specified, as an instrument of therapy. This means only for a specified time, not permanently. It means using slower rates of speaking in order (1) to observe carefully and (2) to produce the new patterns voluntarily. It may be said that the aim at first is to produce patterns without distortion *except* for rate. Excessively slow rates are ordinarily not employed except perhaps in some cases for brief periods for some specific purpose of the moment. The particular rate desired usually is forthcoming from the way the therapist talks in setting the pattern.

3. *Details of sound production.* This aspect also has received detailed emphasis in the field so it will not be described in detail here. It is assumed that the reader has already had a background of phonetics and can analyze speech for changes which need to be made.[13] One point only will be emphasized.

When changes to be made are charted it is not to be assumed thereby that the changes will be brought about only through direct instruction on each sound unit, and certainly not to be assumed that "tongue exercises" constitute a prerequisite change to be effected. This point is stressed here to emphasize the influence which hidden assumptions about part-functions in isolation have had on therapeutic procedure and to emphasize the importance of conscious assumptions of part-functions in relationship to other aspects of behavior.

[13] For persons without such knowledge a brief presentation will be found in Ollie Backus, *Speech in Education: A Guide for the Classroom Teacher.* New York: Longmans, 1943, chaps. 2 and 6.

Chapter 4

The Individual's Present Situation

Analysis of goal region and paths to the goal were presented first because they involve largely a background of knowledge about human behavior. Analysis of a particular individual's present situation requires both that the therapist have such knowledge and that he have skill in applying it in a given case. This chapter is concerned then with the question: How can the speech therapist analyze an individual's present situation from the broad point of view presented in Chapters 2 and 3? In answering this question it presents the thesis that the speech therapist should be guided by the procedures known as *scientific method*. The steps in scientific method may be stated briefly for this purpose as follows:

1. Ask clear, answerable questions
2. Observe
3. Describe
4. Evaluate

Two features of scientific method serve to point up its potential contribution to the task at hand.

Scientific method seeks to find out by experimentation rather than by verbal definition. When a speech therapist examines a child only to the extent of being able to attach a label such as "stuttering," "hearing loss," "cleft palate," he is apt to infer the person's total present situation more by what that label represents to him than by what the individual himself really shows in behavior. The limiting effect of verbal definition has been particularly marked in use of the terms *functional* or *structural*. All too frequently the label "structural defect" has limited therapeutic considerations to appliances and drill on speech sounds with little provision for analyzing and changing other aspects of behavior. The limiting effect of verbal definition has been marked also in regard to I. Q. and social adjustment. Children have sometimes been excluded from speech therapy altogether because of verbal reports which have not been checked by direct observation, because of inferences made about the child's *future* ability on the basis of what he did on *one* testing occasion.

Scientific method, by its requirement of experimentation, stresses the need for what is termed *a-historical* as well as historical data about a given client. Historical data refers to reports by someone else about the individual's past behavior. Such data is certainly useful in establishing probability for trends in behavior, in suggesting clues to look for; but it cannot characterize or explain present behavior by itself. Something which happened in the past can only exert an influence upon present behavior if it exerts a force in the *present* situation. For example, early poverty in the home or rejection by a parent may suggest the possibility that feelings of insecurity may characterize a person's behavior in a particular present situation, but whether they actually do or not depends upon the person's *present perception* of the situation in terms of those past events. This needs to be established by observation of behavior in various situations, i.e., by a-historical study.

Let us turn now to a brief consideration of each of the steps of scientific method in order to suggest how the speech therapist should proceed.

1. *Ask clear, answerable questions.* This first step has great importance inasmuch as the kind of questions asked determines the direction of the therapist's behavior in following through with the subsequent steps.

The kind of questions asked depends upon the basic assumptions discussed in Chapter 2: the questions will not be limited to speech mechanism of the client but will include also those which relate to interpersonal relationships involved. Assumptions about whole-part relationships will affect the order in which different questions are asked. The whole, conceived of as more than the sum of the parts, cannot be explained by an additive process, but rather by a process more like multiplication, i.e., a resultant of interacting forces. Applied to human behavior this means that analysis begins (1) with person-interacting-with-environment, (2) proceeds then to person-as-a-whole, which would be considered a part-function, (3) then proceeds to one aspect of the person or one system of organs, which would be considered as a smaller division or sub-part. Thus the questions to be asked would be asked in that order: e.g., (1) What sort of interpersonal situation is he now engaged in? What differences in behavior occur when he is relating to peers, to persons in authority, etc.? (2) What adjustive techniques does he use? How does he use speech? (3) Does he have a hearing loss? How well can he effect closure of the soft palate?, etc.

Questions should not be framed to imply a "yes or no" answer which is related to the value concepts of the observer. For example, when one asks the question "Does this client have (or not have) a speech defect?" it is assumed that people can be put into two classes: those who have speech defects and those who do not. The boundary between the two depends upon the judgment of the examiner as to what constitutes defective speech. A similar implication exists in the commonly asked question, "Does this client have (or not have) a personality problem?" Rather, the questions should be asked in this way: *What sort of speech behavior does this client show? What sort of personality structure does he have?* Then it becomes possible to tell more about the *client* and less about the standards of value of the examiner.

Questions should not contain the word "is" with nouns or adjectives, because such questions likewise depend for answers upon the standards of value of the examiner. For example, take the following questions: Is he lazy? Is he stupid? Is he cooperative? Is she a moron? Is she a neurotic? Is she a behavior problem? In each case the answer depends upon the value concepts which the examiner attaches to the word, rather than upon his observations of what the client does. Even if the question were worded "How lazy is he?"

it would still depend upon value concepts about the word lazy. (This will be discussed further in respect to step 3.)

Questions should be structured in such a way that their answers can be found through step 2, i.e., the act of observing. The simplest questions for the speech therapist to formulate at first will be those which can be answered in terms of the number of times or to what extent a thing or process can be observed in a given situation, e.g., how many times (or to what extent) does he volunteer in class? To what extent does he join in activity on the playground?

The therapist will also find useful those questions which refer to *differences* in what the child does in two particular situations; e.g., what differences in behavior are shown in the classroom and on the playground? What differences in behavior are shown when one interpersonal situation involves another child and another situation involves an adult? Such questions lead to observations which in turn can be patterned for making significant inferences about what is producing certain behavior.

2. *Observation.* Observation takes place at silent levels. There are no words. The observer uses his sense organs — chiefly eyes and ears — for observing behavior. Having asked a question in step 1 which will direct what he looks for and listens for, he will try to pick out of the situation as many details as possible. At best, human sense organs are rather gross structures, capable only of abstracting from the situation a relatively few details. Nevertheless, the observer can increase markedly the details which he abstracts if he has formulated a clear, answerable question, if he consciously prolongs the observation step and if he increasingly looks for *differences*.

Much of the layman's life, comparatively, has been directed to observing only similarities in events, ignoring differences. Yet observed differences offer important clues to an understanding of behavior, clues to the changes that must be made in the therapeutic situation. Take, for example, a client who is observed to have spasms in tongue muscles when the interpersonal situation involves persons perceived as "authority figures," but no spasms when the situations involve persons with whom he feels on an equal basis. Such differences suggest that speech therapy should be directed to changing perceptions of authority relationships. Or take as another example a child who in a speech class one day showed a great deal of random activity, yet in class the next day, where the activity was simpler and more carefully structured, showed very little random activity. Such observations suggest that for that child a change in the structure of the teaching situation should be fruitful in controlling his behavior. Such inferences will not be made, of course, concurrently with observation — they must be made only later in step 4; but they serve to point out right here the importance of observing differences as well as similarities.

3. *Description.* Scientific method specifies that after observation on silent levels comes the translation of those observations into words. At this point sources of error often appear which distort the observer's perception of his own actual experience in observing. The most common source of error lies in the confusion between words which describe and words which evaluate.

The term *description* means mapping in words those features of the situation which the observer abstracted through looking, listening, etc. *It tells more about the thing or process observed than about the observer himself.* For example, consider the words, "The child did not respond when the teacher asked him a question." Since this tells something about the child, it is called *description.* Now consider the words, "The child is not interested" (or "is stubborn," or "is not paying attention"). Since this tells more about the observer, i.e., what he thinks about the child's behavior, it is called *evaluation.*

To describe, the observer must tell what the person *has* or *does.* He needs to avoid the word "is" with nouns or adjectives, since these denote his own evaluation. Use of such words means that the observer has skipped step 3 of description and gone directly to step 4 of evaluation — though not a very useful sort of evaluation.

Scientific method prescribes a certain order for proceeding, i.e., description should come *before* evaluation. Let us explore the importance of this. Suppose a therapist uses the words, "The child is stubborn." Since the words he uses, in speech or in thinking, influence his subsequent behavior with the child, these words will probably influence him to try to overcome the "stubbornness" through nagging, and if that is not successful, to dismiss the youngster from speech therapy. When "the child is stubborn" is taken for description, he may honestly think his senses reported that as fact; hence he will not consider the possibility of any other explanation for the behavior of not responding. Thus those words not only influence his attitude toward the child, but limit the probability of his making further observations which might modify that evaluation.

Now let us suppose that the therapist uses descriptive language to map his observations. "Each time so far that I have asked this child a question, he has not responded." Then as he makes an effort to describe more of the details of the behavior he saw, he may recall further to describe the child's behavior by saying, "He lowered his eyes," "showed some increase of tension in the shoulders." When he moves to step 4 (evaluation), instead of seizing upon one explanation he will consider *several possible explanations*. He might think of "stubbornness" first because that had represented an explanation he had used frequently before, but he would also consider the possibility of fears of various sorts. When he considers the possibility of "fear" his attitude and subsequent behavior toward the child will be very different from what it was when he considered only the one explanation "stubbornness."

The therapist who is just beginning to use scientific method as a way of analyzing a person's present situation must consciously work then to change his own behavior in two ways:

(a) *to delay evaluation* in order to describe what he has actually observed.

(b) *to change his use of language* from "is" to what the person "has or does."

4. *Evaluation.* Evaluation in scientific method represents an attempt to pattern the data, i.e., to establish relationships in order to explain behavior.

Several assumptions are involved:

(a) What one can observe about a situation, person, or process through the senses represents only a small portion of the functioning whole, such portion consisting of only surface manifestations. Yet the really critical processes governing behavior take place at deeper levels. The level of surface manifestations has been called by Lewin [1] "phenotypical behavior," by Korzybski [2] "macroscopic"; the deeper levels have been called by Lewin "genotypical," by Korzybski "sub-

---

[1] Kurt Lewin, *Dynamic Theory of Personality.* New York: McGraw-Hill, 1935, p. 11.

[2] Alfred Korzybski, *Science and Sanity.* Lancaster, Pa.: International Non-Aristotelian Library Publishing Company, 1933, pp. 386 ff.

microscopic." However one may wish to designate in words these differences in levels of behavior, the surface levels can be observed directly, hence can be described; the deeper levels cannot be observed directly but only inferred, or evaluated. For example, one can observe the following phenomena about an individual: he turns away, trembles, has drops of perspiration on forehead, etc.; from these observations one may infer that he feels fear. Similarly, anger, feelings of inferiority, perceptions of others cannot be observed directly but only inferred from the pattern of phenotypical behavior.

(b) Inferences about structure, or relationships which exist on the deeper levels must be made in language of some sort. In the more fully developed sciences, such as physics and astronomy, the language of mathematics is used predominantly; in the newer science of man the language of words still has to be relied upon to a large extent. But the language of the layman, with verbal forms such as "is stubborn," implying the existence of static traits, has had to be modified. New verbal forms — or *constructs*, as they are often called — have been introduced so that inferences about structure can be formulated in terms of relationships in total situation. Word maps about genotypical levels are constructed in terms of *needs, goals, perceptions of self-others, values, adjustive techniques, fear, anger, anxiety*, etc.

Let us take, for example, the descriptive statement used previously: "The child did not respond on a number of occasions when the teacher spoke to him in class." What inferences can be made, using the newer constructs which denote relationship within whole situation?

"He perceives this situation as threatening, as identical with one he formerly experienced in which he was laughed at, possibly punished. He fears what appears to him as certain failure if he speaks; his goal is represented as the need to avoid the threat, the failure; so he uses what for him constitutes a familiar adjustive technique: withdrawing, not participating in the group activity."

Such an analysis of a situation has value because it gives clues to the variables which need to be changed in the individual's behavior. To infer that "he is stubborn" or "he could if he wanted to" or "he's just naturally a nervous child" not only does not square with modern research findings regarding the dynamics of human behavior; it also does not offer predictions about the changes that need to be made nor does it suggest how to proceed in making them.

It is of the utmost importance to recognize that science operates upon assumptions of *probability*, not certainty. Thus evaluations should be made tentatively, as representing what has been observed *under given conditions* (called *indexing*) at a *specified time* (called *dating*). The therapist who is just beginning to practice scientific method in his work must check himself repeatedly to see that he affixes to his statements a date and some limiting phrase indexing the situation. He also needs to affix dates and indexes to the statements of other people regarding children. For example, a child was described as scoring an I. Q. of 65 on a psychometric test. The report mentioned the presence of marked symptoms of anxiety on the part of the child during the test, yet the evaluation of the results made no mention of this as a possible explanatory factor, simply made an explanation in terms of "lack of intelligence." Then making a prediction for all time in the future, as it were, the report recommended institutionalization for the child. Fortunately in this case, the speech therapist did some dating and indexing on his own and accepted the child for therapy on an exploratory basis. When the child was retested a year later, his I. Q. was listed as within normal range, and his reading level slightly above the norm for children of his age. Had the previous report been taken as predicting the future with certainty, the child would doubtless not have been accepted for speech therapy, and might even have been institutionalized. This example has been mentioned, not to discredit psychometric tests, which have great value, but to point out the need for dating and indexing statements in step 4 of scientific method — not only the statements of others but one's own as well. Because children with speech disorders often make low scores on such tests, this particular area serves as a useful example.

The therapist who is just beginning to use scientific method for analyzing an individual's present situation will find that it takes time and discipline to master the procedure. He will need to modify the kind of questions he has been accustomed to ask himself; he will need to observe extensively, more accurately; he will need to change his use of language in order to describe; he will need to adopt new constructs in order to make inferences for the explanation of behavior.

Chapter 5

Basic Design for Therapy

Therapeutic activities cover a wide range of endeavor. They include attempts to modify parts of the environment through consultation with significant persons in the client's environment; modify parts of the person through surgery, hearing aids, prosthetic appliances; modify part-functions through direct instruction for the client in clinic classes. Certainly such direct instruction constitutes the most extensive area of activity in speech therapy. For the vast majority of clients it is the only known instrument at present for bringing about changes in speech behavior. Even for those who have had surgery and/or appliances, clinic instruction is usually needed in order to increase the effect which change in part-function can have on the functional whole, e.g., in order to help a person with a hearing aid assimilate that instrument as part of himself so he can function more normally in interpersonal relationships. Likewise for those who will benefit from changes in the environment on the part of parents, teachers, and others, clinic instruction can contribute significantly. It can help the client to modify adjustive techniques and it can show parents and teachers by actual demonstration how to modify their behavior in dealing with the child. In the discussion which follows, the term *speech therapy* will refer especially to the process involving direct clinic instruction.

The assumption has been made that the teaching situation itself constitutes the most important instrument in such instruction for

41

bringing about changes in behavior. It is not merely the devices or techniques which the therapist uses for teaching speech, but also and more especially, what goes on in the interpersonal relationship which constitutes the teaching situation. The problem of how to change behavior then may be considered in two parts: (1) what the basic design or framework of therapy should be; (2) how this basic design should be utilized by the therapist for therapeutic purposes. This chapter will be concerned with the former; the next chapter with the latter.

Group instruction should form the core of speech therapy. Therapy in speech by its very nature involves changing behavior in interpersonal relationships. It must be changed by a process of *doing,* which requires a succession of "present" times. Thus the most useful framework would appear to be one which would provide those very interpersonal relationships which form a significant aspect of the client's day-to-day living. Individual instruction, composed of one client with teacher, offers the possibility of structuring one sort of interpersonal situation; but group instruction, composed of a number of clients with teacher, offers the possibility of structuring a *variety* of interpersonal situations. In a group each child is interacting not only with an adult viewed as "one-in-authority," but also with peers. Moreover, in a group it is possible to structure real speaking events — real in the sense that they can actually take place in the present instead of being merely preparation for some event which will occur in the future.

The term "group" refers to something over and above the mere presence of numbers of persons assembled in a room; it represents a process of welding those persons into a larger whole, i.e., developing and maintaining *a group structure.* Such a group structure provides an atmosphere for the development of feelings of belongingness, relatedness to others, impulse to speak, recognition of abilities of each person, experiencing of success.

Clearly group instruction is not advocated as a mere labor-saving, mass production device. On the contrary, it involves greater complexity, requires greater teaching skill than does individual instruction. The value lies in its potential superiority for meeting individual needs. Within a group structure it is possible to be working on several different things at the same time with numbers of people or with one person: e.g., building a feeling of belongingness, increasing feelings of personal worth, developing social skills, modifying speech patterns, changing production of particular consonant sounds. The group should be composed ordinarily of eight or ten children — large enough to permit the building of group structure, small enough to meet adequately the various needs of individual members within a usual class period of thirty to forty minutes.

To consider group instruction as the "core" of speech therapy does not preclude the possibility or desirability of individual instruction. It means that the group structure constitutes the whole, from which individual instruction emerges and to which it leads back. The group structure makes possible a different kind of teaching, changes the structure of the individual teaching situation in that it is now conceived as a supplementary function rather than an isolated entity.

Group membership should be non-segregated in respect to kind of speech symptoms. The assumption is made that it is not only possible but desirable to have the group composed of persons with various kinds of speech disorders. For example, in a particular group the following speech disorders might be represented:

1. cleft palate	5. articulation (s-z)
2. hearing loss	6. articulation (r-l)
3. stuttering	7. delayed speech
4. cerebral palsy	8. vocal quality

The older practice of segregating clients for training according to type of speech disorder stems from the assumption that there is a different type of therapy for each different type of disorder. This in turn stems from an implicit assumption relating to classification: namely, that persons who have one set of symptoms in common are alike in all other ways, and that persons with different symptoms are therefore different in all other ways. In point of fact, workers in the field have long recognized that no two persons within a given classification present identical patterning in speech symptoms, nor in functional organization. Absolute sameness simply does not exist among people who stutter, or among those who have cleft palate, or cerebral palsy, hearing loss, or other disorders. Workers in the field, however, have not so clearly recognized that similarities exist among persons in *different* classifications. A number of similarities become apparent when speech behavior is charted in terms of what the person *does*, instead of what class he is in, i.e., when it is described in terms of force patterns, blending, facial grimaces, etc. Force patterns need to be modified in most cases of stuttering, cerebral palsy, cleft palate, severe hearing loss, or voice; so with blending, so with facial grimaces. Furthermore, in respect to functional organization, such as readiness for learning or fear of authority figures, a person with cleft palate may have much more in common with a person who stutters than he does with another who has cleft palate, or vice versa. Thus the basic postulates underlying the practice of segregating clients on the basis of speech symptoms do not appear warranted. It seems desirable then to abandon the concept of a homogeneous group, accept the fact of heterogeneity and create the sort of teaching situation which capitalizes upon it.

Clinical investigations lend support to the belief that persons with different kinds of speech symptoms not only can be but *should* be together for group instruction. Such a mixed group offers a great potential advantage. It may be utilized in avoiding the possibility of trauma which results from "labelling" a child by saying, "He is a stutterer," "He is a cleft-palate case." This is done frequently not only by family and friends but by speech therapists themselves. The act of putting a child who has cleft-palate speech into a group class composed only of other children with cleft-palate speech shouts very loudly to him that they are set apart from others as "different" because of that one characteristic. In a non-segregated group, however, where positive rather than negative aspects of producing and using speech are stressed, the members see a range of problems among them which must be solved. It is important to stress "what's right" about speech as well as what needs to be changed. Such a group allows each child to get recognition for being able to demonstrate for someone else an acceptable pattern of speech production or use. A child who stutters can demonstrate clear vocal quality for one child, a sharp "s" sound for another; then those children in turn can demonstrate for him smoothness of pattern or speaking with less force. Such a structuring of the situation permits the development of greater objectivity, greater matter-of-fact recognition of the job to be done.

The idea of a non-segregated group does not preclude the possibility of having small groups meet together at times to work on a common problem of the moment; the therapist might easily have a special session with two or three who are working to improve voice quality or a particular consonant sound. Such a sub-group would be serving a particular purpose at a particular time, but would exist as supplementary to the larger group. Persons with severe hearing loss, and those with cerebral palsy need a great deal of specialized instruction to meet common needs; but they should also belong to a larger mixed group for the sort of instruction which only such a group can provide effectively.

The teaching situation should be structured to provide corrective "emotional" experience. Were it not for the fact that procedures in therapy have been influenced so largely by the hidden elementalistic assumption that learning takes place on verbal levels as a result of "intellectual" exercise, such a term as corrective "emotional" experience would not be needed. This term emphasizes the non-elementalistic nature of learning as an intellectual-emotional process. The assumption has been made that an individual's perceptions of self and others, his needs, his values, his adjustive techniques have been acquired in previous interpersonal experiences. Changes in such aspects of behavior will come about by a *living through* of significant experiences in the *present.*

This has been recognized to some extent whenever a speech therapist has engaged in conferences with parents and classroom teachers about the need for modifying their interpersonal relations with the child. It has not been recognized to any great extent, however, that in the interpersonal relations which constitute his own clinical teaching he should be demonstrating how such a process of corrective "emotional" experience can be brought about. While some children have found such therapeutic experience in classes where the therapists themselves were not conscious of how such changes were taking place, it seems evident that so important an aspect of therapy should not be left to chance but should be planned consciously in structuring the teaching situation.

This aspect of speech therapy is not to be considered equivalent to the process termed psychotherapy as practiced by psychiatrist or psychologist. The two forms of therapy — speech therapy and psychotherapy — are viewed as two specialties, each with its unique contribution to make, but sharing also a common area of endeavor, along with other fields dealing with human relations. In some cases speech therapy alone would be sufficient to solve problems of adjustment; in some cases psychotherapy alone would be sufficient to meet speech problems; in some cases a combination of speech therapy and psychotherapy would function most effectively. The important thing is for the various fields to be rooted in a common scientific base so that their procedures will complement rather than oppose each other.

Each field has its own limitations as well as its own potentialities in promoting corrective "emotional" experience. In respect to permissiveness — giving the child freedom to react in the situation in ways which meet his needs — speech therapy by and large would lie on a continuum part way between public school education and psychotherapy. It does not have as much permissiveness as a psychotherapeutic situation, but has considerably more than the usual classroom situation. The greatest potentiality of speech therapy appears to lie in *the use of speech as an instrument for creating significant interpersonal relationships,* in which the child can experience real group belongingness, rational authority relationships, acceptance of himself as he is by both authority and peers, gain recognition, learn social skills, so that he can participate more satisfactorily in interpersonal relationships. Another potentiality of speech therapy appears to lie in the possibility of *demonstrating to parents and classroom teachers* how they can modify their relationships with a child.

The teaching situation should be structured in terms of those interpersonal relationships which involve conversational speech. Such a relationship would be integrated for instance by the act of welcoming a guest at the door. Someone knocks; a child goes to the door and opens it; guest and host say "Hello" or "Hi ——"; host says "Come in," then "Have a chair"; guest says "Thank you." Another such relationship involves serving refreshments in the group. One child passes cookies, saying, "Will you have a cookie"; the other person may say, "Yes," and take a cookie, or he may take a cookie and say, "Thank you." The particular speech patterns used in any given situation are determined by the goals of the particular lesson. For example, the pattern might be "Have a cookie" or even just "Have one" for children who are not yet ready for the longer response.

"Yes" would be used if a one-syllable answer were desired or if "s" sounds were being emphasized; "thank you" would be used if a two-syllable answer were desired, if blending, or "th" sounds, or "k" sounds were being emphasized.

The interpersonal situation is viewed as constituting the whole; speech behavior as a part-function of the whole; mechanics of sound production as a sub-part. It is significant to note that the latter is handled within the larger framework rather than as an isolated entity. *Use* of speech precedes and then goes concurrently with mechanics of sound production, instead of following it. This type of procedure has a number of advantages over procedures which consist of drill on nonsense syllables, word lists, "drill" sentences, oral reading of printed material. These advantages will be described briefly as follows.

1. *Use of conversation patterns applies the principle that learning proceeds from whole to parts by a process of differentiation.* A child does not develop speech by building first sounds, then syllables, then adding them to form words, then adding them to form sentences, then adding appropriate movements to use speech in real situations. There seems to be no valid reason then for attempting to teach speech clinically in such fashion. In the case of persons with speech disorders the learning of speech is difficult at best; certainly that process should not be made more difficult by procedures which are contrary to the order in which learning appears to take place. The fact that many children have been able to learn by procedures which go from parts to whole, does not preclude the possibility of their learning more easily and more productively by procedures which go *from whole to parts*. The possibility exists too of obtaining more satisfactory results with the individuals who have not progressed adequately with the older procedures. Proceeding from whole to parts means that the children experience a given situation, participate in some fashion, at least by the very fact of being present even if not actively at first; they participate in an activity such as distributing or accepting a toy even if no speech accompanies the activity at first; they use speech patterns even though the patterns are not phonetically accurate at first.

2. *Use of conversation patterns provides the therapist with a single instrument for a three-fold task, — bringing about changes in functional or-*

ganization, in social skills, and in mechanics of speech production. It should be understood that we are concerned with speech not only as something to be changed but also as an instrument for bringing about changes. In respect to functional organization conversational speech is used to build group structure, to change perceptions of self and others, meet needs, etc. In respect to social skills it is used to give the client himself an instrument for developing more satisfactory interpersonal relationships. In respect to mechanics of speech production conversational speech constitutes material for practice which is as useful as older materials in that it can be kept carefully controlled, simple, offers the possibility of repeated performance; it is more useful in that it is richer in meaning, more closely associated with general bodily activity, more interesting to work on. Conversation patterns can well be used by a therapist who wishes to restrict plans for therapy to mechanics of speech production. Their particular merit, however, will be evident to therapists who wish to plan for therapy broad enough in scope to include the aspects above mentioned.

3. *Use of conversation patterns applies the principle that learning involves the perceptual organization of new wholes, not merely repetition of an activity per se.* Kohler [1] has stressed the importance of organization of the whole in which a part is embedded. He points out that the learning of nonsense syllables is difficult not so much because of lack of meaning as because organization does not take place as readily. Lewin [2] points out that while repetition may cause small units to be organized into larger groups, large amounts of repetition have been shown by experiment to cause breakdown of larger wholes with loss of organization. He emphasizes progress of meaning as having more significance than repetition per se. In the field of reading the application of this concept has meant that in primers the same words are presented numbers of times on a page but embedded each time in a different whole. In speech therapy a given speech pattern is used again and again but each time embedded in a different interpersonal situation. For example a child passes out articles one by one saying, "Have one," but saying it each time to a different person in a different

---

[1] Wolfgang Kohler, *Gestalt Psychology.* New York: Liveright, 1947, p. 273 footnote.

[2] Kurt Lewin, "Behavior and Development as a Function of the Total Situation," in *Manual of Child Psychology,* ed. Carmichael. New York: Wiley, 1946, chap. 16, p. 825.

interpersonal context. Thus if a particular goal in such a case is to learn a "v" sound, the child is exposed to that sound in only one response — called a key response — rather than to many syllables or words containing that sound. Instead of repetition in the sense of drill on isolated part-functions, he engages in a series of experiences in which the one part-function remains constant, but the structure of the situations is varied.

4. *Use of conversation patterns provides a means of handling the problem of transfer of training.* In older procedures when a client practiced on a particular sound in a list of syllables or words he was engaging in an activity that occurred only in a clinic practice period, not in real life. The problem of transfer of training was thus left to the individual's own resources or to parents or to chance. When, however, he works on a real speech response, e.g., "Yes" in an actual question-answer situation, the whole in which that speech activity is embedded occurs very frequently in similar form in everyday life outside the clinic. It has been demonstrated repeatedly both by direct observation and by reports of parents and teachers that as the use of such a response becomes established in the clinic it is soon used outside as well. For example, one boy had learned to respond to the greeting "How are you" with the pattern "Fine," using a normally-produced "f" sound. His mother reported that a neighbor had asked him this question one day, soon after he had begun speech therapy, and was very much impressed when he made the new response. An eight-year-old girl who had had no speech began saying at home to her father and brother, "Have some" as she passed candy and cookies. In her case also the listeners were impressed. Numbers of parents report that children start using "Thank you" in situations at home where the parents had worked in vain to get them to remember even to say it at all, let alone say it within normal range of accuracy. As the key response becomes relatively automatic, other responses are included in the instruction. Experience has shown that many children of their own accord will begin to extend the production of a given sound to other speech responses; that other children do so with very little help.

It has been pointed out that learning must occur as an active process, that motivation — the impulse to change behavior — must come from within. In terms of consequences, those procedures are preferable which result in greater use of new speech patterns through the child's own motivation, rather than by "reminding," "nagging" behavior on the part of someone else. Furthermore, when a child behaves in such fashion outside, his behavior has an effect upon other persons in his environment; people are pleased with him, show approval, treat him more as a person who is capable of improving. This in turn makes that environment more conducive to further development.

Chapter 6

Procedures in Utilizing Basic Design

The basic design for speech therapy has importance only to the extent to which the speech therapist utilizes it for building an inter-personal relationship in which growth in the direction of the goal becomes possible. The assumption is made that it is possible to create an environment in which children can so respond, that the behavior of the therapist is of crucial importance in this process. His behavior constitutes the major influence in developing what Lewin [1] terms "atmosphere" and what Porter [2] calls "psychological climate"; it is gradually supplemented by the influence of the group behavior itself.

We shall consider first how the therapist sets out to build such a psychological climate; second, how he promotes the development of social skills; third, how he brings about changes in mechanics of speech production.

Developing Psychological Climate

1. *Aspects of the therapist's behavior.* Inasmuch as a therapist's basic assumptions play so important a part in determining behavior

---

[1] Kurt Lewin, *Principles of Topological Psychology.* New York: McGraw-Hill, 1936, p. 19.

[2] E. H. Porter, Jr., *An Introduction to Therapeutic Counseling.* Boston: Hough-ton Mifflin, 1950, p. 46.

let us mention briefly some aspects on the perceptive side as he approaches the therapeutic situation. He should understand that it is quite possible for him both to function scientifically in appraising the needs of each child and in manipulating forces for his learning, and yet at the same time to interact with each child warmly. He should see a whole-child-interacting-in-an-environment, not merely a given set of speech symptoms; he should seek always to see each child as that child is, not as a type which fits some preconceived verbal definition in his own perceptive system. Moreover, his perceptions of his own dynamics should be as free from distortion as possible. Children as such should not arouse anxiety in him, nor should the behavior of particular children constitute a personal threat to him. He must not only respect each child's uniqueness as a human being, but must like each one as a person even though he may not like some aspects of behavior. Almost anyone finds it easy to like children who behave according to one's own personal standards; but a therapist must also be able to like those who "get in people's hair," if he hopes to help them change behavior. In order to react in such a way he must refrain from making the old value judgments such as, "The child is bad, is lazy, is stupid"; he should instead make inferences in terms of the child's perceptions or needs. He should recognize the probability that the children in the group — by their very presence there with disorders of speech — have had less experience in group relatedness, enjoyed fewer satisfactions from such interactions, developed fewer skills, been subjected to greater pressures at home, formed more distorted perceptions of self in relation to others. Instead of focusing merely upon the frequently more conspicuous liabilities in the child, the therapist should search in each one for assets, potential as well as real. Then he will be able quite sincerely and with genuine warmth to show interest, acceptance, pleasure toward each one.

On the motor side, his own level of muscular tension should be kept low. While this is most effectively achieved through the development of rational attitudes toward the situation at hand, it is perhaps reassuring to the beginning therapist to know that this can be achieved in some measure too through conscious control: relatively slow movements, relatively slow speech. For example, a teacher can decrease noise level in a group more effectively by speaking more slowly and more quietly than he can by trying to raise his voice above it. His own slowness of movement and speech can decrease level of tension in other members of the group. Such behavior is in no way incompatible with the showing of animation and enthusiasm.

2. *Developing group structure.* In order to develop a group structure — i.e., a relationship which will be perceived in terms of "we" rather than "I" — the therapist will set out to integrate a situation (*a*) in which each child will be encouraged to participate, (*b*) in which his participation will be in relation to another person as part of the whole group, and (*c*) in which he will experience feelings of acceptance and success.

The situation must contain the opportunity for each one to DO something — such as look in a box, take out an object, exchange it with someone. The situation must be simple enough so that members of the group can grasp the pattern of the whole, can understand their role well enough to engage in it, and can succeed in actually carrying out the activity. It should be simple in the sense that the therapist can present it by *showing* rather than by long verbal instructions (e.g., "I'm going to say 'Hello' to each one, like this"); he performs the act, then says, "Now, Jack, you come with me and do it.") It should be simple too in the sense that the particular activity as a part-function of the whole interpersonal situation can be repeated by the children one by one.

The therapist can encourage participation in a number of ways. He can introduce some mild degree of suspense — enough to focus attention and stimulate interest in the object without directing attention too strongly away from the speech activity to be engaged in. For example, he can hold up a brightly colored box saying, "I have a surprise for you today. What do you suppose is in it?"; then he can rattle the box, sometimes even let them make some guesses. He can get the activity going as he wants it by choosing first a child who is relatively more able or willing than the others; then others will follow more readily in that pattern. His use of language also influences willingness to participate: "Do you want to . . ." invites the answer "No"; "John, you do it next," said quietly but with the expectation that he will, produces more positive response. To a child who hesitates he can say, "I'll help you," or to one who refuses a turn he can say, "O.K. We'll come back to you after Betty has had a turn." Such children will be encouraged to participate also by the recognition given to others who precede them. However, a child's wish not to participate should be accepted unemotionally, without pressure, without comparing him unfavorably to others, and without urging him in the name of "pleasing the therapist."

It is particularly important for therapeutic purposes that a child's participation should involve another person, and that this sub-group twosome should exist in relation to the group as a whole. Too often in situations which have been structured in terms of "drill" or "games," the child participates only when it is his turn, and then performs the act by himself. But in situations where he gives a toy to another child, saying to him "have one" or "do you want one" he is participating in a situation which is interpersonal in character. Such a situation has the potentialities mentioned previously for actual use of speech, experience in social skills, and corrective "emotional" experience. The degree to which such a two-person interaction occurs as a matter of attention and participation by the whole group depends upon the skill of the therapist in welding individuals into a whole and maintaining that whole. He can keep the interest of the group centered on the activity in a number of ways: "Let's listen carefully as Tommie says 'Thank you' "; "What did you like about it?"; "Jack, show Mary how you say it"; "I liked that, Susan; let's clap for her." Relatively short but frequent participations, and allowing the children to choose who shall participate next also contribute toward this end. Sometimes so apparently simple an act as changing seating arrangement also makes for greater group participation; for example, a child who tends to be "on the fringes" in the psychological field can participate more actively if he is moved from an end seat, i.e., from the fringes in physical space. Managing to separate two children who are apt to form a sub-group apart from the lesson, can sometimes result in greater participation of the whole membership.

Finally, for each individual to experience feelings of acceptance and success has importance in establishing an atmosphere of security and belongingness. How well the therapist succeeds in this depends in part on the simplicity of the lesson he has chosen, in part on the low level of tension which exists, and also on his own attitude to the child's participation: his attitude as manifest in both visible and audible behavior. The skilled therapist uses an abundance of praise, warmly given. But the praise is used consciously and discriminatingly to lead a child forward toward greater growth. For example, he will say to one, "I liked that, Tommie; you took your turn along with the rest this time"; to another, "I liked that because you looked at Jean more this time"; to another, "I could understand better today"; to still another, "Kennie, you got that just right; say it again for us so we can listen again; wasn't that fine?"

Praise should be used discriminatingly too in the sense that it should put no undue pressure on the child. One mother, for instance, reported praising her son for getting a mark of 100 in spelling. The boy had been having a great deal of trouble in that area and could not routinely achieve that grade; but he had a very great need for approval from his mother, who gave it seldom; so he started copying from another child's paper in order to get the 100. That mother came to see, as therapists also need to, that she should use more praise for behavior that conceivably can be repeated successfully. Care should be taken, too, to restrict praise to the child himself and *not* to link it up with competitive performance such as, "Well, you did as well as Mary that time." Like any other instrument a therapist can use, praise is neither good or bad in itself, but is extremely useful if skillfully employed.

While a child's feeling of success will come at first from the behavior of the therapist, it should soon begin to come also from the group itself. Children will take their cues from the therapist's behavior as he brings them into the response, saying, for example, "Let's clap for Kennie." The lessons built on expressions of appreciation, where children tell each one something they like, serve a similar purpose. If one has ever observed the responses to this sort of activity — the smiles, the expression in the eyes of the child to whom the speech is directed — he will recognize its potentiality in structuring a group atmosphere of friendliness, security and belongingness among the members. Gradually children who have experienced this sort of procedure will praise a child of their own accord, or members of the group will clap spontaneously when one has achieved what for him is a particularly difficult task. Such approval by peers has even more potent effects in changing perceptions than approval by the therapist. Children can readily learn that the particular goals are different for different individuals within one lesson, that each one competes only with himself, and they learn to make their evaluations discriminatingly. For example, one child said about another child's performance which was improved but not yet within normal range, "That's good for him *today*"; about another's, "I think you can do better than that today if you try again." Another child was being held mistakenly for a response more difficult than the one he had made, and responded matter-of-factly, "I'm not ready for that yet." Such evaluation by the group does not come automatically or magically but it can come if the therapist sets out to develop it.

3. *Permissiveness based upon assumptions of rational authority.* The degree of permissiveness considered desirable for group classes in speech therapy has been expressed roughly as lying on a continuum somewhere between that found in psychotherapy and in public school education. In order to specify what the speech therapist should do in order to achieve permissiveness within such range, it is necessary first to specify some basic assumptions regarding authority. Fromm [3] has clarified some issues on this subject by making a distinction between *rational* and *irrational* authority (representing extremes at either end of a continuum). He points out that the question is not whether there should be authority or lack of it, but rather *what kind* of authority there should be. He characterizes rational authority as based on competence, as limited to the performance of a particular function for a particular duration of time, as leading rather than dictating, helping rather than policing; irrational authority as power for the sake of power (whether conscious or non-conscious), demanding blind obedience with implications of infallibility and rejection of criticism. Applied to speech therapy, assumptions of rational authority would enable a teacher to play an active role in group activity — planning lessons and manipulating forces in the environment; would require that he have as much knowledge as possible about the needs of each individual in order to help him develop his potentialities; and would require that he exercise all possible skill to bring this about in the teaching situation. But it would also mean that he would invite active participation from members of the group, would respect their integrity and ability to collaborate; he would not wield power over them in the sense of "you will because I say so," or

[3] Eric Fromm, *Man for Himself.* New York: Norton, 1947, p. 9.

"having ordered this I must be obeyed in order to preserve my own integrity." Because so many of us in our culture have been exposed to irrational authority both at home and at school, it is probable that most speech therapists will need to examine their behavior consciously and carefully over a period of time in order to weed out behavior based upon assumptions of an irrational sort, in order to develop behavior based on assumptions of a more rational sort.

The therapist who operates on assumptions of rational authority will give freedom enough to enable individuals to use the relationship for meeting their particular needs of growth. At the same time he will establish a situation (a) with conformity enough to provide stability of structure for the sake of individual security, (b) with flexibility enough for the variety of needs within the group membership, and (c) with substance enough for the demands imposed by the nature of the instruction, in this case speech education.

4. *Setting limits.* The therapist has a responsibility to structure the situation so that the children can know what is expected of them in the particular situation, and beyond what limits they may not go. A situation too loosely structured actually induces or increases anxiety. This is particularly important to consider in the beginning of therapy when children will come largely with a background of experience with authority which has been characterized by rigidity, inconsistency, and irrational components. They will need to develop perceptions and adjustive techniques to handle greater amounts of permissiveness. Although the therapist may exert more authority at first, it should still be of the rational kind. The setting of limits will not be conceived of as incompatible with permissiveness if it is viewed as structuring of freedom within the boundaries. The therapist should help the children perceive the limits not so much by talking as by doing, *showing.* Order and regularity of procedure constitute an important way of structuring. Praise constitutes another way, e.g., "I like the way Bobby is sitting, comfortably, quietly"; "I like the way Henry is watching." A child who has not been watching can usually be induced to do so by hearing the therapist say in this way what he likes by way of behavior.

5. *Helping children to succeed.* The therapist can frequently prevent the occurrence of behavior he does not want by anticipating possible action well enough ahead of time to take measures which

will avoid it. For example, he can say to a child who frequently
shuffles his feet or sticks out a foot to trip another child, "Douglas,
let's have you change to this chair today. I think it will be more
comfortable. Then I'll bet you can keep those feet more still. I'm
going to help you too by sitting near you today." He can also help
a particular child to succeed by waiting to call on him until after
several have performed an act so that it will seem less strange to
him; by choosing children with less ability to perform some of the
simpler tasks which they can perform well at a particular time. When
the therapist perceives his role as one of helping rather than as one
of policing or punishing, many such ways of handling problems will
occur to him.

6. *Accepting feelings.* In a situation characterized by irrational
authority, some children do not dare to recognize or accept in themselves feelings which are different from or against the authority; if
they do, they are apt to experience guilt reactions. In a situation
characterized by rational authority, a child's behavior may not be
acceptable, but HE is. Simple acceptance of his feelings can be
stated matter-of-factly; one can say, "You were afraid maybe you'd
fail, weren't you?" or "You want to do it and you don't want to do
it, isn't that it?" The child is not penalized for *having* the reactions.
The therapist does *not* say, "Don't be a baby" or "You're a naughty
boy." Rather, after accepting the feeling, he would say, "I'll help
you," or "Let's see if we can help Alice." Sometimes no verbal
mention is made, yet feelings are accepted; for example, if Alice does
not want to participate, the therapist says, "We'll come back to you
later so you can do this," or "I think Alice will want to join in
tomorrow."

7. *Giving choices.* This constitutes one of the most important
ways of offering permissiveness in a teaching situation of this sort.
Many children have really not been able to make many choices at
home or at school, and the experience of doing so in the clinical
situation gives a sense of freedom from restraint, induces more active
participation, promotes greater independence of action, helps to
develop a different sort of perception of authority relationships. For
some children the process involves chiefly a becoming-able to make
choices; for others it provides an outlet for aggressive needs; for others
it involves a growing sense of discrimination of where one may exert

choice and where none is permitted; for those who may not need such corrective "emotional" experience it involves simply a way of participating.

Freedom of choice must be real freedom, not merely *saying* to a child that he may choose, but with a preference clearly implied by the authority or with a threat clearly in the perception of the child if he were to exercise his real choice. At the same time freedom of choice can be structured within certain limits. For example, in a given activity the statement is made that the box may be placed "on the window sill, on the desk, or on the chair," with the possibility of choice within those three alternatives. Or in another activity where children are requesting crayons, they may ask for the color they want from those represented, "the red one," "the blue one," etc. Children can also exert choice in selecting a child to engage next in an activity. The therapist may say to a child beforehand, "Let's see, Jane hasn't had a turn yet, and Jimmie hasn't; you may want to choose one of them." This should be done by way of suggestion rather than by way of a command, however. Group choices can also be made in such matters as refreshments. The therapist may give them a choice for example of having tomato juice or orange juice, as the two things available. At other times he may be able to give more freedom of choice, as for example, when a group of children on one occasion decided to serve hot dogs at a morning party for their mothers, and were permitted to do so.

Some children appear to have need for choosing to make some negative responses. Perhaps the thing most dreaded by inexperienced therapists is that very thing, "What do you do if a child says 'No'?" If the therapist is ready for the possibility so that he can let a child decline to participate, and accept that response unemotionally, the child usually soon stops doing it. Once in a while one negative response may start a chain of them throughout the group. The therapist can laugh with them and say, "You've each had a chance to say 'No'; now we'll each have a chance to say 'Yes.'" Experience has shown that giving more opportunity for choices and accepting some negative responses matter-of-factly, decreases the extent to which such responses occur.

8. *Keeping the teaching situation speech-centered.* In concluding this discussion of developing psychological climate, it should be

emphasized explicitly that such climate should be *speech-centered*. Such a term relates to speech in its broadest sense. When it has been narrowly conceived as meaning only mechanics of speech production, then quite properly there would be circumstances in which one would not wish a group atmosphere to be so centered, e.g., for children with delayed speech, those who stutter, or those with other kinds of speech symptoms who are not yet ready for such rigorous and detailed training. But where speech is broadly conceived to include use in interpersonal relationships then quite properly speech therapy — as indeed speech education for any group — should have the characteristic of being speech-centered.

Within an atmosphere such as has been described, the term *speech-centered* also means that it is quite possible and desirable for children to know that they are attending a speech class, to know that they are working to develop skills in speech, to know in most cases at any given time what those skills consist of.

Lastly, the term *speech-centered* should serve as a criterion for the therapist in structuring teaching situations. When activities or materials in a lesson are so absorbing or distracting that the speech behavior becomes secondary, that lesson should be discarded or restructured. The goal in planning is to structure a lesson sufficiently simple in design and of such a nature that it is the speech behavior which constitutes the chief core of interest.

Developing Social Skills

The development of social skills, as pointed out in a previous chapter, serves as an instrument for the therapist in modifying functional organization and also provides the child with an instrument for improving his interpersonal relationships. In the discussion which follows certain aspects of procedure will be outlined.

1. *Ability to follow conventional social patterns.* To have the situations *real* constitutes the most important point of procedure. This cannot be emphasized too strongly; it is in fact relatively simple to accomplish once the therapist understands what the term *real* implies. It can best be defined by a series of examples. Let us consider as a situation welcoming a guest at the door. The situation is not structured to pretend that there is a door nor to pretend that someone is knocking; a child really goes outside and knocks. He

does not pretend to be someone else, he is himself and is welcomed as such. The whole project involving the welcoming of a guest may occupy several lessons and may include plans for having some guests come from outside the group, several days hence. That future event may well be mentioned early in the project, but the important thing is the *present* situation with its reality of the children who are there now. Similarly, introductions are structured with the people who are actually present in the group at the time, who are considered as themselves and not some mythical figures whose reality lies in some future time. So it is too with ordering in a restaurant. It is not enough to "get ready" or "practice" for a trip to a real soda bar "tomorrow" or "the day after." The children actually do the ordering with their own refreshments. Interest in an activity must come from the reality of the present, not from promises of something real in the future.

Another example may be found in situations which involve asking permission. This sort of interpersonal relationship has importance in the clinic program because it occurs commonly in life outside the clinic and because it often has forces which produce strong feeling, as when a request is denied. When the clinic situation is structured as pretending to ask permission of a teacher or parent or some other person, it becomes little more than an exercise devoid of the feeling which is part of a real event. It is so much more effective — and very possible — to structure a lesson so that the children ask permission for real things right in the clinic: "May I open the window?" "May I close the door?" "May I get a drink?" "May I sit in your seat?" etc. The choices made by the children in responding create conditions similar to those found in situations outside the clinic. How this may be worked out is demonstrated in an illustrative lesson in Part Two.

2. *Ability to win acceptance and support from others.* The most important points of procedure concern the choice of situations for the teaching situation, together with the utilization of the psychological climate for facing realistically and unemotionally the problems of behavior involved. Many children — and especially those with defective speech — do not know how, or have adjustive techniques which prevent them from getting the acceptance and support which they need from others. Take for example the boy who

wanted desperately to be liked by others but succeeded only in alienating himself through behavior characterized by tripping, pulling at hair, and making fun of others. Because the therapist had been creating an atmosphere in which the group talked frankly about problems, he could bring up this problem for discussion. It was introduced quite casually in connection with the general topic of things we like and things we don't like in the behavior of others toward us. The assumption was made — not that the child was "bad" or "was a disciplinary problem" — but that here was something he had not learned to handle, that there were others with some difficulty also and that the group had better work to help each other solve such problems. Children and therapist listed ways in which it is possible to show another person that you like him, such as saving a chair, choosing him for an activity sometimes, inviting him to go with you to get a drink at the fountain. Then such behavior was practiced in the group.

Another example is that of a boy who on the playground would consistently grab the ball and run in the other direction whenever it came his way. While this was not a situation which involved social skills in direct relation to speaking, it offered something very tangible for that boy to illustrate a characteristic way of behaving which showed up also in speaking situations. The group talked about the consequences of such behavior, how it made the others feel, how it made the boy himself feel when the others did not like to play with him. Then they demonstrated how to play ball, how you wanted it to come your way so you could choose someone to toss it to. The boy received praise for the more appropriate behavior, had the experience of trying out a new adjustive technique, tested out the difference in consequences. Gradually he became able to adopt that sort of technique in other situations. At the same time the other children learned a new adjustive technique — how it is possible to help a member change behavior which they do not like.

One very common event in a group situation where chairs are unassigned, is that of one child finding that someone has taken what he considers his chair, whereupon he behaves with some irritation frequently stirring up considerable feeling. Such a circumstance suggests a useful and very real teaching situation to the therapist. In such a lesson children take chairs purposely; a child says quietly and pleasantly, "You have my chair," or variations of such a pattern; the other child responds, "I'm sorry, I didn't know it," or "I was just fooling, here it is," or "O.K. You may have it." They discover that through speech — the words that are said, the tone of voice used — it is possible to handle a situation like this more easily and pleasantly.

Other situations which children frequently need to learn better ways of handling involve offering-accepting help, giving-receiving praise, meeting situations in which a sense of failure is experienced. These should be selected for class activity when the group is ready to face the problems involved. The direction of procedure for bringing about these changes is suggested in respect to offering-accepting help by the following: development of group awareness and acceptance of the belief that each person both needs help from others and can give help to others; perception of helping as a pleasant way of interrelating without involving an evaluation that to need help is to be inferior; exploration of ways of offering and accepting help; practice on the adjustive techniques involved so that the organization of such behavior becomes familiar.

In respect to situations involving giving-receiving praise the procedure has a similar pattern: of utilizing group structure, of "doing" in day-to-day activities, of analyzing and evaluating performance. As individuals become accustomed both to giving and to receiving praise in an atmosphere of warmth, friendliness and objectivity, such interpersonal behavior ceases to produce anxiety or embarrassment. In situations involving evaluations of succeeding-failing, a child learns that one act at one time does not represent *all* of him, that while he may experience "failure" in one respect that does not mean that HE as a whole person has failed.

3. *Ability to share attitudes.* Several points of procedure should be indicated, of which the most basic one relates to permissiveness in the acceptance of feelings, as described previously. The child needs to experience again and again both in respect to others and himself, that one is not penalized for expressing certain attitudes. The point of view is accepted and stressed in the group that it is quite possible to both like and dislike something or someone — that everyone has such responses at certain times. Two scientific principles are applied in this connection: (1) *non-allness*, i.e., that disliking someone or

something does not represent all of one's feelings, nor does it tell all about the object; (2) *multi-valued orientation*, i.e., that evaluations such as liking-disliking can more accurately be described on a range or many-point scale than on only a two-point scale. One does not in reality have "total like" or "total dislike." One activity for the group to engage in involves setting up, say, a four point scale: "like very much — like quite well — dislike somewhat — dislike greatly." Members use it first in telling about foods, games, and the like; later they work into topics which are more heavily loaded with feeling, such as things at school, actions of a sister or brother, or things feared.[4] The therapist must understand that many persons find it difficult at first to engage in this. He will need to verbalize for an individual at first: "You want to and you don't want to, is that it?" "You want to do it but at the same time you're a little scared to, aren't you?" Changes that ensue in an individual's ability to share attitudes appear to come about from a combination of having some new criteria for evaluating, together with the experience of actually expressing attitudes.

4. *Development of greater flexibility in role-taking.* The chief point of procedure here relates to the use made of the real speaking situations which have been selected. In almost any activity the roles of leader-follower are involved, with certain children playing predominately one role. Members of the group need to understand that in our culture one does not always lead nor should one always follow. Greater flexibility is developed by giving each person experience in playing the less familiar role, experience in the feelings of satisfaction and success from so doing.

Situations which involve asking permission, with the uncertainty of whether or not the request may be granted, offer possibilities for developing flexibility in behavior. The discussion may begin with comments about the frequency of this use of speech with parents, teachers, playmates. It is pointed out that while many times a request is granted, sometimes it is not. The children discuss how a refusal should be accepted. As they ask permission of different members of the group to do various things they get practice in responding appropriately to whatever response the other person makes. Fre-

---

[4] For more detailed explanation of these scientific principles the reader is referred to the sources on general semantics in the bibliography.

quently they gain insight into the consequences of their own behavior by seeing it in someone else. For instance one boy had frequently indulged in negative responses when a child who was collecting materials would ask him, "May I have it?" Usually he said, "No." One day when he was assuming the role of collecting materials and asked that question himself a child said, "No" to him. His expression changed, with increase of tension as if he were about to become angry. Then suddenly he smiled and said, "O.K." Later he said, "Gee, that's what I do lots of times." He did not give so many negative responses after that but when he did he smiled and made evident the fact that he was not serious about it.

Modifying Aspects of Speech Production

1. *Perceptual organization.* It has been pointed out that in the sort of learning involving motor skills some sort of perceptual organization takes place in the individual. He gets "a notion" of the patterning of the process he is attempting to perform, some awareness of difference between what he was doing and what he is trying to learn to do. If he had been saying "yeth" for "yes" he gets some awareness of difference between the muscular action of protruding the tongue and putting it in proximity to the alveolar ridge. A widely used method in speech therapy for developing such perceptual organization has been called "ear training." This involves spending long periods of time bombarding the child with sound stimuli before he even starts to try to produce such sounds in practice. One can easily make observations which call into question the validity of such a procedure, however. Children can very quickly tell the difference — usually after only two or three attempts — when the therapist produces two sounds, the one "normal," the other "defective." The real problem in discrimination lies in the individual's ability to tell the difference when HE is making the two sounds.[5] But before the child can get practice in this he must be able to produce both sounds. Thus an order of procedure which makes discrimination come first and motor production second appears to have little validity.

The practice of "ear training" appears to be based upon the assumption that parts of an organism function in and of themselves,

[5] Furthermore, in almost every case people learn to discriminate through a sense of kinesthesia before they can hear the difference.

as if perceptual organization came about from "training an ear." Granted that some clients have improved in ability to discriminate in their own performance through such procedure, it appears that such improvement must be postulated as resulting from other factors than the one consciously held.

A non-elementalistic, non-additive view of perceptual organization has been formulated by Meyers.[6] He points out that sensory, motor, associative functions are always inextricably bound up in responses of the organism, that what one sees or hears through sensory channels is always influenced by the motor patterns which have been developed. He says "We take to be 'real' that to which we have developed relatively adaptive behavior patterns of response." So it is that an individual who protrudes the tongue in making an "s" sound in "yes" will hear the sound in someone else as similar to the one he makes. Thus in changing the sensory aspect of behavior it is necessary to change also the motor aspect of behavior. There appear to be no clear cut additive steps, therefore, in teaching a child to make particular speech sounds. One can follow some sort of progression but the parts or steps need to be interrelated.

The therapist starts with a speech pattern in context, in a situation; an example is "Do you want one?" with the response "Yes." Attention is called to the response "yes"; to the "s" at the end: the way it sounds, the way it looks when someone says it, the way it feels when one makes it. Several attempts to produce it are made by various members in the group, some directions are given in the attempt to help a given person produce it. Some children will achieve that in a given lesson, some will not; but all will use the response, with whatever "s" sound represents his ability at the moment. As the children observe each other they learn to evaluate the attempts honestly and matter-of-factly, yet with comments tempered according to the ability of each: "I like that — that's what you're after"; "That's coming — you're getting the idea"; "That's fine for you today — we'll keep working on it." Thus the process of perceptual organization is promoted by procedures which combine emphasis upon the sensory, motor, associative (evaluative) aspects of behavior.

---

[6] Russell Meyers, M.D., "Perceptual Response and the Neurology of Abstraction," *Etc., A Review of General Semantics*, Spring, 1949, Vol. VI, No. 3.

2. *Order of presentation in teaching consonant sounds.* Older procedures followed a so-called "developmental" order, that is, those consonants which occurred first in the process of normal speech development were presented first in clinical teaching. There seems to be no valid reason, however, for supposing that the situation of a five-year-old child with delayed speech is the same as the situation of a child in his second year who is developing speech normally. Hence there seems to be no valid reason to suppose that such an order of presentation has importance as a clinical procedure. Of greater relevance it would seem would be considerations such as ease of learning for a particular child at a particular time or the needs of the group. It will be noticed in Part Two that the "th" sound as in "thank you" and the "v" sound in "have one" are presented early. These are relatively simple to produce; many children can make them normally already, and for those who cannot such material constitutes a first task at which they are most likely to succeed. Hence these sounds are useful in helping the children learn procedure for working on speech sounds. The "s" sound is usually presented next but for a different reason. It is more difficult to produce but because of its frequency in speech, changes in manner of producing that sound result in markedly improved intelligibility. Moreover, because it is so frequently distorted it represents a need in numbers of children in the group.

Clinical experience provides ample evidence that acquiring the ability to produce a number of consonant sounds is not an additive process. For example, a child who has had a number of sound substitutions and has had to work for some time on "th" and "s" sounds, will later learn to make "r" and "l" sounds quite rapidly even though he was unable to make them on early trials. The learning involved on such early sounds appears to facilitate later learning. A therapist need not feel anxious over spending ample time at first on a particular sound, just because he sees that the child has a long list to acquire.

3. *Phonetic characteristics of practice material.* The assumption that repetition per se constitutes the most important feature in motor learning has been criticized as lacking validity, yet this assumption appears to have had marked influence on traditional procedures in speech therapy. Material for practice in the form of word lists and

drill sentences has been loaded with many occurrences of a given speech sound. The procedures presented here call for speech responses which contain at first but *one* occurrence of a given sound. This is based upon the assumption that perceptual organization constitutes an important feature in learning, along with repeated experience in producing the motor response. The very fact that a child is to work on a particular sound means that its production is difficult for him. One occurrence of that sound in a response would appear to offer difficulty enough at first. Perceptual organization on the part of the child is facilitated by proceeding from the simple to the more complex, from what he can succeed with to what he will be better able to succeed with later. Thus for work on final "r" (i.e., in regions where that sound is used) "You're welcome" is preferable at first to "Where are you going" because the sound occurs only once. The repeated experience comes from using the one response with its one occurrence of the sound in question in a variety of situations, as previously described.

It is desirable that the speech pattern have phonetic simplicity in respect to other sound substitutions which the children may have. For example the response "For you" would be preferable to "You're welcome" since it does not contain "l" and "k" sounds which, if also defective, would cause the whole pattern to appear distorted. When a choice must be made, however, between a response that has phonetic simplicity and one that has the possibility of frequent and appropriate use in real activity, then the latter is chosen. For example, while "Thumb" is phonetically simpler to produce, it is discarded as a key response in favor of "Thank you," which can be made so much more meaningful in a real situation. Any distortion which may be present on the "k" sound is ignored for the time being in most cases.

4. *Practice on sub-parts.* Special work on a single sound needs to be done in many cases in this type of teaching as in others. But the way in which this is structured assumes importance: it is not done in isolation from a whole pattern or from the whole situation, but rather imbedded in context. For example, suppose that a child needs special help to get the "k" sound in the response "Thank you." The whole pattern is used first, then scrutinized carefully as it is said slowly; then just the "kee-you" syllable combination is practiced by

the group; then it is put back into the whole pattern; then the pattern is used again in the situation, even though that particular child may not yet be able to make it correctly. The order followed is whole — part — whole. Many children who show a delay in learning to produce a sound normally nevertheless are acquiring some perceptual organization, e.g., they give evidence of awareness of where the sound should occur in various responses, even though they cannot say it adequately, and later are able to put the correct sound in quite readily.

5. *Speech production for the child who stutters.* Special comment should be made in answer to the frequently asked question, "But what do you do about the child who stutters?" This will serve as an explicit summary of what has been expressed implicitly in both Parts One and Two. The point of view is held that the problem of stuttering is amenable to treatment by a speech therapist in a teaching situation, as are most other problems in speech; that the teaching situation should undertake to change behavior in its broadest aspects as well as in its details as needed: e.g., functional organization, social skills, mechanics of speech production. Relatively general agreement exists among workers in the field that stuttering represents a symptom of "emotional" conflict, that it occurs as a result of disturbances in interpersonal relationships; that treatment for it should be concerned with reducing conflicts along with the accompanying anxiety, with changing evaluations of self in relation to others, with developing social skills, with modifying mechanics of speech production in the direction of more acceptable patterns.

The fact that goals for a child who stutters are related more especially to modifying functional organization and developing social skills and less upon mechanics, in no way constitutes a problem of structuring therapy for him in the sort of group described here. In the first place the other children also have goals to reach in respect to functional organization and social skills. In the second place although some of them have goals also in respect to learning consonant sounds, the speech patterns which serve as material for such practice serve also as the instrument for modifying functional organization and developing social skills; hence no cleavage in class activity is required. In the third place the very ability of the child who stutters to demonstrate aspects of normal speech which some others cannot produce is utilized as an instrument for modifying his perception of himself or his speech problem. In the fourth place he too needs to work on mechanics of production, but — as in the case of the others too — to do it in a positive rather than a negative way. This means focusing upon desirable characteristics of speech: relatively slow rate, sufficient loudness to be heard easily, relatively little expenditure of force, grouping together words that belong together, blending sounds within a phrase, etc. What is being taught is "normal" speech, not "stuttering" or "cleft-palate" speech; hence it is possible for persons with various kinds of problems to have a common instruction. Different therapists have different opinions about the best techniques to use for details of speech production. This is true in respect to stuttering as well as other kinds of speech disorders. But these can be used within the therapeutic framework presented here. For example, the writers use the more general techniques of working on the speech characteristics just described; some workers use voluntary stuttering as one special technique, others use a process known as "the bounce," i.e., a controlled number of voluntary repetitions. Any of these can be utilized as a way of handling problems of mechanics for a particular child, as other members of the group are working on special techniques for specific aspects of their problems.

In the case of the young child who stutters, it is the belief of the writers that the question is not "Should he or should he not be enrolled in a group for speech therapy?" but rather "What kind of speech therapy should he — or any other child for that matter — have?" This book represents our effort at this date to formulate an answer.

Part Two

Illustrative Lessons in Group Therapy

INTRODUCTION

Procedures suggested in the lesson material contained in Part Two are intended to indicate broad direction rather than specific formulae. The detailed description at best can be considered only a framework within which the speech therapist will make adaptations, modifications, and inventions to meet the demands of her particular teaching situation. The resource material in itself has no intrinsic quality for insuring successful teaching. The value resides rather in the use the therapist makes of it, the extent to which she makes it come alive as she attempts to help children grow and develop.

The lessons for the primary and intermediate age levels are grouped into three divisions: Unit I. Developing the Therapeutic Relationship; Unit II. Acquiring Speaking Skills; Unit III. Increasing Facility in Use of Skills. This is done not to designate separate steps in the process but to emphasize three different aspects which characterize all phases of therapy.

The format of each lesson indicates the structure first in terms of the whole, i.e., interpersonal situations, then in terms of the parts, i.e., the speaking aspects growing out of such situations, the variety of particular speech patterns to be selected and used, the sounds to

71

be emphasized as needed, and such equipment as may implement the lesson.

The section in each lesson designated "Procedures" indicates ways of teaching; the section designated "Notes" presents ramifications and explanations of these particular procedures. Supplementary suggestions to further broaden or narrow the lesson for work on particular sounds follow most of the lessons. A summary of the plans precedes each section. An index of key responses for reference purposes is found at the conclusion of the first two sections in the primary and intermediate lessons (pages 219–220 and 378–380).

A similarity of speaking events and speech patterns forms the bases of the work for the three age levels, modified at the younger age levels by wider use of concrete materials, increased opportunity for motor activity; at the older age level by more group planning and somewhat more complex participation. Since the greatest share of speech therapy done in the elementary schools is at the primary level, and the next greatest at the intermediate level, the material is presented in this order. The pre-school material follows in briefer form, inasmuch as it parallels closely the previous work and is used somewhat less extensively. Suggested adaptations of these lessons in group therapy for work with an individual child conclude Part Two for the benefit of numbers of workers in the field who teach children on an individual basis.

Chapter 7

Primary
Illustrative Lessons

UNIT ONE

DEVELOPING THE THERAPEUTIC RELATIONSHIP

A. INTERPERSONAL SITUATIONS WITH THEIR SPEAKING ASPECTS

73

B. SUMMARY OF ACTIVITIES

C. SUMMARY OF SPEECH PATTERNS *

Lesson 1. "Hi . . . . (first names)"   "May I have it?"

"Is your name . . .?"   "For you."
"What is your name?"
                               "Thank you."
"Have one."   and others   77
"Have a . . . ."

Lesson 2. "Hi . . . . (first names)"

"Is your name . . .?"
"What is your name?"   "For you."

"Have one."   "The . . . ."
"Have a look."   "In the . . . ."
"May I have it?"   "That one."
"What do I (you)
   have?"   "Thank you." . . .   82

Lesson 3. "Hi . . . . (first names)"   "For you."

"Is your name . . .?"   "The . . . ."
"What is your name?"   "In the . . . ."
                               "That one."

"Have one."
"Have a . . . ."   "Thank you."
"May I have it?"   "With mine."
"What one do you
   have?"   "Come . . . ." . . .   88

Lesson 4. "Hi . . . . (first names)"   "The . . . ."
           "Have one."   "In the . . . ."
           "Have a . . . ."   "That one"
           "May I have a . . . .?"
           "May I have it?"   "Thank you."

* In referring to these responses it should be remembered that functional use
is considered here before phonetic accuracy.

"With mine."

"For you."

"I like your . . . ."   95

Lesson 5. "Hi . . . (first names)"   "For you."

"Will you come to

"Come in."   our party?"

"Thank you."   "It's on Thursday at

"Meet my friends."   two o'clock.

"This is . . . ."   "It will be in the
                                  lunch room."

"Have a chair." or

"Sit by me."   "I liked the party."

"Have a . . . ?"   "I had a good time."   102

"May I have a . . . ?"

D. SUMMARY OF EQUIPMENT

Unit I · Lesson 1

1. *Interpersonal Situations:* getting acquainted; exchanging toys

2. *Speaking Aspect of Situation:* exchanging greetings; obtaining information about names; requesting, distributing, acknowledging a toy

3. *Particular Speech Patterns:* "Hi . . . ."

   "Have one."

   "For you."

   First names

   "May I have one."

   "Thank you."

   "Is your name . . . ? "

   "What is your name? "

4. *Sounds Emphasized:* θ ð f v

5. *Equipment:* color cone (separate wooden discs of various colors mounted on one base) in large box

PROCEDURES	NOTES
THERAPIST: We often begin to get acquainted by finding out each other's names. Let's see if I know your names, and if you know mine. You will know some names better than I, and you will need to help me.	*Whatever responses children make are acceptable here. A child may make a verbal response, lower his head, or refuse to take a turn. He can be praised for listening, sitting quietly, learning one name. Another child, more ready, may be chosen early to set the pattern of asking each child a question. The teacher can expect and accept different degrees of participation.*

(*Enumerates children's names by asking,* Is your name . . . ? *or* What is your name?)

It's going to take time to learn everyone's name. How many of you know the name of the person sitting next to you? How many know the name of one other person? Let's say them slowly together.

You may have a turn now. Let me show you how. (*Turns to one child and says,* Is your name . . . ?) (*Turns to another child and says,* What is your name?) In this way I can talk to everyone here. Jack, you may do it first.

CHILD: (*Rising and going to each member of the group*) Is your name . . .? *or* What is your name?

THERAPIST: I liked the way Jack talked loudly enough so we could hear easily.

(*This activity can be continued until each child who wants to take part has had a turn.*)

It will be fun seeing these new friends each day. As you learn their names you will want to say "Hi" or "Hello" when you see them in the halls or on the playground or here in speech class. Like this: "Hi, Ann." One of you go to each boy and girl and show us. What will you do if you forget a name? That's right. We all forget names sometimes, and when we do we just ask, "What is your name?"

CHILD: Hi, Ann, *or* What is your name? Hi, Ann.

(*Continue until each child who wants to take part has had a turn.*)

THERAPIST: It's fun to get acquainted, isn't it? We'll do some more of this tomorrow.

I have something in the box. It's a surprise; you will want to have a look. After you have had a look in the box what can you say? That's right. Watch how I say it. "Thank you." When do you use "Thank you"?

On an even more simple level, one child may go around the group saying "Hi" to each one, who in turn responds with the same pattern, "Hi." A child with markedly delayed speech may be taken by the teacher to each group member. The children say "Hi," to this child even though he makes no verbal response. In this way he gradually acquires some idea of the two-way process in communication.

This lesson is structured to promote participation; to encourage one child talking directly to another. Phonetic accuracy need not be emphasized. It is structured to increase a child's confidence in his ability to use speech, increase perceptions of his own personal worth. Such goals will be furthered by the comments of the therapist directed toward praise, recognition of such qualities as smiling, looking at people, talking loudly enough to be heard, etc.

CHILDREN:* When mother bakes a cake, ties my shoe, gives me a penny. When my teacher reads me a story, gives me paints or crayons, plays the piano for me, etc.

This discussion gives the therapist opportunity to observe each child's facility in the use of speech as a social tool, as well as sounds that may be defective.

THERAPIST: Yes, you use it in many ways. Listen to the way I say it. "Thank you." Do you notice that my tongue comes out a little when I start? "Thank you." Try the sound by itself. "θ."

CHILD: "θ"

THERAPIST: Now let's say "Thank you."

CHILDREN: (*Each one has a turn.*) Thank you.

THERAPIST: (*Extending the box which the child can open.*) "Have a look."

CHILD: Thank you.

(*Continue until each child has looked in the box.*)

THERAPIST: I'll take the color cone out now, and you may each have one part of it. Watch what I say as I give it to you. "Have one." That's easy to say. Look at me again while I say it. Do you see how I tuck my lower lip under my upper teeth? Let's practice it first.

While there are many speech patterns which could be used in extending the box, the therapist, by using "Have a look," controls the response, using it numerous times. In later lessons as the children initiate the activity, they may be guided to use other patterns as "Do you want to see?" "Look in," etc.

CHILD: Have one. (*Each child has a turn.*)

THERAPIST: (*Comments as each child gives responses*) Ann, I liked that. Jimmie,

* The term "children" as it is used throughout these lessons designates a number of children in the group responding one by one.

let's try it again.　Watch me first.　That's coming better.

Roger, you may pass out the discs so that everyone gets to hold one.　What will you say when you do it?

CHILD: (*Distributing the discs*)　Have one, *or* For you.

CHILDREN: (*Acknowledging the disc*) Thank you.

THERAPIST: Kathie, you may collect the discs.　It will be fun putting them on the stick.

The therapist will want to begin patterning the needs of children in these early lessons, i.e., a need for belongingness, participation, recognition, permissiveness, success, etc.

CHILD: (*Extending base of cone while each child in the group replaces a disc, saying,* "Have one." *As each group member adds a disc to the cone she acknowledges it.*) Thank you.

She * needs to establish the feeling in each child that he is liked by the therapist, that there are many things he can do well, and that she is there to help him.

THERAPIST: (*Interrupting after first or second turn*)　Watch Kathie as she replies "Thank you" to you.　She is remembering to put her tongue out just a little.

THERAPIST: What things have you worked on today in speech?

CHILDREN: Getting acquainted; saying "Hi," "Have one," "May I have one?" and "Thank you."

Supplementary Suggestions

The situations which are suggested in this first lesson may serve as the basis for meeting various individual needs as developing a feeling

* For purposes of simplicity and clarity in language structure the therapist is designated by the pronoun "she," the child by the pronoun "he."

of belongingness, encouraging participation, giving recognition, etc. Children who have particular speech needs other than those indicated in this lesson do not necessarily have to begin working on sounds immediately since their first classes are conceived of as a readiness period for such work . . . a time in which they become aware of some of their abilities in speech, as well as a time for developing a sense of satisfaction through participating in the experiences provided.

It is understood that a child may come into speech class with some anxieties and insecurities concerning this new experience. This is especially true if he is entering speech class at the same time he is making a new adjustment in a classroom to a different teacher and a strange group of boys and girls.

The therapist needs to recognize and accept behavior indicating such feelings. The child will need warmth and support, reassurance, emphasis on assets, not stressing of liabilities. If he does not volunteer to enter into these first lessons he should not be forced or penalized, but given time to be more ready to take part. She may take his turn with him for a time, or let another child help him.

One child may come with excessively high levels of aspiration determined to do everything "perfectly," be easily upset when he does not meet his own standards. The therapist will want to guide him in achieving satisfaction by doing better than he was, getting a response more adequately than he did previously. She will want to praise him for willingness to take his turn, listen to others, etc. She may help him understand that everyone in the class needs assistance from time to time, that everyone has some things he can do more capably than others, and thereby allow him to accept a less high standard of performance.

Another child with an excessively low level of aspiration is undoubtedly struggling with feelings of inadequacy and inferiority, feelings that there is no use in trying, that he is not liked, not wanted, etc. Here the therapist can begin by noticing areas in which he merits praise, even for such a simple task as arranging the chairs, helping her carry materials. She may see that he receives recognition from the group for taking part in any limited way that is possible for him at this stage of his development. She may structure his turn so he is able to succeed and from that guide him in increasing perceptions of his own personal worth.

Unit I · Lesson 2

1. *Interpersonal Situations:* getting acquainted; exchanging toys

2. *Speaking Aspect of Situations:* exchanging greetings; obtaining information about names; requesting, distributing, acknowledging a toy

3. *Particular Speech Patterns:* "Hi . . . (first names)" "Have one."
   "Have a look."
   "Is your name . . . ?" "May I have one?"
   "What is your name?" "What do I have?"

   "For you." "The . . . ."
   "In the . . . ."
   "That one."

4. *Sounds Emphasized:* θ ð **f** **v**
   "Thank you."

5. *Equipment:* dolly pull (a small wagon with eight or ten blocks that can be removed) in a large box

---

PROCEDURES	NOTES
THERAPIST: Let's begin by seeing how many people you know by name. You can do it in two ways, asking, "Is your name . . . ?" or "What is your name?" Ann, you may have the first turn.	*Use of this activity also encourages both participation and functional speech. Phonetic accuracy can be promoted where children are ready for it. A child with delayed speech or very distorted speech may be encouraged to get proper over-all syllabification, if he is ready. Sounds may then be stressed later for him.*
CHILDREN: (*Several take a turn going to each member in the group.*) Is your name . . .? or What is your name?	
THERAPIST: It will be fun now to say "Hi" to the children. Who would like to do it first? I'm glad you want a turn today, Kenny. Let's wait until everyone is listening and watching.	*In an instance like this, the therapist may utilize the child's volunteering as a basis for warm, sincere praise. The child's willingness to take part may give him a place in the group even though his speech is inadequate.*
CHILD: (*Going to one group member, addressing him, accepting a reply, moving on to another.*) Hi.	

82

THERAPIST: Now you may choose some-
ne else to do it. (*In the process of choos-
ng the teacher can guide choices by saying,
"Ann has had a turn; let's pick someone
lse." Or, "Let's see, I don't think Roger
r Kathie has had a turn.")*

THERAPIST: You have had fun greeting
riends. Today I have a different sur-
rise in the box for you. You may each
ave a look. Do you remember what you
ay when you get a turn to look in the
ox? Yes. "Thank you." Remember
ast time Ann said it loudly enough for us
o hear, Jimmie smiled, Mary looked
ight at us when she said it. Kathie
vatched the "θ." You can't remember
o do all those things, but we can help
ou with one. Let's practice it now.
Listen to me first. Watch me. "Thank
ou."

CHILDREN: (*Each has a turn and gets indi-
idual help from the teacher as needed.*)
Thank you.

THERAPIST: I'm going to give each of
ou a look because you are wondering
vhat I have in the box. I'm going to
give you a look for another reason, too.
t will give you a chance to use "Thank
ou," saying it with your tongue coming
ut just a little as you have been prac-
icing. (*Extends box to each child indi-
idually.*) "Have a look."

CHILDREN: Thank you.

THERAPIST: (*When she comes to a child
vho has been having some difficulty with*

*The structure of these lessons
is similar in many respects.
There is security for children
in a patterned routine. It is
important, also, for children
to have many experiences using a few simple speech patterns in similar situations.*

*Here the therapist should
mention some positive asset
of each child thus promoting
his sense of personal worth,
ability to perform certain
tasks, etc.*

*In the pattern "Thank you"
particular attention is paid
to the "θ." Some children
will need help and be ready
for use of the medial "k."*

this response she may say, I'm going to wait just a minute so you can get set to make that "θ" right the first time. Are you ready? Watch me. "Thank you." Try it. "Thank you." Now, "Have a look.")

CHILD: Thank you.

THERAPIST: Fine; you can do that better than you could yesterday. Make it again for Ann. Now for Joe. (*Turning to the group*) Shall we clap for Kenny?

Clapping is a way of expressing approval which children enjoy giving as well as getting. It serves to keep group members a part of each activity, and gives individual children recognition from their peers. This promotes group belongingness, feelings of success, etc.

THERAPIST: Now let's take the wagon out of the box. There are many parts to this wagon. They come off. You may have one if you can hold it quietly in your lap. Jean, you are making "have" better than you were. Try it for practice. Each of you show her how you say it. She will give you a piece from the wagon saying "Have one." What will you reply?

CHILDREN: Thank you.

CHILD: (*Passing out parts of wagon*) Have one.

OTHER CHILDREN: (*Individually acknowledging receipt of a part*) Thank you.

In some instances a child may be able to produce the "v" more easily in "have a" than in "have one." In such cases the pattern used may be "Have a piece." "Have it" is another possibility.

THERAPIST: (*Interrupting*) Joe, I think you can do better when you say "Thank you." Let me help you. Watch. "Thank you." That's fine. Jean, give Joe another chance.

THERAPIST: Now that you each have a part of the wagon, you can have fun putting it back together again. While Kenny holds the wagon you may put your part back on, saying to him "Have one." Practice it first. What will he say to you? "Thank you." Show us you can do that, Kenny.

CHILDREN: (*Replacing parts of wagon*) Have one.

CHILD: (*Accepting parts*) Thank you.

THERAPIST: (*Interrupting*) I believe Roger should keep his piece a little longer. He has shown us before that he can say "Have one" better. You go back to him after you have given Kathie a turn.

Even when children are carrying on the activity the therapist should follow it closely, giving help where indicated. In this instance she does not penalize the child, merely gives him some help and another opportunity to take part.

THERAPIST: Now I have all the parts of the wagon here. Watch. As I put each part on the table, I will tell you the name of the color: "The red one," "The yellow one," etc. (*If many of the children have difficulty discriminating colors, the therapist may use "The big one" and "The little one" to designate the different parts.*) When mother says, "What do you have in that bag, you may say, "The wieners you sent for." If the teacher asks, "What book do you have?" you may reply, "The one about Jim and Judy." When else do you use "the"?

The therapist should place the object on the table, allow time for the children to look at it, then say the pattern "the red one" as the children's attention is focused on what she is saying, not on the object.

CHILDREN: The ball and bat; The boy; The dog, etc.

THERAPIST: Do you notice the word "the" begins something like "thank you." See that your tongue comes out a little when you say it. Watch "the." You use the word often. You've been

It is probably unnecessary to differentiate between the voiced and unvoiced sound except through giving the pattern, guiding the child to imitate it.

getting the sound well in "Thank you."
Let's each one try saying "the." Watch
me. My tongue comes out just a little.
"The." Now you do it.

CHILD: (*Each child has a turn saying "the";
therapist gives individual help as needed*)

THERAPIST: (*Picking up a red block*)
When I ask "What do I have?" you will
answer, "The red one."; (*picking up a
blue block*) What do I have, Ann? "The
blue one." (*Each child gets a turn to
respond, and is held for the best sound he is
capable of making at the present time. One
child who needs experience giving a longer
response or working on the "v" sound may
substitute for the teacher and lead the activity,
asking the question "What do I have?"*)

*Children gain experience here
in shift of role, sometimes
leading an activity, directing
a question; other times following the activity, answering a question, children who
want to lead all the time
need to be guided to follow
part of the time. Children
who are reluctant to lead need
to be encouraged to do so.*

THERAPIST: You liked holding the parts
of the wagon. You may do it again, but
this time you choose the part you want,
and ask for it this way: "May I have a
red one?" What do you have to watch
when you ask? Yes, the "v" in "Have
a." For practice, each of you ask for the
red one. If you remember to tuck your
lower lip under your teeth then you will
each get a turn asking for whatever part
you'd like. If someone else gets your
favorite part, you may ask him instead
of me for it.

CHILDREN: May I have a red one? (*Each
child gets turn practicing. The therapist
gives individual help where indicated.*)

*The therapist should take
care here that the child is
blending "v" in "have a. . . ."*

THERAPIST: Each of you is holding a part
of the wagon again. When you put it
back this time, you will get practice using

*If a child is reluctant to re-
linquish his piece he should
have freedom to hold it longer.*

that new word "the" differently. Listen. I'm going to put mine "in the wagon." I will say it again: "In the wagon." Hear the word you have been working on. Each of you try it first.

As he becomes more secure he will have less reason to retain it, and will also learn in order for group activities to go on he will want to follow actions of others.

CHILDREN: (*Each has a turn. Therapist gives help as indicated.*) In the wagon.

THERAPIST: Where will you put yours, Roger?

CHILDREN: (*Each one replies, then replaces part in the wagon*) In the wagon.

(*If children are acquiring use of this sound fairly easily the therapist may want to expand responses to use of "that one" by asking the question "Which one do you want?" to which the child points to one piece and says "that one." This may be introduced in a way similar to the one used for "the. . . ."*)

Here the therapist will accept from each child the response he is capable of and ready to make. One child may merit praise for merely taking his turn, placing the part in the wagon; another for using four syllables; another for smiling; a fourth for including the "ð" sound.

THERAPIST: What have you had fun working on today? What things are you saying better than you were? Let's see, all of you used "Thank you" several times; some of you are using the "θ" sound now in it. Each of you used "the" in two ways: some of you with the sound "ð." And you can say "Have one," too. In addition I noticed that Roger sat in his chair today without touching the person next to him. That's hard for him to do, and I'm proud of him. Mary took her turn each time. Jean watched the other boys and girls when they had a turn.

The therapist needs to begin developing awareness in the child of his job in speech class regarding both what speech responses he uses adequately under guidance and the responses on which he requires help and practice. At first she will point this out rather specifically at the conclusion of each lesson. Later the children will do more of it themselves.

Unit I · Lesson 3

1. *Interpersonal Situations:* welcoming a friend; exchanging toys; guessing

2. *Speaking Aspect of Situations:* exchanging greetings; requesting, distributing, acknowledging a toy; asking and answering questions

3. *Particular Speech Patterns:* "Hi ... (first names)"

"Is your name ...?"
"What is your name?"

"Come."

"Have one."
"Have a look."
"May I have one?"
"What one do you have?"

"For you."

"The ...."
"In the ...."
"That one."
"Thank you."
"With mine."

4. *Sounds Emphasized:* θ ð f v

5. *Equipment:* small colored cubes in box

PROCEDURES	NOTES

THERAPIST: You have been coming to speech class for several days. You know the names of some of the other boys and girls here. You know how to greet them. Doesn't it make you feel good when someone says "Hi" to you? You like saying "Hi" to others, too.

I have noticed that when Nancy says "Hi" she smiles. When Jimmie says "Hi" he looks right at you. When Marilyn says "Hi" she says it loudly enough for you to hear. Jack said "Hi" to me in the hall upstairs, and waited for me to answer before he went into his room. I liked that.

Legitimate, sincere praise should constitute an integral part of each lesson. It contributes to developing a child's sense of confidence, belongingness; makes him better able to profit from help; gives him status in the group.

88

Karen told me she wanted to be first today to tell you "Hi." Watch and listen as she does it. See what you like about the way she does it.

CHILD: Hi. . . .

THERAPIST: What did you like?

CHILDREN: She knew everyone's name but Jimmie's and she asked him; she smiled at me; she waited for my answer; etc.

THERAPIST: (*May designate other children for a turn, or have children choose the one to follow. She will encourage similar comments regarding specific phases of the speech performance.*) Each one of you sounded differently as you said "Hi." Who said it somewhat faster? somewhat slower? Whose voice was higher? lower? Whose speech was louder? softer? Whose speech was easy to understand? not as easy? Everyone's speech is different in some ways from everyone else's. Your teacher and I do not talk exactly alike. Your mothers do not all sound the same. Neither do your two brothers.

You do not come to speech class to learn to talk exactly like everyone else, but you do come to learn to talk better in some way.

Let's listen as each of you count to eight. I will help you. Some things you say just like everyone else. Some things you say differently enough that you need some help. Can you tell where?

The praise which the therapist gives in specific terms helps set standards which the children can go by later in evaluating each other's speech. They can be encouraged to begin right now.

Notice that values of "good" or "bad" are not included here, but rather the beginning of a concept of "similarities" and "differences."

(Therapist calls attention to something she likes as each child counts — one child smiling, etc. She may go on to specify one child putting his tongue out slightly on "three," another saying "four" with his lower lip tucked under his upper teeth, a third child saying "six" and "seven" with his tongue behind his teeth, etc.)

This is done largely to give additional recognition to each child for something he says well. It also serves to begin developing the children's awareness of likenesses and differences in speech.

I have a new surprise in the box for you today. Can you guess what it may be?

CHILDREN: *(Individually)* Colored wheels? A wagon? Candy?

THERAPIST: You were close, but you didn't guess it. Nancy, suppose you show each boy and girl what the box has in it, first saying, "Have a look." You can say "have a" easily if you take it slowly and watch. Practice it first. "Have a look." *(Turning to other children)* What will you say when Nancy gives you a look?

The response "Have a look" has been used previously, in some instances for communication, in others for emphasis on the "v." It can also be emphasized for a child needing work on the "l."

CHILDREN: Thank you. *(Each one has a turn, with individual help where indicated.)*

CHILD: *(Opening the box and showing the contents to one child at a time)* Have a look.

CHILD: Thank you.

Since the children are familiar with the procedure of looking in the box, replying with "Thank you" the therapist first gives them practice on the response, pointing out parts for them to watch, parts they do well. This keeps the work speech centered.

THERAPIST: There are lots of blocks in the box. There are enough for you to have four or five if you watch your speech when it is your turn; if you listen when someone else is having a turn.

Jean, you may give each one a block,

The therapist may vary this

saying "Have one," this way. What will you say when she gives you a block? (*Turning to other children*) Thank you.

CHILD: (*Distributing blocks*) Have one, or Have a block.

CHILD: Thank you.

THERAPIST: (*May interrupt to help a child make the response correctly, comment regarding a correct response, etc.*)

There are more blocks for you here. You may have another by asking for it this way. "May I have it?" What is easy for you there? What do you need to watch? Try it first.

CHILDREN: (*Each having a turn*) May I have it?

CHILD: May I have it? (*Each child then requests a block from another child or therapist.*)

THERAPIST or CHILD: Yes, *or* Here. (*Possibly* "All right.")

CHILD: Thank you.

THERAPIST: Look at the blocks I have here. "The red one." "The green one." "The blue one." Watch me while I say that again. Notice that my tongue comes out on "the." What do I have?

CHILD: The red one. (*Continue until each child has answered, therapist giving help where needed.*)

procedure sometimes giving the leader his choice in which colors to distribute, other times allowing the child to designate the color he would like. A child may not like the color he is given, and should be free to request another. If this slows down the work of the group too much, the therapist may place limits on it.

If children find the "v" and "ð" confusing, they need not be attempted in the same lesson, but the "ð" may be worked on at a later time. Usually, if the two sounds are worked on in separate parts of the same lesson, little difficulty is encountered.

THERAPIST: You are holding two blocks. Put one under your chair. Hold one in your hand, but cover it. See if you can tell me which one you have in your hand remembering how to say "the. . . ." — What one do you have?

CHILD: The. . . .

THERAPIST: Since I still have more blocks here, you may have another one by telling me which one you want — "the red one," "the green one," etc.

THERAPIST: What one do you want?

CHILD: The . . . one. (*Continue until each child acquires another block.*)

THERAPIST: On the table here I have three blocks that belong to me, and three that do not. Watch where I put the ones that are not mine. Listen to what I say. "With mine." I will do it again. "With mine." "With" has a sound in it something like "Thank you." Try "with mine."

CHILDREN: (*Individually*) With mine.

THERAPIST: Now say "with." Now "with mine." (*Children each have a turn saying this, therapist giving individual help where needed.*)

THERAPIST: Now you are ready to get another block. Where will you put it?

CHILD: With mine.

THERAPIST: What have you had fun doing today?

These variations of the same activity provide ways of meeting individual needs: (a) The child who shows stuttering symptoms may use any of the phrases suggested for purposes of adopting a somewhat slower rate, pausing between phrases, blending within a phrase, reduction of force, etc.; (b) Child with symptoms of delayed speech may simply hand out articles, or accept one given him without vocalizing. The therapist may repeat the appropriate speech responses for him, or call his attention to ways other children use speech in this connection. At first any vocalization is accepted and praised. Later particular sounds can be encouraged.

CHILD: Saying "Hi" to people; listening to ways in which our speech is different; working on "Have one," "Have a look," "May I have one?" "The red one," "In the box," "Thank you" and "With mine."

Supplementary Suggestions

THERAPIST: Watch where I'm going to put one of my blocks. Now listen as I tell you where I put it — "In the box." What part of that is easy for you? What part do you have to watch carefully? Try saying it.

CHILD: In the box. (*Children each have turn saying this, therapist giving individual help where needed.*)

THERAPIST: Where will you put one block?

CHILD: In the box.

Here, the therapist would not correct the child for errors in making the "k" or "s" if he is just acquiring correct use of the "ð" sound. Some children can be guided to include them, however, just by imitating the pattern set for them.

THERAPIST: (*Comments after various ones have taken turn*) I liked the way Jimmie stopped a minute before he said that to make sure he would say "the" the new way he is working on. I liked the way Kenny said it a little louder this time. I liked the way Jean took her turn, etc.

(*If use of "ð" is becoming easier a similar procedure may be employed in setting up the response "that one"*)

THERAPIST: What block will you put in the box?

CHILD: That one.

Such responses as "up," "on top," or "down" may be substituted for "in the box" if some children in the group need work on the plosives. These responses are functionally complete as are the patterns "Come" and "Go" for the child with delayed speech, as well.

THERAPIST: Mary, I believe that word "come" which you say differently from the other boys and girls you can say better with some help. Jean, show her how you say it. Jimmie, Jack, Kenny. . . . Listen to me, and watch. "C . . . ome." Now you try it.

CHILD: Come.

THERAPIST: Mary, choose the people to "Come" to the door, this way. "Come, Jean." Think each time before you begin.

CHILD: C . . . ome, Jack. (*Continue until she has designated each child who is to come to the door.*)

The responses on this page may not all be utilized in one lesson. The therapist may decide on one or two she is going to establish, such as "up" and "down." She may take a group of blocks herself, put them "up" (on the box) or "down" (in the box) one at a time, slowly saying the pattern after she has placed a block. She may then hold a block, ask a child "Where shall I put it?" and follow his direction of "up" or "down." She may give a block to a child asking him
"Where will you put it?" When the children become familiar with the two responses to be used, as well as the activity, the teacher may give individual help where indicated on particular sound elements, then give the children opportunity both to answer the question and participate by dropping the block in a box. In the early lessons the children make similar responses; later on each child gains facility in using patterns on which he is working whenever it is appropriate.

Unit I · Lesson 4

1. *Interpersonal Situations:* welcoming a friend; exchanging toys; expressing appreciation

2. *Speaking Aspect of Situation:* giving greetings; requesting, distributing, acknowledging a toy; giving and receiving a compliment

3. *Particular Speech Patterns:* "Hi .... (first names)   "The ...."
                             "Have one."   "In the ...."
                             "Have a look."   "That one."
                             "May I have one? "   "Thank you."
                             "What one do you have? "   "With mine."

                             "For you."

4. *Sounds Emphasized:*   f   v   θ   ð

5. *Equipment:* several coins such as pennies, nickels, dimes; coin purses.

PROCEDURES	NOTES
THERAPIST: It is easy for most of you now to tell your friends here in class "Hi," or "Hello." Nearly everyone has had a turn doing it. Mary, I'm going to take your hand and help you today as you go around saying "Hi" to the boys and girls. That will be fun for you, and to make it even easier you may just say "Hi" and not worry about names since this is your first turn. (*Turning to other children*) You know Mary's name, though, and you will want to say "Hi, Mary," to her. That will help show her how it is done.	*The child who tends to withdraw needs to be encouraged and helped to participate, not forced into it. As the therapist takes this child with her she is assisting the little girl in being a part of an interpersonal situation, relating to other children. Their responses to her, friendly and pleased, will serve to reduce the child's fears and anxieties toward her peers, make it more possible for her to feel secure with them.*

CHILD: (*Going to each child in the group*) Hi.

CHILDREN: Hi, Mary.

THERAPIST: Didn't you like the way Mary looked at each of you when she said "Hi"?

95

You often need to ask your mother, daddy, or teacher for something, don't you? What do you say if you want a blue crayon? a bread and jelly sandwich? an ice cream cone? some money?

CHILDREN: I need a blue crayon. I'm hungry for a sandwich. I'd like an ice cream cone. May I have a nickel?

THERAPIST: "May I have . . .?" is one way of asking. We are going to work on that today. You will have fun asking for what I have in the box. What do you suppose is there this time?

CHILDREN: Wagon? Discs? Blocks?

THERAPIST: You didn't quite guess it. Nancy, you show the boys and girls again how well you said "Have a look" when you had a turn to show them what was in the box. Say it for them again. I liked the way you tucked your lip under your teeth. Jimmie, see if you can say it, too, well enough to take the box around today. Wait, and watch how I do it first. "Have a look."

CHILD: Have a look.

THERAPIST: Say it three more times to make sure of it.

THERAPIST: (*Turning to children*) What will you say when Jimmie gives you a look?

CHILDREN: Thank you. (*Each one has a turn with therapist giving individual help where needed.*)

Repeated experience here helps the child gain awareness of the pattern, centers his attention on the speech to be used in the activity.

CHILD: (*Opening the box and showing the contents to one child at a time*)   Have a look.

CHILDREN: (*Individually*)   Thank you.

THERAPIST: You will have a good time today asking for, getting, and giving away the money in the box. The money belongs to me and I use it in other classes, too. So you will take good care of it, I know. There is enough here for you to have several coins if you watch your speech when it is your turn, and listen when someone else is having a turn.

Often at a party you pass cookies, or something cool to drink to your guests. Sometimes mother may let you pass around napkins, or sandwiches. When you do you often say pleasantly to your visitors, "Have one," or "Have a napkin." Jack, you may give each one here a coin now in something of the same way. "Have one." (*Turning to other children*) What will you say when he gives you some money? "Thank you."

This response represents one which the child has frequent occasion to use in his classroom and at home. However, use as made of it here in the immediate present is a situation real to the child.

CHILD: (*Distributing coins*) Have one, *or* Have a . . .

CHILDREN: Thank you.

THERAPIST: Jack, you put your new sound in four times without any help from me. I liked that. Everyone of you said "Thank you," carefully, just as it should be said.

A child may refuse to answer "Thank you," or make little attempt to include the new sound. The teacher will be guided by her understanding of the child's dynamics in handling such a situation.

He may have been held to rigid standards of performance and have a great need at the moment for permissiveness to "do it wrong." He may feel insecure, wanting the therapist to like him, not sure she does, and be testing her to see if he can keep her love even though doing something of which she will not approve. Likewise he may be testing his relations with one or several members in the group.

Whether the therapist chooses to ignore the behavior, accept it, or suggest the child's doing differently she will be careful not to reject him, label his behavior "bad" or punish him.

As the child grows in his feelings of security and belongingness he will be more ready to be guided in acceptable forms of behavior, and will learn to act in terms of consequences for himself and the group.

(Another child or two may distribute coins in similar fashion.)

THERAPIST: Do you notice how quietly June is keeping her money in her hand? When she holds it like that it isn't so apt to slip to the floor. It also makes it easier for us to hear the person who is talking. See if you can hold your money quietly, too.

Small coin purses are sometimes useful here and make it more possible for the children to take care of the coins as they get several.

Sometimes when you are playing with a friend you give one toy to your friend to play with. If you have two pennies to spend, you may give him one. If I need a penny to buy a post card, and have no change, I may ask a friend for one penny, this way: "May I have it?" I think I will ask Kathie that way.

THERAPIST: *(Looking at the child's coins, pointing to one)* Kathie, may I have it?

CHILD: Yes.

THERAPIST: Thank you.

THERAPIST: Kathie, let's see how you might ask for one.

CHILD: May I have it.

THERAPIST: Try it again.   Watch me

Here the therapist should "set the pattern" slowly. Children should have attention called to the way "have" looks and sounds. This basic technique of the teacher's performing an activity, waiting until the child is watching her face, then saying it, has many values in speech therapy: slowing the tempo for a child who needs to slow his rate in order to include a sound, speak with less jerkiness, force, etc.; giving visual as well as auditory patterns; keeping child's attention centered, etc. It promotes eye contact in communication, as well. Children also soon begin to wait until others are watching before speaking.

first. Be sure and put that new sound in.
"May I have it?" That was better.
Make it three times, and then you may
have a turn requesting one coin from each
boy and girl.

CHILD: May I have it?

CHILDREN: Yes.

*(One child may reply "no" to the request.
The therapist should accept the "no" by
such comments as:* "Sometimes when
someone asks you for money, you can't
give it away, or you may not want to, or
you may have a special use for it. You
may say "no" to Kathie if it seems best
to you to do so. Then you will probably
want to give it to the next person who
asks for it. And, of course, some of you
will want to give Kathie a coin because
then soon you will have a turn; also,
everyone is to get more money later.

*The child should feel some
freedom to use the response
"no," refuse a request occasionally. The therapist
will need to set some limits,
however, as saying "no"
twice, and then saying "yes,"
or suggesting that when he
gives a coin to someone who
asks for it, then he will get
the next turn, etc.*

*(Other procedures and responses may be
utilized here — distributing the coins:*
"Have one," *and* "Thank you"; *requesting a coin:* "May I have it?"; *enumerating
the coins:* "the dime," "the penny"; *putting the coins together:* "with mine"; *putting the coins away:* "in the box"; *indicating a specific coin:* "that one.")

THERAPIST: You have put all the coins in
the box and I have told you "Thank you"
for taking such good care of the money.
I noticed that you remembered to say
"Thank you" each time someone gave
you some money, too.

There is another time when you use

*As these responses are used
the therapist will begin to
develop different standards
for individual children. She
may on certain occasions
withhold a coin, for instance,
if a child who is now using
"have" with a fair degree of
ease doesn't use it when he
requests a coin. There should
be no thought of "punish-
ment" but rather suggestion
such as, "You need some
help on that. I will come
back to you in a minute.
Perhaps you can surprise me
and get it the first time."
Other children may receive
the coin on the basis of having
asked for it slowly, imitating*

"Thank you." Sometimes Mother tells you she likes the way you hung up your coat, or helped with the dishes. Your teacher may tell you she likes your pretty pink dress, or your new brown shoes. Each time someone tells you something that makes you feel good, what do you usually say? That's right. "Thank you." You say it very well now. I'm going to tell each of you something I like. How will you reply?

THERAPIST: Jimmie, I like the big pocket in your jeans.

CHILD: Thank you.

THERAPIST: Notice how many things the children are wearing that you like. Telling someone what you like is often called a compliment. Can you give a compliment to two people?

CHILD: I like your blue bows.

CHILD: Thank you.

CHILD: I like the cowboy picture on your sweater.

CHILD: Thank you.

THERAPIST: You give compliments because they make others feel good, and because sometimes you like to receive a compliment, too.

(*Continue until each child has received one compliment.*)

THERAPIST: What have you worked on in speech class today?

over-all syllabification, etc.

One child who may find the production of a sound especially difficult may begin to become aware of differences in his former sound and the new one he is striving to acquire before he can actually produce it within normal range. As he begins to develop an awareness of phrases in which he should incorporate that sound, as he uses the phrases functionally incorporating the sound as well as he is able to at this stage, he becomes more ready for the final stages of incorporating the correct sound automatically. This might be true, for instance, in the "k" in "Thank you," the "l" in "I like," the "k" in "Come," the "r" in some of the patterns suggested in ensuing lessons. Of great importance also is the therapist's utilization of particular abilities the child has along with recognition of difficulties he is encountering.

CHILDREN: Saying "Hi," asking for money.

THERAPIST: In what ways did you ask for money?

CHILD: "May I have it?" or when you asked "What do you want?" we said "The penny," or someone passed the money out saying, "Have one."

THERAPIST: What did you say when you got some money?

CHILD: Thank you.

THERAPIST: When else did you use "Thank you"?

CHILD: When someone gave us a compliment.

THERAPIST: Perhaps you can find someone else today to whom you may give a compliment and if someone compliments you, remember to use "Thank you."

Compliments serve a valuable means-end in speech therapy, helping the child modify perceptions of self when someone notices his jeans, his shoes, his smile; helping him modify perceptions of his environment as "I guess they like me if they like my belt"; satisfying needs for being noticed, liked, recognized; promoting interrelatedness as he in turn can compliment others.

Unit I · Lesson 5

1. *Interpersonal Situation:* giving a party

2. *Speaking Aspects of Situation:* exchanging greetings; making introductions; issuing invitations; passing and accepting refreshments; leave-taking

3. *Particular Speech Patterns:* "Hi . . . . (first names)."   "Have a chair," or
                                                               "Sit by me."
      "Come in."
                                                           "Have one."
      "Thank you."   "May I have one?"

      "Meet my friends."   "For you."
      "This is . . . ."

4. *Sounds Emphasized:*   f   v   θ   k

5. *Equipment:* straws, napkins, paper cups, fruit juice; tray, napkins, spoons, dixie cups; milk, graham crackers

---

PROCEDURES	NOTES

THERAPIST: (*Having arranged the chairs fairly close to and facing the door*) When someone knocks at the door, you often go to the door, open it, and greet the person who is standing there. If you are having a party, the people who knock will be coming to your party as a rule, and you will invite them in. Jimmie, you go outside the door, knock, and I will show you how it is done.

CHILD: (*Goes outside the door, and knocks.*)

THERAPIST: (*Walking to the door and opening it*) Hi, Jimmie.

CHILD: Hi, Miss . . . .

THERAPIST: Come in.

A party provides opportunity for learning simple social patterns; winning acceptance and support from those invited; shift in roles as preparing refreshments, answering the door, giving invitations; modifying certain unsocial adjustive techniques into behavior acceptable at a party.

These speech responses should be set up carefully, patterned very simply, with more emphasis on their use than on phonetic accuracy, although the latter should be encouraged whenever the children are ready for it.

Two or three lessons may be thought of as preparation for the party. If more than this the children are apt to lose

CHILD: Thank you.

THERAPIST: Each of us said two things. What were they? Yes, we each said "Hi." I said, "Come in," and Jimmie said, "Thank you." Let's practice those for a moment, and then you may each have a turn, both going outside the door and knocking, and greeting someone at the door.

CHILDREN: Come in; Thank you.

THERAPIST: "Thank you" is fairly easy for you now. Jack, what do you have to watch when you say it? Each of you say it for Jack. "Come in" is one Mary has done some work on. Most of you say it with a "k" sound that isn't different. Say "Come in" for Mary. Now you try it, Mary. See if you can say it carefully three times so that it sounds all right to us.

Now you will practice knocking at the door and being greeted. (*This should be done until each child has had several turns.*)

After your friend comes to your party, you will want to see that he meets your friends. In two days you are going to have a small party here and each of you may invite a friend. This will help you know what to do on the day you have guests. I will show you first.

(*To child after he has knocked at the door and been greeted*) "Meet my friends." "This is . . . ." (*Continue until he has been introduced to each child.*)

That will be fun to do because you know

interest, lose a sense of relationship between what they are working on and its application in the real event. However, the preparatory lessons should involve real doing as well. For instance, one child actually knocking on door, another answering it, etc.

The goals of this party situation are reduction of anxiety, building self-confidence, increasing group belongingness, participating through using speech to the best of the child's ability at this time. They are concerned with details of speech production only as individual children show a readiness for it.

In this way the child is not only changing in broad fundamental ways necessary for learning, but also is experiencing the very situation for which he will develop a need for more accurate production of speech. Assuming also that experiencing success makes the child more eager and able to go on succeeding at harder tasks, the party gives him the possibility of succeeding right from the first, as answering the door, even though he cannot then use speech; using speech in that act even though he cannot yet say the pattern correctly; finally, when he can use the pattern correctly in such a situation, solving the problem of transfer of training from production to use.

each other's names so well. But if you do
forget someone's name, what can you do?
Yes, you can ask, "What is your name?"

CHILD 1: (*Goes outside the door, and
knocks.*)

CHILD 2: Hi, Ann.

CHILD 1: Hi, Jimmie.

CHILD 2: Come in.

CHILD 1: Thank you.

CHILD 2: Meet my friends. This is . . . .

CHILDREN: (*Greet each other, saying "Hi."*)

THERAPIST: I liked the way Ann looked
at each person she was introducing. I
liked the way you looked so pleased to
meet Jimmie, as if you were glad he came
to the party. I noticed that Jimmie got
his "θ" sound in in "Thank you." I
was surprised to notice that Jimmie got
the sound in twice when he used "This"
and he hasn't even worked on that yet.

After you have welcomed your guest, and
introduced him, you may want to invite
him to sit down so that you can talk with
him later. What could you say?

CHILDREN: Sit down. Sit by me. Have
a chair.

THERAPIST: Since you have been working
on the word "Have," practice saying
"Have a chair."

*This is all that should be
undertaken in one lesson.
Practice in passing refreshments, giving invitations,
may be undertaken in a second lesson, and the third
lesson may involve actual
inviting.*

CHILDREN: Have a chair. (*Continue until each child has had a turn, therapist giving help where indicated.*)

THERAPIST: Let's put the whole thing together now — greeting at the door, introduction, and invitation to sit down.

CHILD 1: (*Goes outside the door and knocks.*)

CHILD 2: Hi, Ann.

CHILD 1: Hi, Jean.

CHILD 2: Come in.

CHILD 1: Thank you.

CHILD 2: Meet my friends. This is . . . .

CHILDREN: Hi . . . (*Exchanging names*).

CHILD 2: Have a chair.

*   *   *   *   *

THERAPIST: When you pass refreshments, such as cookies at the party, what can you say that you have worked on?

CHILDREN: Have a cookie.

THERAPIST: What will you watch especially? You might also say "For you." Then what will you watch? If someone forgets to pass you a napkin, what could you say? Yes, "May I have a napkin?". And, of course, when someone gives you something you will know about thanking them, won't you?

The children may decide to have their mothers as guests, a friend from their own room, a brother or sister. They may decide to hold the party after school and invite their teachers. The speech therapist will want to make some previous arrangements before this project is undertaken, talking it over with the classroom teacher first so that plans can be worked in with the regular school program.

(Give individual practice on each response as needed. A tray with napkins or empty dixie cups will be useful in making the work more real.)

THERAPIST: Why do you suppose you are having a party in speech class in two days? Yes, to have fun, and to eat cookies, and to invite a friend. Most important of all, the party is a chance for you to *do* things as they are done at a party — welcoming someone at a party, introducing them to your friends, passing refreshments, and using speech in different ways.

*   *   *   *   *

Perhaps you should work on what you will say in inviting your friend to the party. Tell me what you would say, Ann? Show us by inviting one person.

CHILD: Will you come to our party?

THERAPIST: You will want to tell your friend what day the party is, what time it is, and where it is. It will sound like this: "Will you come to our party? It's on Thursday at two o'clock. It will be in the lunch room."

The invitation patterns given here provide somewhat longer responses for the children who can handle them. The patterns may be shortened for some of the other children as "Come to our party."

I will invite two people that way, to help you. Then you will each have a turn. *(Therapist uses above pattern twice.)* Practice what you will say first.

CHILDREN: Will you come to our party?

THERAPIST: That is easy for most of you. It has the word in it that Mary is working on. The next part has more difficult sounds. Some of you will be able to get one sound you have learned to make better in "Thursday." Listen first. "It's on Thursday at two o'clock."

CHILDREN: It's on Thursday at two o'clock."

THERAPIST: Next you will want to tell them where it is. Listen: "It will be in the lunch room."

CHILDREN: (*Each child has a turn practicing the response first, teacher giving individual help where needed.*) It will be in the lunch room.

THERAPIST: Now you are ready to put the invitation together. Who would like to give the first invitation? Jean, you may invite someone. You can watch that "come" and "Thursday." You can think about talking loudly enough for us to hear, too.

CHILD: "Will you come to our party? It's on Thursday at two o'clock. It will be in the lunch room."

Ideally the actual invitations should be given in speech class. The children who are coming to the party may come in for their invitations, or the whole group may go to the teachers they are inviting.

(*Continue above until at least several children have had a turn issuing the invitation.*)

THERAPIST: I believe you are ready for the party now. Let's see, what have you learned how to do?

CHILDREN: Greet someone at the door, introduce him to our friends, invite him to sit down, pass out the surprise, *and* invite him to the party.

Leave-taking can be pointed up and used at the conclusion of the party: "Thank you for the party"; "I liked the cookies."

THERAPIST: There are many ways you use speech to have fun, aren't there?

Chapter 7

Primary Illustrative Lessons

UNIT TWO

ACQUIRING SPEAKING SKILLS

A. INTERPERSONAL SITUATIONS WITH THEIR SPEAKING ASPECTS

108

B. SUMMARY OF ACTIVITIES

C. SUMMARY OF SPEECH PATTERNS

Lesson 1

Lesson 2

"Yes" or "No."   "May I have one?"

"Both."   "Read it."
"Both of them."   "Here" or "There."
"Thank you."   "One more."

"That one."   "Lay it down."
"With mine."   "Have a look."

"Can you . . .?" 126

Lesson 3

"Yes." "No."   "May I . . . go?"
                        have a . . .?"
"Both."   look at . . .?"
"Both of them."
"Thank you."   "Here." "There."
                     "Right."
                     "Write . . . ."

"Come . . . ." 131

Lesson 4

"Yes." "No."   "Lay it down."
                     "Have a look."
"With mine."   "Look at my . . . ."

"Thank you."   "Do you want a ticket?"
                     "Can you . . . hold it?"
"May I have one?"   get one?"
"Have one."   take one?"
"For you."   give me one?"
"Reach it."
"Here." "There."   "Get a ticket here." . . . 136

Lesson 5

"Yes." "No."   "Look at it."

"Yes, I . . . do, can . . . ."   "Have a look."
"Hit or miss?"

                                  "Can you . . .
"For you."   catch it?"
"May I have . . .?"   throw it?"

"Reach one."   "Thank you." 141
"Here" or "There."
"Ready?"
"Right."

Lesson 6

"Yes."
"What do you miss?"   "Reach the . . . ."
"What else?"   "Here" or "There."
                                  "Ready?"
"For you."
"May I have a . . .?"   "On the . . . ."
                                  "In the . . . ."
"With a . . . ."   "The . . . ."

                                  "Look what I have."
                                  "Have a look."

                                  "Thank you." 148

Lesson 7

"This is . . . ."   "Right."
"Hi . . . ."
"Miss . . . ."   "I'm thinking of . . . ."   155

"Yes."
"Who else?"
"Guess again."

Lesson 8

"Yes."   "For you."
"On the house."   "Have one."
"What do you miss?"   "May I have the . . .?"

"Dinner."

"Hide your eyes."
"Open your eyes."   "That's right."
"Yes." "No."   "Ready?"   197
"It's . . . ."
"Guess again."
"See." "Look."

Lesson 18

"Hide your eyes."   "Where is the . . .?"
"Open your eyes."   "Is it in the . . .?"
"Hello."   "Yes, it is."
"Who was it?"   "No, it isn't."
"Was it . . .?"

                           "Who has it?"
                           "Does . . .?"

                           "Reach in and get it."
                           "Show me . . . ." 200

D. SUMMARY OF EQUIPMENT

Unit II · Lesson 1

1. *Interpersonal Situations:* exchanging articles indicating a preference
2. *Speaking Aspect of Situation:* asking and answering questions
3. *Particular Speech Patterns:*

"Yes" or "No."   "Reach it."   "Can you . . . hold it?"
                    "Here" or "There."   get one?"

REVIEW   take one?"

"Both." or   "Lay it down."   give me one?"
"Both of them."   "Have a look."
"Thank you."

"With mine."

"May I have one?"

4. *Sounds Emphasized:*   s   θ   ð   r   l   k
5. *Equipment:* a pack of trading cards

| PROCEDURES | NOTES |

THERAPIST: If your mother says to you, "Do you want a piece of cake?" you will probably say, "Yes." Your teacher may point to a book saying "Do you like this book?" to which you will often answer "Yes" or "No," or perhaps, "I liked one of the stories in it." When mother asks if you will go to the store, your answer may be "Yes." You use "yes" in many ways. Can you think of some?

CHILDREN: (*Individually*) When my daddy asks if I'd like him to read the funny papers to me; when a friend asks if I'll come outdoors and play; when my mother asks if I'd like to go to the show . . . .

THERAPIST: I have a pack of trading

The "s" which is apt to be difficult for many in the class, requiring considerable time and care in teaching, will give opportunities for success and recognition of the child who stutters or the one who is working, primarily on an "r," "k," "ð" and others. It cannot be emphasized too strongly that continuously giving these children the feeling that they have assets in certain directions makes them more ready to learn in an area which poses some difficulty for them.

Some children make the sound "s" through imitation fairly easily. These

118

cards which Bill brought. They are a part of his collection. There are enough of them for you to make a collection, too, during class, although Bill will want them back. If you want one now, I will give it to you. However, I have a special reason for giving one to each of you. I want you to hear each other make the new word "yes" since that is something many of you will be working on. Watch as each person has a turn . . . see if everyone's word sounds the same, or if you see and hear some differences.

THERAPIST: Ann, do you want a card?

CHILD: Yes.

THERAPIST: (*May give each child one turn without commenting on production.*) She may give the children each another turn making such comments as the following:

Jimmie keeps his teeth together when he says "Ye . . . s." That keeps his tongue back.

Ann's tongue comes forward when she says "Yes . . . ."

Bill says "Yeah" without a "s" sound in it. Some people do it that way. You remember we are finding out that no one talks exactly like everyone else.

Kathie's "Yes . . . ." has a "bubbly" sound which means the air is coming out of a different place from Ann's and Jimmie's.

(*It should be noted here that first comments*

children should begin immediately incorporating it in the response "Yes" under careful guidance.

Others will be able to produce it partially better; that is, a child who has a marked lingual protrusion may have an "s" in which his tongue is back, although the sound is not yet sharp. If the sound is going in the direction of normal, he, too, can be given assistance in including it in the one response. Each time the child makes the response, the therapist should say in what ways it is better than his former sound, and in what ways it needs more work. For the child who may have to work on the sound in isolation for some time before he gets a semblance of a normal sound — such as a child with a cleft palate, one with a markedly lateral sound, etc., — there are a number of alternatives. The therapist should be sure that along the way he receives recognition for other sounds he makes easily that some other children are working on. He should be given the opportunity to use the response "Yes" also in an activity since his awareness of where the "s" should be included will begin to develop in that way along with his hearing the other children use it.

do not include an evaluation of "right" or "wrong," but simply call attention to differences.)

THERAPIST: "Let's try making it this way now. Listen. Watch. "Ye...s." Listen to just this part. "s" Try it.

It may be advisable to separate the pattern first as "Ye...s" in order to prevent reoccurrence of a former defective pattern. This practice should be kept to a minimum. Care should be taken, too, to prevent too much force on a newly acquired sound.

CHILDREN: "s" *(Each child has several turns.)*

THERAPIST: *(Makes comments as the following where necessary. In so far as possible, it is desirable for these children to learn the "s" through imitation rather than through direction pertaining to tongue movement. In some cases giving some specific direction proves to be helpful, however.)*

Jimmie makes the sound as most people do. It is easy for him. Jimmie, go to each boy and girl and show him how you do it.

There are a number of speech patterns included here which give children requiring work on sounds other than "s" opportunities for speech in the same activity. A child who has numerous defective sounds should be held only for the "s" at first. Since this sound occurs frequently in speech, and often requires a longer time to learn it is considered more important at this stage in therapy.

Ann, if you keep your teeth together that will help you put your tongue back further.

Bill, listen first. Now try it. I like that.

Kathie, begin saying "he" out loud ... now whisper it, now put your teeth together and whisper it ... Now go from "he" to "s" like this. *(One way of directing the air stream centrally. Other techniques which the teacher finds useful may be used here.)*

THERAPIST: More of you are making the "s" alike now. Most of you are making it well enough to use it in one easy word, "Ye...s" Try it first. Listen to me.

CHILDREN: (*Individually*) "Ye ... s"
(*Where needed the therapist may give a direction first before the child says* "Yes," *as* "Ann, watch me ... see my teeth are together at the end" ... , *etc.*)

THERAPIST: You may have a card now if you want one, providing you watch how you use the "s" in "Ye ... s."

THERAPIST: Do you want one?

CHILDREN: (*Individually*) Ye ... s. (*Continue until each child has had a turn.*)

THERAPIST: (*To one child not making the "s" well enough to include it in the response yet*) That "Ye ... s" is still hard for you. Try just "s" ... , etc. You have learned to use "Thank you" so well, suppose you tell me "Thank you" when I give you a card. — Here is a card for you.

Child makes "s" a number of times in isolation as the therapist gives directions which enable him to begin establishing proper movement and direction for an "s." As soon as the sound is going in the direction of normal, the child should begin incorporating it in a response.

CHILD: Thank you.

THERAPIST: Jimmie, that "Ye ... s" is easy for you. You need to practice on the "r." Try it. Listen to me first. Remember that your tongue must come up.

CHILD: "r"

THERAPIST: I liked that because your tongue did come up when you made it. The end of the sound you made sounds more like the one most people use. Try it again. See if you can make it four times just that way .... The word you are working on is "R ... each it." Try it.

CHILD: R ... each it.

THERAPIST: Ann and Jean, this sound is easy for you. Show Jimmie how you say "Reach it" — you may take some of these cards — by answering my question correctly. See how many cards you can get. What will you do to get a card?

CHILD: R . . . each it. (*Continue until this one child has acquired several cards.*)

THERAPIST: You have many cards now. You may give one to each boy and girl by telling him, "R . . . each it."

CHILD: (*Distributes cards one at a time by giving the direction, "Reach it." Teacher checks critically on production of "r" in the response. Children reach out and choose a card.*)

THERAPIST: Let's go ahead now, giving more of you practice on "s" as you add another card to your collection. Do you want one?

CHILDREN: Yes. (*Continue until each child has had a turn.*)

(*Another child who is able to include an "r" sound more easily in the responses "Here," and "There" may answer the question, "Where will you get a card?" replying "Here" or "There" as he points to a card on the table. He may then give the direction, "Take a card here," or "Take a card there," to the other children.*

The child working on "l" may use the response "Lay one on the table," giving the direction a number of times to various children as a means of getting the cards together again.)

THERAPIST: Each of you has three cards now. I have three cards, too. Watch where I put the next card that I get. "With mine." Watch where I put the next one. "With mine." In a short time, you will get another card. Where will you put it?

CHILDREN: With mine.

THERAPIST: What sound do you have to watch?

CHILDREN: "ð"

This sound in "with mine" can be taught as a voiced or voiceless fricative depending on prevalent use in the community.

THERAPIST: Let's see if you can each say it. Then you will all have a turn to get a card.

CHILDREN: With mine. *(Continue until each child has said it once or more adequately, depending on the need for practice.)*

THERAPIST: Where will you put it?

CHILD: With mine. *(Continue until each child has had a turn.)*

THERAPIST: I have two cards here. This time you may choose two cards that you would like. Watch me. I'll take "Both." Listen again. "Both." What sound do you need to watch?

CHILDREN: "θ"

THERAPIST: Try it first. "Both."

CHILDREN: Both. *(Continue until each child has practiced it some, therapist giving help where needed.)*

THERAPIST: (*Holding out two cards*) What one do you want?

CHILDREN: Both. (*Continue until each child obtains two cards.*)

THERAPIST: Each of you has had some special help today, some with "Yes," some with "With," some with "Reach" and "Lay one on the table." Kathie, these sounds were all easy for you. What one is it you need some help on? Yes, the "k." Try it by itself. Do it four times. Listen to me first. Take it easy; don't push too hard.

CHILD: "k"

THERAPIST: Try it in "Can you ...." Listen. Going slowly will make it easier. Dividing it will keep that old sound from creeping in. "C ... an you ...?"

CHILD: "C ... an you ...." (*Practices several times.*)

THERAPIST: I liked that because you are taking it slowly, and thinking first of your sound. You rest for a minute and let the other boys and girls show you how they do it. Ann, Bill, and Marion — who have had to work very hard on the "s" sound — make this one easily. (*Children demonstrate this sound.*)

THERAPIST: Listen how I'm going to collect the cards: "Can you put one on the table?" (*Therapist directs this question to each child, emphasizing the "can" as she repeats the question. She may choose to do some work on the "Ye ... s" response, also as the children reply, placing one card on the table.)* Now, Kathie, it's your turn. You are going to ask the boys and girls the same question I did. You will have fun collecting cards, and also it will give you many chances to use that word "can."

CHILD: Can you put one on the table?

CHILD: Ye . . . s.

(This response can be utilized in other ways, such as distributing the cards asking, "Can you hold one?" or collecting them asking, "Can you give me one?" The latter response includes two difficult sounds and should be used with care, as does "Can you take one?" or "Can you get one?" Some children, however, will be ready for this early.)

THERAPIST: Now all the cards are back on the table. What do you tell Bill for letting us use them today? What speech have you worked on today while you were having fun with the cards?

CHILDREN: Yes.   Reach one.   Both. Thank you.   Lay it on the table.   Can you . . .?

THERAPIST: That's right, and some others, too. You have worked especially on the new word "Yes." You will be using that some more in class. Listen when other people say it. See how many differences you can hear.

Unit II · Lesson 2

1. *Interpersonal Situation:* exchanging articles; indicating a preference
2. *Speaking Aspect of Situation:* asking and answering questions
3. *Particular Speech Patterns:*

"Yes" or "No."   "Reach it."   "Can you . . .?"
"Here." or "There."
"One more."

REVIEW

"Both." or "Both of them."
"Thank you."   "Lay it down."
"Have a look."
"That one."
"With mine."

"May I have one?"

4. *Sounds Emphasized:*   s   r   l   θ   ð   k
5. *Equipment:* several sets of eight colored crayons (preferably primary size)

PROCEDURES

NOTES

THERAPIST: The last time you were here you worked especially on the "s" sound in "Yes." You got trading cards by replying "Yes" when I asked you if you wanted one. Have you noticed how differently people say "Yes"? Sometimes they simply nod their heads meaning "Yes" without saying anything. Sometimes they use "un-huh" or "yeah." If you say "Yes" when you will do something but don't want to very much it sounds different from saying "Yes" when you want to do it very much. But, for the most part, when people say "Yes" the last sound in it is much the same, regardless who says it. What many of you are going to be working on is making your "s" sound more like other people's. Listen to me now, and see if you can tell

126

which "Yes" that I make is better, the first or the second one? Can you tell why?

(Therapist gives several series of "Yes" in sets of two, one of them made with a lingual, lateral, or whistling "s," the other within normal range. Children differentiate between them. Therapist helps them both see and hear differences.)

THERAPIST: I have something in the box for you. Before you can see it, you will want some practice on making that new sound. Listen first. Watch it. Try it.

CHILDREN: "s"

THERAPIST: Now try it in "Ye ... s."

CHILDREN: Ye ... s.

This suggestion for "ear-training" can be utilized as needed in context with the various speech patterns which are used. As soon as possible it should be developed in such a way that the child evaluates his own sound as well as that of another.

(At the introduction of this lesson the therapist may also give practice on other sounds which certain children need, such as the " θ," "f," "v," "r," "l," and "k"; she may incorporate these sounds in responses which she plans to use in the lesson.)

THERAPIST: *(To child who stutters)* Eddie, you may take the box to each one saying, "Do you want a look?" "Do you want a look?" Let me help you say it slowly and easily without pushing too hard. Say it with me. "Do you want a look?" Each time you say it to someone, wait a minute before you begin so you don't get in too big a hurry. *(To other children)* In order for you to get a look at the surprise in the box you will watch "Yes" very carefully.

If the teacher is maintaining a relatively slow tempo in the class, it is easy to suggest that the child pause a moment before making a reply in order to consciously include the newer sound. This will reduce the number of times a child makes an incorrect response and has to repeat it. Praise should be given for a response which is within normal range on the first attempt, although a child need

CHILD: Do you want a look?

CHILDREN: Yes.

THERAPIST: (*Interrupting*) If you answer Eddie as slowly as he is asking you it will be easier for you to make an "s" sound that is the best one for you. Eddie, I like it so much because you are waiting a minute before you begin. I like it, too, because you are looking at each person and smiling. (*Continue as above*)

THERAPIST: There are lots of crayons in the box, aren't there? Let's see if you can get them away from me by using your best speech.

THERAPIST: Do you want one?

CHILDREN: Ye . . . s (*Continue until each child has received a crayon.*)

THERAPIST: This time you may decide on a special color which you want. If you decide you want a red one, and I hold out a blue one to you, what will you say? "No." That's right.

THERAPIST: Do you want this one?

CHILDREN: Yes *or* No. (*Continue until each child has had a turn, and received an additional crayon.*)

THERAPIST: Jimmie, what can you tell the boys and girls in order to get practice on your "r" and in order to give them each another crayon?

CHILD: R . . . each one. (*Therapist gives additional help on the "r" where needed.*)

not be penalized for not suc- ceeding the first time, but rather helped to do better the next time.

In stressing the "s" in "Yes" the therapist should be careful to accept "No" as an appropriate response' also. Children need not reply parrot-like with "Yes" each time a question is asked or an article extended to them. Freedom to express dislike or respond negatively should be granted him. On the other hand, the teacher can structure the lesson so that most of the time the children will want to respond posi- tively.

THERAPIST: Jimmie, listen to the way I start this. Then you will have a turn. The other boys and girls need to listen, too, so they will know what to say.

THERAPIST: Do you want one?

CHILD: Yes.

Here the therapist sets the pattern by "doing" instead of explaining.

THERAPIST: Reach it.

CHILD: Thank you.

(Therapist may repeat this several times so children hear the sequence.)

CHILD: *(With "r" difficulty)* Do you want one?

CHILDREN: Yes.

CHILD: Reach it.

CHILDREN: *(Individually)* Thank you.

THERAPIST: You have had many more chances today to use your new sounds. What are some of the things you worked on? "Yes." "No." "Both." "With mine." "Thank you." "That one." "Reach one," etc.

Jimmie, what do you have to watch in "Reach one"? Ann, what do you have to remember to do when you say "Yes"? Mary, what do you need to remember in "That one"? Eddie, what did you do today each time before you began to talk?

Supplementary Suggestions

By now the children have several crayons in their possession. The crayons may be collected and put in the box in any way which gives certain children experience using particular responses on which they are working.

One child may collect one set by asking, "May I have it?" to which the children reply "Yes," and he acknowledges receipt by using "Thank you."

Another child needing work on "θ" and "ð" may collect crayons two at a time — the last two the children are holding by asking "May I have both?", or he may use "Put yours with mine." The first response is better in some ways because it elicits "Yes," which the therapist should be checking on continuously whenever it occurs.

If all or several of the children are needing more work on "tʃ" the therapist may collect the crayons, asking "Which one will you give me?" (A child needing work on the "g" may also initiate this activity) to which the children reply "That one."

"Can you put it in the box?" and "Lay it on the table" are other ways of collecting the crayons.

Once the crayons are all in, the therapist may redistribute them as she did earlier: have one child do it; give the children opportunity to request a special crayon, "May I have the red one?" (She may hold them responsible for the "ð" in "the" here), etc.

Unit II · Lesson 3

1. *Interpersonal Situation:* requesting and granting permission
2. *Speaking Aspect of Situation:* asking and answering a question
3. *Particular Speech Patterns:*

"Yes."	"May I get . . . ?"	"Here" or "There."
"No."	have a . . . ?"	"Right . . . ."
	look at . . . ?"	"Write . . . ."
REVIEW		"Come . . . ."
"Both." or		
"Both of them."		
"Thank you."		

4. *Sounds Emphasized:* s θ r v l g k
5. *Equipment:* none

PROCEDURES	NOTES

THERAPIST: There are many times when you need to ask permission of your mother, daddy, or teacher to do something special; you ask permission to bring a friend home from school, to go outdoors and play, to paint at the easel when your work is finished, to be excused from school early to go to the dentist.

Sometimes you don't like to ask permission because you are afraid that mother may not let you do what you want to do. That happens to all of us. One time I wanted to be excused a day early from school to start on a long trip. I didn't like to ask because I was afraid I wouldn't be permitted to go. When you ask to be given permission you need to expect sometimes to be refused. Then you won't feel too upset if you cannot do as you ask.

Today you are going to work on speech you use in asking permission. You will

131

have fun doing it because part of the time
you will ask for permission, and part of
the time you will give the permission.

You may ask any of the four things.
Listen carefully. You may be able to do
several of them.

May I write my name on the board?
May I sit by . . . ?
May I open the door? (or close the door)
May I get a drink?

Let's practice each one first; then you
may choose the thing you most want to
do. Listen. "May I write my name on
the board?" Listen again. (*Repeat*)
What sound in there do you need to
watch, Jimmie? Bill?

CHILD: The "r" in "write," the "ð" in
"the."

(*Each child repeats this question, with help
given to the children having difficulty with
the "r," and the "ð." A somewhat slower
rate should be emphasized here and phrasing
"May I write my name . . . on the board?"*)

(*The second question, "May I sit by . . .?"
should have similar practice. Attention may
be called to the presence of the "s" in "sit,"
but in most instances the child just beginning
work on that sound in "Yes" should not be
held responsible for it here. It is well for him
to develop some awareness of it, however.*)

(*The third and fourth "May I go open the
door?" "May I get a drink?" should be
introduced in similar manner. These provide work on the "g" and "ð" sounds.*)

For the child with almost totally unintelligible speech, these simple patterns give practice in over-all syllabification. Each child should have at least one opportunity — more if necessary — to say the above as preparation for actually getting to do the things.)

THERAPIST: Now before you have a turn, you will need to practice the answer you may give when it is your turn for someone to ask permission of you. What choice of answers do you have? Which one is more difficult? Why? Yes, that "s" sound is one on which many of you are working to make better. Try it. Listen first.

CHILDREN: "s" *(Therapist gives each child an opportunity to say this a number of times; children with more skill show the others. Children with less skill are given directions, encouragement, praise. This sound should be combined then with "Yes" and additional work given on it.)*

THERAPIST: Now you are ready to ask permission. Remember, someone may say "No" to you, in which case you will get another turn later, and you will remember that it is often necessary to say "No" and to accept it without feeling upset. Jimmie, you may ask permission of Bill. You can easily choose to ask for the thing which will give you practice on your special sound. Which one was that? Later, if you like, you may ask for one of the others.

CHILD: May I write my name on the board?

CHILD: Yes.
CHILD: Thank you.

Now, Bill, you may choose someone to ask permission of Jimmie.

CHILD: May I sit by . . .?
CHILD: No.
CHILD: Thank you, anyway.
CHILD: You're welcome.

THERAPIST: Ann, you didn't get to do what you asked, but you know you will get another turn. Jimmie, you may choose someone to ask permission of Ann.

Kathie, when you ask you will want to watch the "ð" sound that comes in "the" when you say either "May I write my name on the board?" or "May I go open the door." Try it.

CHILD: May I go open the door?
CHILD: Yes.
CHILD: Thank you.
CHILD: You're welcome.

THERAPIST: I notice each one of you has said "You're welcome," to the person who said "Thank you" to you. I like that. The "Yes" is still hard for you to get in when you answer without thinking. Before the rest of you have a turn, let's stop and practice it again.

CHILDREN: Yes.

(*For children needing individual help other than that included above, such special responses may be included as "May I sit by both . . . and . . .?" or "May I sit with . . .?*

This interchange of asking and granting permission can be continued until each child has had several turns. This offers opportunity to ob-

"May I have chalk to write my name on the board?" *and* "May I go open the door and look out?" *provide work on the "v" and "l" in responses similar to those which children have had previously, as does* "May I write my name here?")

THERAPIST: What have you had fun doing today? Yes, you have asked permission. Sometimes you got to do what you asked, and sometimes not. Which would you rather do, ask permission, or be asked? You have to do both many times during the day.

What sounds did you work on? What did you say to get practice on the "s," "r," "l," "g," "θ"? Do you want to do this again?

serve the children interacting with each other (choice of person to sit by, choice of person to have next turn, choice of activity). It will be interesting to note children's reaction to a refusal, their "role" in the person of authority who can grant permission or not as he chooses.

Unit II · Lesson 4

1. *Interpersonal Situation:* exchanging articles
2. *Speaking Aspects of Situation:* requesting, distributing, acknowledging an object
3. *Particular Speech Patterns:*

"Yes" or "No."   "Reach one."   "Do you want a ticket?"
                     "Here" or "There."   "Can you ... hold it?
               REVIEW   get one?
                     "For you."   take one?
"With mine."   give me one?"
                     "Look at my ..."   "Get a ticket here."
"Thank you."

"May I have one?"
"Have one."

4. *Sounds Emphasized:* s r l θ ð f v k g
5. *Equipment:* small pieces of construction paper cut to resemble tickets; stapler

---

PROCEDURES

THERAPIST: You get a ticket of admission to most places where you must pay to enter. You buy a ticket for a show, for a concert, for a basketball game, and for a church supper. For what other things do you buy tickets?

CHILDREN: (*Individually*) For a bus, train, or plane trip; for a football game; for a play; etc.

THERAPIST: You don't often get a chance to keep tickets. You give it to the ticket taker. Sometimes you sell tickets to things, and then you start out with many tickets and end with few. Today you are not going to buy or sell tickets, but you

NOTES

This lesson can be introduced as the ones previously with "Have a look," etc. The therapist may have one set of tickets fastened together so that the children see what they will have when they leave class.

136

are going to have fun working on your speech and collecting tickets. Before you go home you may fasten the tickets together and make a book of tickets, like this one. (*Therapist shows her tickets.*)

Before you get your tickets let's see if you can make the new sound in "Yes." After all, if you want a ticket you will have to be able to answer when I ask you, and the more times you answer with a sound that is like the one you are learning, the more tickets you will get. Listen to me first. Watch. "s" What are some of the things you need to remember to do?

CHILDREN: Keep my tongue back. Keep my teeth together. Not push too hard. Keep the air coming through the middle.

THERAPIST: Let's watch Kathie do it. (*Turning to other children*) What did you like about her's? Make it again for them.

CHILDREN: "s" (*Each child has a turn to produce the "s" sound. The teacher calls attention to the ones that are made satisfactorily, gives help where needed.*)

THERAPIST: Now put the sound in "Yes," being careful to make it just as you practiced it.

CHILDREN: (*Individually*) "Yes." (*Children have several opportunities to say it.*)

THERAPIST: I will give each of you a ticket if you make the "s" sound in "Yes" the very best you can. If you have trouble I will help you first before you get the ticket.

The therapist, by using specific comments herself in appraising a child's sound gradually establishes standards by which the children can evaluate each other. The teacher may ask, for example "What did you like about Kathie's sound? Did she keep her tongue back?" etc.

Since the tickets are easy to handle and the children like acquiring them the above patterns can be used a number of times. In fact, each child may have a turn distributing tickets. The teacher may wish to center chief emphasis during this lesson on the "Yes" response, giving each child a number of occasions on which to use it. However, she may easily provide special practice for the children who have needs other than "s" by use of the responses suggested in Lessons 1 and 2, Unit II.

*   *   *

One child may distribute the tickets using the response "R . . . each it," or "Get a ticket here."

Another one may ask "Can you hold one?" or "Can you hold one more?" for work on the "k." "Can you take one?" or "Can you get one?"

THERAPIST: (*Looking at one child*) Do you want a ticket?

CHILD: Yes. (*Continue until each child has had a turn.*)

THERAPIST: Mary, you may have a turn asking each boy and girl if he wants a ticket. It will be a chance for you to look at each person as you ask him, go slowly without hurrying, and make the "you" right. Try "you" by itself.

CHILD: You.

THERAPIST: Now try the whole thing. Listen to me first. "Do you want a ticket?"

CHILD: Do you want a ticket? (*Child may need help before beginning activity.*)

THERAPIST: Now you are ready to give a ticket to everyone.

CHILD: Do you want a ticket? ("*Do you want one?*" *may be substituted if "ticket" is too difficult, or the first pattern may be used for the child who needs work on the "k" and has made a start on it in the responses suggested previously.*)

CHILDREN: (*Individually*) Yes.

* * * * *

THERAPIST: This stapler works very easily, and is fun to use. Watch how I do it. You will each get a turn to use it. You will each watch the "s" sound very carefully when you answer my question.

may be used if the child is ready for two difficult sounds in one response.

Some child may distribute the tickets by saying "Have one" or "For you" for work on the "f" and "v". Each child may request a ticket with the response "May I have one?" to which one child who is gaining ... or needing to gain ... some facility in use of "Yes" may reply as he gives the tickets out one by one.

One child may ask each child as he gives out the tickets "Where will you put it?" to which the children answer "With mine."

"Thank you" should accompany receipt of all the tickets ... for use of the "θ."

One child may show the others his tickets using the response "Look at my red ones." "Look at my blue ones." etc.

THERAPIST: Do you want to staple your tickets?

CHILDREN: (*Individually*) Yes. (*Continue until each child has fastened his tickets together in a book.*)

THERAPIST: You had fun today collecting tickets. What speech did you work on in order to get the tickets?

CHILDREN: Yes. With mine. Thank you. May I have one? For you, etc.

THERAPIST: When someone asks about your book of tickets you can say that you got them when you were working on speech. You may even show your mother how well you are making "Yes" now.

Additional Supplementary Suggestions

Since the "s" is defective more often than any other sound, and since it is felt that the child should establish a new sound in a few responses well, "Yes" should be emphasized until it is almost automatic before undertaking new responses.

The following suggestions can be utilized for an entire lesson, and varied to meet the needs of individual children in ways which have been suggested previously.

For speech responses emphasizing "Yes" in answer to the question "Do you want . . .?"

Do you want to make a hole? (Use of paper punch)
Do you want to use a staple? (Use of stapler)
Do you want to put a stick on the ladder? (Use of blackboard and chalk)
Do you want to put a ball on the ladder? (Use of blackboard and chalk)
Do you want to put an eye (etc.) on the pumpkin? (Use of blackboard)
Do you want to put a pumpkin on the fence? (Use of blackboard)
Do you want to put an egg in the basket? (Use of blackboard)

Do you want to put an apple on the tree?   (Use of blackboard)
Do you want to put a piece in the puzzle?   (Use of an eight or
ten piece puzzle)

For speech responses emphasizing "Yes" in answer to the question
"Do you have . . .?", material similar to that listed above can be used.

For speech patterns emphasizing "Yes" in answer to the question
"Can you put . . .?", material similar to that listed above can also
be used.

Unit II · Lesson 5

1. *Interpersonal Situation:* playing a game

2. *Speaking Aspect of Situation:* choosing, taking a turn, asking and answering a question

3. *Particular Speech Patterns:*

"Yes" or "No."	"Reach one."	"Can you . . .
"Yes, I . . . do, can . . ." etc.	"Here" or "There."	catch it?"
"Hit or miss?"	"Ready?"	throw it?"
	"Right."	
"For you."		"Thank you."
"May I have . . .?"	"Look at it."	
	"Have a look."	

4. *Sounds Emphasized:* s   r   l   and others as needed

5. *Equipment:* A target painted on cardboard that may be placed on the floor; a target drawn with chalk on the floor; a bean bag

---

PROCEDURES	NOTES
THERAPIST: You have worked on speech which you use in passing out and collecting cards and tickets, inviting someone to a party, making an introduction. You have worked on speech you use when asking permission of someone. You often use speech in playing a game, too. When boys play baseball they choose sides, for example, and yell when it's a "home run" or an "out." In football the players call signals. In jump rope the girls jump to rhymes that they say. Games call for different speech. Today you are going to have fun working on speech in a special game that will be fun for several reasons — both fun to do, and fun to work on special sounds you use.	*Note here that the conversational speech patterns used in playing the game are kept the chief core of interest. This differs from traditional use of games as a "motivating device."*

Do you like throwing a bean bag? Practice it for a minute.

141

THERAPIST: (*Tossing the bean bag to one child*) Can you catch it?

CHILD: Yes.

THERAPIST: Can you throw it?

CHILD: Yes.

THERAPIST: When you have a turn, what sound must you watch in "Yes"?

CHILDREN: "s"

THERAPIST: Let's stop for a minute and practice it, to see if you are getting it better.

CHILDREN: (*Practice "s" individually, with the therapist giving help where indicated.*)

THERAPIST: (*Resumes tossing bean bag after children have worked on "s" in isolation and in the response "Yes."*) "Can you catch it?" (*Therapist should withhold tossing the bean bag until the child has responded with "Yes," using the best "s" of which he is capable at that particular time.*)

CHILDREN: Yes.

THERAPIST: Can you throw it?

CHILDREN: Yes. (*Continue until each child has had one turn, or several, depending on the need.*)

(*This exchange of the bean bag can also be adapted for meeting other needs in the way*

This activity can be done fairly rapidly since the children should have some skill in use of the "s" in "Yes" by now. On occasion the therapist may withhold the bean bag, if a child does not produce an "s" as well as he is able at this particular time, saying, "I'm coming back to you. I think you can do better."

As the children begin establishing the "s" within normal range more easily, the response "Yes" should be extended to "Yes, I do," or "Yes, I can." Some children will be ready for this before others.

of practicing on particular sounds. One example is given, but others may be substituted.)

THERAPIST: Jimmie, you have been working on the "r" in the word "r . . . each." Try it by itself. Now in the word. That is so much better than you were doing. I believe you are ready for some practice in putting it in a different response, like this. R . . . eady? (*As the therapist says this she indicates that she is about to toss the bean bag. When the child responds "Yes," she does toss it.*) "Now Jimmie, it's your turn to toss it to me, and in order for you to get practice on your sound you ask me the same thing. Listen first. Ready?

CHILD: R . . . eady?

THERAPIST: Yes. (*Child tosses bean bag.*)

THERAPIST: Ready?

CHILD: Yes. (*Then tosses bean bag*), etc.

(*This activity should be continued several times between the child and the therapist so the children hear the entire pattern several times.*)

THERAPIST: Now, Jimmie, you may give each person a turn, tossing the bean bag to him, and asking "R . . . eady?" I want you to notice if each child when he answers you is checking himself on his "s." You, in turn, must watch your "r."

CHILD: Ready?

CHILDREN: Yes.   (*Jimmie tosses bean bag.*)

CHILDREN: Ready?

CHILD: Yes.   (*Continue until each child has had one or more turns.*)

(*Other responses which may be introduced in similar fashion and which utilize the same situation are as follows:*)

CHILD: Have a look.   (*Tosses the bean bag.*)

CHILDREN: (*Individually receive the bean bag.*) Thank you.

*   *   *   *   *

CHILD: For you.

CHILDREN: (*Individually*) Thank you.

*   *   *   *   *

CHILD: Here.   (*Tosses the bean bag.*)

CHILDREN: (*Individually*) Thank you. (*Receiving the bean bag.*)

*   *   *   *   *

CHILD: May I have the bean bag?

CHILD: Yes, you may.

*   *   *   *   *

CHILD: Can you catch the bean bag?

CHILDREN: (*Individually*) Yes, *or* Yes, I can.

*   *   *   *   *

THERAPIST: Take a look at the target on

the floor. Do you see the bull's eye? When the bean bag is all the way on the bull's eye, you call it a "hit." If it is slightly off the bull's eye, or entirely off, like this, you call it a "miss." I'm going to stand right next to the target, and ask you some questions to be sure you know what is called a "hit" and what is called a "miss."

THERAPIST: (*Dropping bean bag on target*) Jean, hit or miss?

CHILDREN: (*Individually*) Hit, *or* Miss. (*Therapist repeats a number of times, emphasizing at first not phonetic accuracy, but understanding of the target.*)

THERAPIST: You can hear that "miss" has a sound in it like "yes." Try it. Watch that you get the new sound in. Listen to it again. "Miss."

CHILDREN: (*Individually*) Miss. (*Each child has several turns saying it, the therapist giving individual help as needed.*)

THERAPIST: Because that is new for you, you will need to practice it more before you have a turn at the target. Let's each ask Ann the question once to see if you are really ready for the game. Listen. I'm going to use Ann's name at the beginning. "Ann, hit or miss?" Listen again. Watch me. Now each of you try it for practice.

The therapist will need to point out that the name should come first in this speech pattern. This keeps the "s" a truly final one and somewhat easier than a medial one in most cases.

CHILDREN: (*Individually*) Ann, hit or miss? (*Children each have a turn, therapist giving help where indicated. Emphasis should be placed on using the name first.*)

THERAPIST: Now you are ready to have a turn at trying to hit the target, and at using certain speech after you have had a try. Will you each hit the target for sure? Will any of you hit the target for sure? That's right, not for sure. You will try, and you will want to hit it, but you may not. That is the way in games; you don't always win even when you would like being the winner. This game is even fixed so that it is extra hard to make a hit, which means you get lots of practice on the "s" in "miss." But you will have fun playing the game anyway. I'll be first. I want to give you an extra chance to see and hear just what I do.

THERAPIST: Billy, hit or miss?

CHILD: Miss.

THERAPIST: Yes. It's your turn now.

(Note that the "Yes" occurs very naturally here in the speech pattern. The therapist may suggest that the child who is working on "r" reply "Right" to the child's response.)

CHILD: Mary, hit or miss?

CHILD: Miss.

CHILD: Yes. It's your turn now.

THERAPIST: Billy didn't hit the target, but I liked the way he watched so carefully before he did it. I liked the way he remembered to get in his "s" sound, too, and used Mary's name at the beginning.

Since this activity is structured so that a hit is not easy, the children usually recognize the challenge and work that much harder to do it. If it becomes too easy so that the children are not having op-

THERAPIST: What new speech have you worked on? That word "miss" you use in many different ways. We will talk about it when you come again. "Ready" is one that comes along often, too. We will talk about it more next time also.

portunity to use the "miss" response, the target can be placed at a greater distance.

Unit II · Lesson 6

1. *Interpersonal Situation:* guessing

2. *Speaking Aspect of Situation:* asking and answering questions

3. *Particular Speech Patterns:*

"Yes."	"Reach the . . . ."	"The . . . ."
"What do you miss?"	"Right."	"On the . . . ."
"What else?"	"Here" or "There."	"In the . . . ."
	"Ready?"	"With a . . . ."
"Can you put the . . .?"		
	"Look what I have."	"Thank you."
	"Have a look."	
	"Hide your eyes."	"For you."
	"Open your eyes."	"May I have a . . .?"
	"Do you want the . . .?"	

4. *Sounds Emphasized:* s l r θ ð f v

5. *Equipment:* a group of assorted toys that are related, such as farm animals, colored blocks, vehicles, desk objects

---

PROCEDURES

THERAPIST: Sometimes when your daddy comes home from work he says to you, "I have a surprise for you. Guess what it is," or mother may say, "There is a surprise in the oven for you. Can you guess what it is?" Then you have fun guessing. Sometimes a boy comes to me and says, "Guess what I have in my pocket," and then I try to decide what he must have in that pocket. When else do you guess?

CHILDREN: We try to guess what's in our packages at Christmas or on our birthday, etc.

THERAPIST: You are going to do some guessing today, but it will be easier because you will have some hints before you

NOTES

The therapist will use three or four items at the outset of this activity, depending on the abilities of the group. The number can be increased to five or six later. There should be enough items so that there is some challenge in checking the one or two items removed. If there are so many that too much time is consumed in recall, then the activity tends to be centered on recall rather than on speech. The items should be related in function, large enough to be seen easily, small enough to be concealed quickly.

try. Watch what I have here. (*Thera-pist takes articles from pocket or box one at a time for children to see, lays them on the table, waits until children have examined the article and are looking at her face, and sets the pattern by saying* "the boat," "the truck," *etc. She can stress a slower rate, pausing between phrases, and includ-ing the* "ð" *sound.*)

THERAPIST: In order for you to know better what is here, let's have several of you name the things just as I did. Listen. "The boat." What sound do you need to watch? Each of you try it first, and then I'll choose some of you to name each thing that is here.

CHILDREN: The boat.

THERAPIST: Ann, you may have a turn now. I believe you can get the "ð" sound in each time.

CHILD: The boat. The train. The car, etc.

THERAPIST: I liked that, Ann, because you used the "ð" sound nearly every time. Jimmie, you may have a turn doing it now, and it will be a chance for you to go slowly, take your time, and talk smoothly. Listen to me. (*Therapist may repeat pat-terns, emphasizing particularly the pause between each phrase.*)

CHILD: The boat, etc.

The following responses may be used for meeting individual needs, and in reviewing previous responses which have been stressed.)

CHILD: (*Distributing articles*) For you.

CHILDREN: Thank you.

*   *   *   *   *

CHILDREN: May I have the . . .?

CHILD: Yes.

*   *   *   *   *

CHILD: (*Drawing articles from a box*)
Look what I have.

CHILDREN: The . . . .

*   *   *   *   *

CHILD: (*Addressing questions to children
holding objects*) Can you put the train
on the table?

CHILDREN: Yes.

CHILD: Thank you.

*   *   *   *   *

CHILD: Reach the . . . .

CHILDREN: Thank you.

*   *   *   *   *

THERAPIST: Where will you put the . . .?

CHILDREN: With the . . . , *or* On the
table, *or* In the box.

*   *   *   *   *

THERAPIST: The last time you worked
on the "s" sound in "hit or miss." In
what different ways do you use "miss"?

CHILDREN: (*Individually*) In a teacher's   *In this discussion here th* name, such as "Miss Smith." When you miss a problem in arithmetic. When you miss a friend who is away. When you miss going swimming in winter.

use of speech is stressed before phonetic accuracy. It helps develop the child's awareness that he is working on speech which he uses often.

THERAPIST: That's right, you use the word in many ways. If you think about it, it is almost as easy as getting it in the word "Yes." Try it. Listen first: "s," "miss."

CHILDREN: "s," "miss." (*Therapist continues giving help where indicated. Special help on other sounds may be included here also.*)

THERAPIST: Look carefully at the four things I have here. Ann, hide your eyes. (*Therapist removes one object.*) Open your eyes. What do you miss?

CHILD: The truck?

THERAPIST: Yes *or* Right.

THERAPIST: Before each of you has a turn, let's see if you can get the "s" in "What do you miss?" Try it.

Therapist repeats this activity several times for children to hear the pattern. She may say, "Notice that when you guess correctly what is missing, I say 'Yes.' That is extra practice for those of you who are working on 's.' If you need work on 'r,' you may say 'right.'"

CHILDREN: (*Individually*) What do you miss? (*Children continue practicing it as long as they need help.*)

THERAPIST: Now you may each have a turn. Listen as Billy takes the first turn. There is something for each of you to watch in your speech.

It is better for the therapist or child leading this sequence to indicate the one child who should close his eyes instead of having the entire group do it. This helps prevent ac-

CHILD: Hide your eyes, Ann. (*Child removes one object.*) Open your eyes *or* Ready. What do you miss?

CHILDREN: The . . .?

CHILD: Right, *or* Yes. *(Continue until each child has had a turn removing an object. The therapist may add to the original group of four objects or change it to add interest.)*

THERAPIST: You had fun doing that, didn't you? And you watched your sounds so carefully that I'm going to let you do it again but will make it harder. This time I will take *two* things away. When I choose you, you will tell me just one thing you miss. Then I'll ask you a question, "What else?" and you'll tell me the second thing you miss. Let's try it.

THERAPIST: Jean, hide your eyes. *(Therapist removes two objects.)* Open your eyes. What do you miss?

CHILD: The plane?

THERAPIST: Yes. What else?

CHILD: The . . .?

THERAPIST: Yes.

THERAPIST: That was fun, too, wasn't it? Listen to the new response, "What else?" Try it, remembering that you use the same sound there which you use in "yes" and "miss."

CHILDREN: What else? *(Therapist gives help where needed. If a child has difficulty with both "l" and "s," only the "s" should be emphasized here.)*

cusations of "peeking" and permits all but one child to be in on the process.

THERAPIST: Mary, you may have the first turn. Name the things first so we can remember everything that is here. Six things are quite a few to keep in mind.

CHILD: The . . . , etc. Hide your eyes, Jack. Open your eyes. What do you miss?

CHILDREN: The . . .?

CHILD: Yes, what else?

CHILDREN: The . . . .

CHILD: Yes.

THERAPIST: Joe, you need to work some on your "r" sound now. Try it alone for me. You're getting it better every time. Put it in "R . . . eady." See if you can make it five times. Now try it in "R . . . ight." I'll take the next turn doing the same things that the other boys and girls have been doing, and you notice how I use your "r" sound.

THERAPIST: Betty, hide your eyes. Ready. What do you miss? The . . .? Right. What else? The . . .? Right. Now you take the next turn. (*Child follows above pattern, being held responsible for the "r" sounds.*)

Sometimes you ask the question, "What's missing?" instead of, "What do you miss?" Later on you will work on that, but right now two "s" sounds so close together make it a little hard for you.

(*Other responses which may be set up and*

utilized in a similar manner are as follows:)

CHILD: Hide your eyes.   Open your eyes.
What do you miss?

CHILDREN: The . . .?

CHILD: Yes.

CHILDREN: Where do you have it?

CHILD: In the box *or* In my pocket *or* In
my hand *or* Here.

*   *   *   *   *

CHILD: Peggy, hide your eyes.   Open
your eyes.   What do you miss?

CHILDREN: (*Individually*)   The . . .?

CHILD: Yes.   Do you want it?

CHILDREN: (*Individually*)   Yes, I do.
Thank you.

THERAPIST: What have you worked on
today?

Unit II · Lesson 7

1. *Interpersonal Situation:* including a friend; guessing
2. *Speaking Aspect of Situation:* making introductions; asking and answering questions
3. *Particular Speech Patterns:*
   "This is . . . ."   "I'm thinking of a . . . ."
   "Miss."
   "Mrs."   "Right."
   "Mister."
   "Yes."   "Hi . . . ."
   "Who else? "
   "Guess again."
4. *Sounds Emphasized:* s   r θ
5. *Equipment:* none

PROCEDURES

THERAPIST: When you had a party here several weeks ago, what did you do after you had welcomed your friend at the door and brought him in? Yes, you introduced him to your friends.

Your daddy and mother may have introduced you at some time by saying, "George, this is my son, Jim" or "Meet my daughter, Ann." You make an introduction when you want one of your friends to meet another. If you bring a friend home from school to play, you usually introduce him to your mother if she doesn't already know him. If you bring a friend to speech class, you will need to introduce him to me and to the other boys and girls. Ann has a friend here today. She will introduce her to you this way: "Jean, this is Billy." Billy, you will say, "Hi, Jean," and she will say, "Hi, Billy." Ann, you may introduce her to the boys and girls now.

NOTES

The therapist can plan to have a friend of a child who is in speech class visit frequently, so that such speaking events as greetings and introductions become an integral part of each lesson. Introductions are somewhat difficult and need to be experienced many times.

Permitting the child to bring a friend to speech class has other desirable aspects. He gains recognition in his own class group for choosing a friend to take with him. He is given recognition in speech class from an outsider for a sound or response on which he is working. Since the speech patterns that are being worked on are those every child has occasion to use, a visitor can fit in easily to the group proceedings.

155

Sometimes you forget someone's name when you are making an introduction. Everyone does that at some time or another. If you do that, then you just ask the person his name.

CHILD: (*Introducing friend to each member of the class*) Jean, this is Jimmie.

CHILDREN: Hi. . . .

THERAPIST: When you introduce your teacher, you have a chance to use the "s" in the very word you have been working on — "Miss," as in my name "Miss Hale." Listen: "Miss Hale, this is Jean." Try "Miss" by itself.

CHILDREN: Miss. (*Each child has additional practice with this response.*)

THERAPIST: When you put it with someone's name, it is more difficult. Try it. "Miss Hale."

CHILDREN: Miss Hale. (*Therapist gives individual help as indicated.*)

THERAPIST: Each of you bring a friend to me and introduce him, remembering to watch the "s" sound.

CHILDREN: Miss Hale, this is Jack.

THERAPIST: Hi, Jack.

CHILD: Hi, Miss Hale.

THERAPIST: Did you notice that Jack got his "s" sound in when he said "Hi" to me, too? I liked that.

The therapist may call attention to the "s" in "this" if she thinks individual children are ready to handle it. As a rule, the "s" in "this" is too difficult for many of them at this stage. In particular instances, however, a child may be ready for help here.

CHILDREN: (*Continue until each child has had an opportunity to introduce one child to the therapist.*)

THERAPIST: Now you will need to work on your own teacher's name. Five of you have a "Miss" for a teacher, and the rest of you have a "Mrs." "Mrs." is harder, but I will give you some help with it. The first part of "Mrs." is like "Miss."

THERAPIST: What is your teacher's name?

CHILD: Miss . . . . *or* Mrs. . . . . (*Continue until each child has had a turn.*)

THERAPIST: You have worked on two things today, making an introduction and using the "s" in "Miss" with someone's name. You will soon be able to surprise your teacher by using the "s" when you say her name.

It should be noted that for children who do not need special work on the sounds mentioned here, the practice in use of speech in performing an introduction is also important.

Supplementary Suggestions

THERAPIST: The other day you worked on saying "What else." Here is a way to get some more practice on it and also on the word "thinking" that has a "θ" in it.

THERAPIST: I'm thinking of two boys.

CHILDREN: Harry?

THERAPIST: No, guess again.

CHILDREN: Jack?

THERAPIST: Yes, who else?

This activity may be continued for some time, the therapist at first taking several turns to set the pattern. If the children reply to her question by saying, "Is it Harry?" she may say, "That is one way of asking. An even shorter way is to just use the name like this — 'Harry?'" Many of the children will be ready to include the "s" sound in "Guess again." She should point this out, give them special help, hold them responsible for the "s" there. Children who are still having particular difficulty with the "s" should be con-

CHILDREN: Jim?

THERAPIST: Yes.

(The pattern may be varied as follows:)

CHILD: I'm thinking of two girls here.

CHILDREN: Ann?

CHILD: Right.   Who else?

CHILDREN: Jean?

CHILD: No, guess again.

CHILDREN: Betty?

CHILD: Right.

cerned with it only in "Yes" and "Who else?"

Unit II · Lesson 8

1. *Interpersonal Situation:* making and responding to an inquiry
2. *Speaking Aspect of Situation:* asking and answering questions
3. *Particular Speech Patterns:*

"Yes."	"The . . . ."	"Here."	"For you."
"On the house."	"With a . . . ."	"Reach it."	"Have one."
"What do you miss?"			"May I have
"What else?"	"Thank you."		the . . . ."
"Guess again."	"You're welcome."		"What do you
			have?"

"Get me the . . . ."

"Can you . . . ."
"Take one."
"Keep it."

4. *Sounds Emphasized:* s θ ð f v r k g
5. *Equipment:* cardboard house with detachable parts as windows, doors, etc., or blackboard and chalk

PROCEDURES

THERAPIST: You often use the word "house" when you say such things as "Come over to my house and play," "Let's play in the house," "I'm going into the house and get my marbles," etc. That word "house," like "yes" and "miss" and "What else?" has an "s" in it. Do you hear it? Listen again. Now again.

I'm going to say it two times. Watch me. Listen. Tell me which one sounds better to you, the first or the second one?

(*Therapist gives several series of the word "house" in sets of two, one of them made with a lingual, lateral, or whistling "s," or with the "s" sound omitted, the other within normal range. Children differentiate between the sounds. Therapist helps them both to see and hear differences.*)

THERAPIST: Try the word "house" by itself quickly to see if you can use the "s."

CHILDREN: House.

159

THERAPIST: (*Pointing to an outline of a house on the board, or to a cardboard replica*) What do you call what I have here? Each of you say it, watching the "s."

CHILDREN: House. (*Each child has several turns saying it in reply to the therapist's question. Help is given where needed.*)

THERAPIST: Tell me some things you do in your house. Tell me some things you have on your house and in your house.

CHILDREN: Eat, sleep, read funny books, play, help mother, etc. Doors, windows, chimney, shutters, roof, porch, steps, bricks, boards, etc. Chairs, tables, lamps, pictures, beds, books, etc.

THERAPIST: I have some parts of the house here that will fit on it. Watch. (*She takes articles from pocket or box one at a time for children to see, lays them on the table, waits until children have examined the article and are looking at her face, and sets the pattern by saying "The window," "The door," etc. She can stress a slower rate, pausing between phrases, and including the "ð" sound.*)

Ann, your "ð" sound is so much better. Let's hear you name each of the things for us.

CHILD: The . . . , etc.

THERAPIST: Jimmie, you may pass out these things so each boy and girl has one. You may ask each one slowly and easily, "What do you want?" Each one who answers will check himself on the sound in "the" as he tells you and in "thank you."

CHILD: (*Holding the articles ready to distribute*) What do you want?

CHILDREN: The . . . .

CHILD: Here.

CHILDREN: (*Individually*) Thank you.

CHILD: You're welcome.

(Other speech responses which may be used in a similar fashion are as follows:)

CHILD: *(Distributing articles)* For you.

CHILDREN: *(Individually)* Thank you.

*   *   *   *   *

CHILDREN: May I have the . . .?

CHILD: Yes *or* Reach it.

CHILDREN: *(Individually)* Thank you.

CHILD: You're welcome.

*   *   *   *   *

THERAPIST: *(After articles have been distributed)* What do you have?

CHILDREN: The . . . .

(The therapist may now direct each child to attach his piece to the house, or she may choose a child to lead the activity.)

THERAPIST: Do you have a door for the house?

CHILD: Yes, I do.

THERAPIST: Where will you put the door?

CHILD: On the house.

THERAPIST: *(Directing question to another child while first child actually places article on the house)* Where is Ann putting the door?

CHILD: On the house. *(Continue until each child has had an opportunity to put his piece on the house.)*

THERAPIST: You often use the word "house" when you invite someone to your house, like this, "Jean, can you come over to my house?"

As you leave today, each of you invite one person to come over to your house, saying it as I did and watching the "s" in your new word.

CHILDREN: Jack, can you come over to my house?

CHILDREN: Thank you. I'd like to.

Supplementary Suggestions

THERAPIST: Jerry has difficulty using the "g" sound, but he can make it easily. Show us five of them, Jerry. Now try it in the word "get." That's right. Do it again. All the pieces are on the house. Perhaps you would like to collect them again. You may do it by asking this way: "Get me the door." Try it. Then to give the children practice on using the new word "house," you may ask, "Where did you get it?" I'll show you first.

THERAPIST: Get me the chimney, Jerry. Thank you. Where did you get it?

CHILD: On the house. (*Child may carry on above pattern until the things are removed from the house.*)

This lesson can be adapted very easily in many ways which the therapist will find helpful. One child who frequently substitutes "me" for "I" may describe to the group what he is going to do in this manner: "I'm going to get the window," "I'm going to get the door," etc. A child working on a medial "k" may answer a question from each child in the group, "What will you do?" with "Pick it off." A child who omits the final "z" sound may use this speech as he takes the things off the house one by one: "The window comes off," "The door comes off," etc.

*　*　*　*　*

CHILD: Reach me the flower box.

CHILDREN: (*Individually*) Here.

CHILD: Where did you get it?

CHILDREN: (*Individually*) On the house.

*　*　*　*　*

CHILD: Ann, hide your eyes. (*Removes two parts from the house.*) Open your eyes. What do you miss?

CHILDREN: (*Individually*) The . . .?

CHILD: Yes, *or* Right. What else? *or* No.
That's not right. Guess again.

CHILD: Can you put the window on the
house?

CHILDREN: Yes, I can.

*   *   *   *   *

CHILDREN: (*Directing this question to one
child who is working on the "l."*)   What
will you do with the door?

CHILD: Lay it on the table.

Unit II · Lesson 9

1. *Interpersonal Situation:* making and responding to an inquiry
2. *Speaking Aspect of Situation:* asking and answering questions
3. *Particular Speech Patterns:*

"On the face."   "Thank you." "Reach it." "Get me the
"Yes, I do."   ...."
"What do you miss?" "With it."
"What else?"   "Can you ... ?"
"Guess again."   "Take one."
                                               "Keep it."

                                               "May I have the
                                               ...."
                                               "Have one."

4. *Sounds Emphasized:*   s   θ   ð   f   v   k   g   r
5. *Equipment:* large cardboard face with slits into which the parts of the face can be inserted, or blackboard and chalk

---

PROCEDURES

THERAPIST: You have been practicing on using better sounds in speech you use often, such as "Can I ...?" "Get me a ... ," "Reach one," "Ready," "Yes," "Miss ... ," "Guess again," "What else?" "Thank you," and others. Another word you use often also has an "s" sound. Listen, "face." Where are your eyes, ears? Where is your nose, mouth? Yes, on your *face.* The sound in that is getting easy enough for many of you so that you can almost make it without any help from me, if you stop a minute before you start and remember what you have to do. Let's see if each of you can make the sound twice as you've been learning to do it.

THERAPIST: (*Pointing to one child's face*) What do you call that? That's right, "a face." Do you hear the "s" sound in it? Listen again. Now again.

I'm going to say it two times. Watch me. Listen. Tell me which one sounds better to you, the first or the second one?

(*Therapist gives several series of "face" in sets of two, one of them made with a lingual, lateral, or whistling "s," or with the "s" sound omitted, the other within normal range. Children differentiate between the sounds. Teacher helps them both see and hear differences.*)

164

THERAPIST: (*Pointing to outline of a face on the board, or to a cardboard replica*) What do you call what I have here? Each of you answer that question when I ask you, making sure to include the "s" sound.

THERAPIST: What do you call it?

CHILDREN: (*Individually*) A face. (*Each child has several turns saying it in reply to the therapist's question. Help is given where needed.*)

THERAPIST: What are some parts of a face?

CHILDREN: (*Individually*) Eyes, ears, nose, mouth, chin, eyebrows, etc.

THERAPIST: I have some parts of the face that will fit on it. Watch. (*She takes parts from pocket or box one at a time for children to see, then says, "Watch where I'm going to put it — on the face."*) (*She continues this until she has the parts all on the face. Care should be taken that the children both listen and watch what she says as well as what she does. She can encourage this by being careful to talk before she performs the activity each time.*)

All the parts are on the face now. You are going to have a turn now to do what I did, but you will need to watch the "s" in "face." Try it once again quickly.

CHILDREN: (*Individually*) On the face. (*Each child uses this, teacher giving help where indicated.*)

THERAPIST: Where will you get the eye?

CHILDREN: (*Individually*) On the face.

(*Child takes part from face, and places it on the table.*)

THERAPIST: (*After all parts have been removed*) Where will you put the eye?

CHILDREN: (*Individually*) On the face. (*Parts are replaced on the face.*)

Supplementary Suggestions

THERAPIST: Do you have a part for the face?

CHILDREN: (*Individually*)   Yes, I do.

THERAPIST: Where will you put it?

CHILDREN: (*Individually*)   On the face.

THERAPIST: (*Directing question to another child while first child actually places article on the face.*)   Where is she putting the nose?

CHILD: On the face.

*   *   *   *   *

THERAPIST: In order for you to get some work on the "g," Jerry, you may ask for the parts of the face in this way: "Get me the eye." "Thank you."   "Where did you get it?"

CHILD: On the face.   (*Child may then direct above activity until things are removed from the face, the therapist guiding child's use of "g" in "Get . . . ."*)

*   *   *   *   *

CHILD: (*Addressing question to one child who needs work on "r" and is holding the various parts.*)   May I have the nose?

CHILD: Reach it.   (*Child obtains part.*)   What will you do with it?

CHILD: Put it on the face.

*   *   *   *

CHILD 1: Ann, hide your eyes.   (*Removes two parts from the face.*) Open your eyes.   What do you miss?

CHILD 2: The . . .?

CHILD 1: Yes *or* Right.   What else? *or* No *or* That's not right. Guess again.

CHILD 1: (*After correct guess was made*)   Where were they?

CHILD: On the face.

*   *   *   *   *

CHILD: Can you put the eye on the face?

CHILDREN: Yes, I can.

(*With the parts again on the table, one child may distribute them so that the children do not see what everyone else is getting.*)

CHILD: Have one *or* Take one.

CHILDREN: Thank you.

CHILD: (*Not the same child as the one who distributed*)   What do you have?

CHILDREN: The . . . .

CHILD: What will you do with it?

CHILDREN: Keep it *or* Put it on the face.

THERAPIST: What have you had fun doing today?   What sound have you worked on?   In what new word can you use that sound?

Unit II · Lesson 10

1. *Interpersonal Situation:* borrowing and lending; giving and carrying out directions
2. *Speaking Aspect of Situation:* making a request; asking and answering questions; making and accepting suggestions
3. *Particular Speech Patterns:*
   "A piece of...."   "Here."   "What do you have?"   "That one."
   "Reach it."   "May I have..."
   "Write...."   "Which one?"
   "Can you...."
   "Yes, I can."
   "In my pocket."

   "Get...."
4. *Sounds Emphasized:*   s   r   v   k   g   ð   tʃ
5. *Equipment:* a box containing articles such as a piece of gum, chalk, paper, puzzle, crayon, pencil, newspaper, money, candy, string; or a number of pieces of candy wrapped in cellophane; a piece of chalk for each child.

PROCEDURES	NOTES

THERAPIST: Today I had a "piece of pie" for lunch. Sometimes I have a "piece of cake." When else do you use the word "piece"?

CHILDREN: (*Individually*)   A piece of watermelon, meat, bread, paper, gum, etc.

THERAPIST: Watch what I have in the box. As I take each thing out, you may be thinking what you would like to have. You may be thinking, too, about the way I use the "s" sound. (*Therapist takes articles from the box one at a time for children to see, lays them on the table, waits until children have examined the article and are looking at her, sets the pattern by saying,* "a piece of gum," "a piece of chalk," "a

The objects selected by the therapist should be real objects, not pictures. Simple things such as gum, small note paper, candy wrapped in cellophane, etc., will provide opportunity for many speech responses.

Care should be taken that the "s" in "piece of" is carefully blended.

168

piece of paper," *etc. She may stress a slower rate, pausing between phrases and the "s" sound in "piece.")* You may each have a piece of something, but first you will want to be sure you can use the "s" sound in the new word. Listen. Watch: "A piece of . . . ." Try it.

CHILDREN: A piece of. *(Each child has several turns doing this. Therapist gives help where needed. She may call attention to the children who make it fairly easily, and call on them to set the pattern for the others.)*

THERAPIST: Saying "a piece of gum" is somewhat harder. You will need to practice it carefully. *(Extending a piece of gum)* What do you call it?

CHILDREN: A piece of gum. *(Continue until children can say it fairly accurately.)*

THERAPIST: You may choose what you would like now. Before you get it, however, you must show me how well you can use the "s" when you ask for it. What do you want?

CHILDREN: A piece of . . . .

THERAPIST: Here *or* Reach it.

CHILDREN: Thank you.

(The therapist may choose one child who needs work on the "r" to lead activity so he can say "here" or "reach it.")

THERAPIST: Mary, listen to the way I'm going to begin collecting the pieces the children have. What do you have?

It is not expected that all children are using a newly acquired "s" automatically yet. There will be constant need for the teacher to set the pattern, show the child how to make it, give him special directions. In such an activity as this she will want to help the child succeed as often as he can. If this response is too difficult, she may work in several ways of eliciting "Yes" from him which will still make it possible for him to take part in the activity. For instance, instead of asking, "What do you want?" for obtaining the response "a piece of . . . ." when it is this child's turn, she may ask, "Do you want a . . .?" to which he can reply "Yes."

CHILDREN: (*Individually*) A piece of . . . .

THERAPIST: Can you put it on the table?

CHILDREN: (*Individually*) Yes, I can.

THERAPIST: Thank you.

THERAPIST: (*Directing her question to the child who is working on the "k."*) Mary, why am I going to choose you to do what I did? That's right, so you can get practice on saying "Can," and the other boys and girls can remember about their "s" in "Yes." (*Turning to children*) When all the things are back on the table, you will have fun choosing something different.

CHILD: What do you have?

CHILDREN: A piece of . . . .

CHILD: Can you put it on the table?

CHILDREN: (*Individually*) Yes, I can.

(*Continue with above pattern as indicated.*)

THERAPIST: You may put what you have left in your pocket. What did you put in your pocket?

CHILDREN: (*Answering the question individually*) A piece of . . . .

THERAPIST: Where did you put it?

CHILDREN: In my pocket.

THERAPIST: "In my pocket" uses the

"k" sound that Mary and Susan are working on. Each of you show them how you say it. Now, Mary and Susan, practice it.

THERAPIST: (*To Mary and Susan*) Where did Jimmie put the piece he had?

CHILDREN: In his pocket. (*Continue until children working on "k" have several opportunities to use this response.*)

THERAPIST: You may put what you have back in the box now. What will you put in the box?

CHILDREN: (*Individually*) A piece of . . . .

*   *   *   *   *

THERAPIST: I have a piece of chalk for each of you. The chalk is in different sizes, but each piece writes well. You may tell me which piece you'd like by pointing to it and saying "That one." Try it first.

CHILDREN: That one. (*Therapist gives help as needed.*)

THERAPIST: What do you say when you want something? Yes, "May I have . . . ." You will use that and also the new word "piece" when you ask.

CHILDREN: May I have a piece of chalk?

THERAPIST: Yes, which one?

CHILDREN: That one.

THERAPIST: Here, *or* Reach it.

CHILDREN: Thank you.

THERAPIST: What do you do with chalk?

CHILD: Write with it *or* Draw.

THERAPIST: The word "write" is one for the people who are working on "r" to practice. Try it. Listen: "Wr . . . ite."

CHILDREN: Write. (*Therapist gives individual help where needed. She calls attention to the children who say it easily and well and has them demonstrate to the children who are working on it.*)

THERAPIST: I have a ladder on the board. Watch, I'm going to begin at the bottom of the ladder and put a number on each step. It doesn't matter what number I write, just so I fill the ladder. That was fun, wasn't it? Would you like a turn? Jimmie will tell you what number to write. He may ask you to write any number between one and five. (*This will depend on the ability and grade placement of the group. First graders can usually write to five, second to one hundred, etc.*)

A set of lines on the board representing a ladder or boxes will keep the children's drawings of proportionate size. In this situation, as in others mentioned previously, the activity is planned to provide for speech and is at all times an instrument to promote speech, not an end in itself. When it becomes too interesting or time consuming then it loses its value.

CHILD: Write a one. (*One child follows this direction.*) Where did you put it?

CHILDREN: On the ladder.

CHILD: What did you use?

CHILDREN: A piece of chalk.

*   *   *   *   *

THERAPIST: Sometimes when I come to school, I have to borrow some supplies

Writing numbers may be used if most of the children

from another teacher. Perhaps I need a piece of chalk, or a piece of brown paper, or a piece of string. I often ask a boy or girl to go on an errand for me and get what I need. When you go on an errand, you need to use speech unless someone writes a note for you to take. But when I'm in a hurry, I do not like to take time to write a note, so you need to ask for the thing like this: "Miss Hale would like a piece of string," or "Miss Hale needs a piece of blue paper." You may practice borrowing this piece of blue paper for me, and when I think you are using the "s" the best you can in my name and in "a piece," I will send each of you on an errand.

CHILDREN: Miss Hale would like a piece of blue paper. (*Continue until each child has had several opportunities to use this.*)

THERAPIST: I'm going to send Nancy over here with some things for you to get. I'll ask Jean to sit by the door with some supplies. I'll have Jack over there.

THERAPIST: Ann, I need some more string to wrap this package. Will you get a piece of string for me from Nancy?

CHILD: Yes. (*Going to Nancy*) Miss Hale would like a piece of string to wrap a package.

CHILD: Here you are.

CHILD: Thank you. (*Takes string to therapist*)

THERAPIST: Thank you, Ann.

in the group have had at least a half year in first grade. If they haven't, such objects as balls and sticks may be substituted.

For those children who are ready, writing numbers gives some opportunity to emphasize production of the sound elements contained in the numbers.

Many children who have speech deviations are reluctant to go on errands which involve speech. The therapist can structure the first experiences very simply as in this lesson. She may then suggest that the classroom teacher see that the children are chosen occasionally for errands. It is also possible for the therapist to gradually increase the difficulty of the errand in regard to speech involved and situation and help prepare the child for it.

The children should be held responsible for the "s" sound only in the responses on which they have worked, unless they indicate readiness for greater complexity of responses.

THERAPIST: (*Directing question to boys and girls*) What did you like about the way Ann went on that errand for me?

CHILDREN: She seemed glad she was going. She smiled. She watched her "s" three times in "Yes," "Miss," and "piece." She remembered to say "Thank you."

THERAPIST: (*Continues until each child has gone on one errand. This provides many opportunities for the children to begin evaluating performance in speech. The therapist should call attention to positive assets in each instance, as well as make suggestions for improvement. A comment such as "What did you like?" structures the situation for praise.*)

What did you have fun doing today? Yes, you worked on several new things: "A piece of . . . ," "That one," and "Write . . . ." You also got some practice going on errands. It wasn't very hard, was it?

Unit II · Lesson 11

1. *Interpersonal Situation:* exchanging articles similar to those at a dinner table; purchasing at a store

2. *Speaking Aspect of Situation:* making a request

3. *Particular Speech Patterns:*

<table>
<tr><td>"Some . . . ."</td><td>"Here."</td></tr>
<tr><td>"Will you pass me . . . ."</td><td>"Thank you."</td></tr>
<tr><td></td><td>"You're welcome."</td></tr>
</table>

4. *Sounds Emphasized:*　s　r　θ

5. *Equipment:* a collection of food which children may have occasion to request at the table, such as milk, bread, peanut butter, crackers, etc.; a set of the small packaged breakfast cereals could be utilized; a group of four or five articles such as children have occasion to buy at the store — i.e., gum, candy, peanuts, pop corn; or trading cards, comic books, pencils, marbles, etc.

PROCEDURES	NOTES

THERAPIST: Take a look around the room. Do you see "some windows," "some doors," "some chalk," "some blackboards"? What else do you see?

CHILDREN: (*Individually*) Some cupboards, some lights, some tables, some shades, etc.

THERAPIST: You use the word "some" in many ways. Listen to it. Watch. What sound do you have in it that you have been working on? Try it.

CHILDREN: (*Individually*) Some. (*Continue practicing until children can do it fairly easily with an "s" that is appropriate for each child at his particular level of progress.*)

175

THERAPIST: Look at what I have here: "some corn flakes," "some krispies," "some puffs." You may have a box by asking, using the "s" in "some." What do you want, Ann?

CHILDREN: (*Individually*) Some . . . . (*Continue until each child has one article.*)

THERAPIST: At the dinner table when you want something, you often ask for it by saying, "I'd like some more bread" or "May I have another piece of meat?" You may also ask in this way, "Will you pass me some bread, please?" Listen to it again. "Will you pass me some bread, please?" What sound do you hear in "some bread"? Yes, you have already worked on that. I wonder if you can use it in "pass," too. That is new. Try it by itself.

CHILDREN: (*Individually*) Pass.

THERAPIST: This will be harder. Try "Pass me some . . . ."

CHILDREN: (*Individually*) Pass me some . . . . (*Continue, therapist giving help as indicated. If children are not producing an "s" easily yet, they should be held responsible for an "s" only in one instance.*)

THERAPIST: If you will hold the food you have so that everyone can see what you have, Jack may choose one thing he would like, saying, "Jimmie, will you pass me some butter?" Then the person from whom he gets something will have the next turn.

CHILD: Jimmie, will you pass me some . . . ?

CHILDREN: (*Giving the article requested to the person who requested it*) Here.

CHILD: Thank you.

CHILDREN: You're welcome.

(*This activity should be continued until each child has had an opportunity to exchange articles once or more.*)

THERAPIST: How many of you sometimes go to the store for your mother? Going to the store for your mother is something like going on an errand for me, as you practiced the last time. Perhaps mother may write you a note. More often she tells you what she wants. Often you go to the store to get something you want yourself. I have here some things you might want. Look. Watch. "Some candy," "some peanuts," "some pop corn," "some gum," "some cracker-jacks."

THERAPIST: (*Extending one article*) What do you call it?

CHILD: Some peanuts. (*Continue until each child has additional practice working on "some."*)

THERAPIST: These things are ones with which you will practice. You will not get them to keep, but if you work very hard on speech that you use at the store, the next time you come to class we will walk over to the little store across the street so that you can really buy something.

Joe, suppose you be the storekeeper for a while, and the boys and girls will come to you to buy. Nancy, perhaps you and I can show them first how to do it.

THERAPIST: Hello, may I help you?

CHILD: I'd like some candy.

THERAPIST: Here you are. That will be five cents.

CHILD: Thank you.

This pattern should be repeated several times by the teacher and one child before two children carry it on. The teacher should call attention to various sounds that need to be checked and give individual help in preparation for buying. Here the speech used should be emphasized more than the situation.

Unit II · Lesson 12

1. *Interpersonal Situations:* requesting and granting permission; obtaining an article; carrying on a conversation

2. *Speaking Aspect of Situation:* asking and answering a question; giving a direction; making a comment

3. *Particular Speech Patterns:*

"May I see what you have?" "Reach in and . . . ." "Go to the window."

"Yes, you may." "Get me the . . . ." "Come back."

"What did you see?" "Will you give me . . . ."

"What else?" "I got the . . . ." "Look out."

"Guess again."

4. *Sounds Emphasized:* **s** **r** **k** **g** **l**

5. *Equipment:* a box with an assortment of small objects

PROCEDURES	NOTES

THERAPIST: After you get to school in the morning, you may say to a friend, "Did you see the fire truck go past this morning?" or "Guess what I saw last night," or maybe you will say, "Come, see what is happening to the bulbs we planted." The words "see" and "saw" you use many times during a day. You can hear the "s" sound there, can't you?

I have some things here in the box. You may each see what I have after you have asked permission in this way: "May I see what you have?" Listen again to the way you will ask. "May I see what you have?" Each of you practice it first.

CHILDREN: (*Individually*) May I see what you have? (*Each child has an opportunity to say this, the therapist giving special help where needed.*)

She may need to have children work on "s" in isolation and in "see" but should begin with whole pattern and work back to it.

THERAPIST: Now you are ready to ask. When someone asks you what you saw, you will only tell one thing so other people can have a turn, although there are many things in the box.

CHILD: May I see what you have?

THERAPIST: Yes, you may. (*After child has looked*) What did you see?

CHILD: A blue boat.

THERAPIST: (*To child who has just looked in the box*) You may choose the next person who will ask permission of you.

CHILD: May I see what you have?

CHILD: Yes, you may. What did you see?

CHILD: A red airplane. (*This activity may be continued until each child has had a turn.*)

THERAPIST: In order for Jimmie to use his "r" today, he may tell each of you what to get out of the box in this way: "Reach in and get the red airplane." Jimmie, practice it first to be sure you are using your best "r."

CHILD: Reach in and get the red airplane. (*Child then directs each child to obtain a certain toy.*)

THERAPIST: Mary and Susan, in order for you to work on the "g" sound, one of you may give directions to the other in this way: "Get me the orange train." If Mary tells Susan that, then she will come

The children should feel permissiveness to say "no" occasionally. The therapist may set limits in various ways, such as suggesting that after a child has refused a request twice, he grant it the next time. She may also point out that "no" is easy but that since "yes" is more difficult, he will need to use it more often.

It should be noted here that the usual conversational pattern used in response to the query "What did you see?" consists of one phrase, such as "a red airplane," "a big block," etc. The children should not be expected to answer in a complete sentence. If they do, the therapist may comment as follows: "Sometimes you use a long answer when someone asks you a question; however, more often you give a shorter answer. If, for example, I point to the window and say, 'What is that called?' your answer will be 'a window' and not 'That is called a window.'"

to you and say, "Will you give me the orange train?" and then take it back to Mary. You will want to practice it first.

CHILDREN: (*Individually*) Get me the orange train. Will you give me the orange train?

THERAPIST: Now both of you are ready to collect the things the children are holding.

CHILD: (*Directing question to another child.*) Susan, get me the blue boat.

CHILD: (*To the person holding the boat*) Will you give me the blue boat?

CHILD: Yes, I will.

CHILD: (*Returning to the one requesting the toy*) I got the blue boat.

CHILD: Thank you. (*Continue until toys are collected.*)

*   *   *   *   *

THERAPIST: Now let's have some fun looking out the window to see how many different things you can see. It will give you a chance to work on several things you do very easily now in speech: "Go to the window. Look out. Come back. What did you see?"

I'll do it first so that you can hear what to say. When you come back you will tell only one thing at first, and then I will ask you "What else?"

THERAPIST: Go to the window. Look out. Come back. What did you see?

After the therapist has set the pattern several times, the

CHILD: A swing.

THERAPIST: What else?

CHILD: A slide.

(*Another possibility of using a similar situation for work on these speech patterns is as follows:*)

CHILD: (*After returning from the window*) Guess what I saw at the window?

CHILD: Did you see . . .?

CHILD: No, guess again *or* Yes, I did.

THERAPIST: What have you worked on today? Yes, you have worked especially on the "s" in "see" and "saw." You have also asked permission and told someone what to do.

children may continue with this activity until they have explored most of the possibilities of things to see outside that particular window. It may add to the interest if the therapist keeps a list on the board of each thing that is seen. The children often have fun seeing how long a list they can make.

Unit II · Lesson 13

1. *Interpersonal Situations:* taking a message; obtaining information
2. *Speaking Aspect of Situation:* relating a message; asking and answering questions
3. *Particular Speech Patterns:*
   "What did Jack say?"   Others as indicated in lesson
   "He said . . . ."
4. *Sounds Emphasized:*   s   r   l   k   g   θ   ð
5. *Equipment:* coins

PROCEDURES

THERAPIST: When you come to speech class, you often tell me something your own teacher said to you, or your mother or your daddy. You may tell me, "My mother said she was coming to visit next Thursday," or "My daddy said he was going to take me to the circus when it comes." "Said" is a word you use almost as often as you do the ones we worked on last time, "see" and "saw."

Think of one thing you might say to the person sitting next to you.

CHILDREN: (*Individually*) I'm going to the show tonight. I'm going up town. I'm going outdoors to play.

THERAPIST: There are three things you can choose from to say to the person next to you, either choose the one about the show or one of the others. Later on you may choose anything you like to tell, but for practice we are going to keep to these three things.

NOTES

This lesson may be worked out according to the abilities and interests of the children. If several of the children have speech that is difficult to understand, the therapist will need to limit the responses so that the group will understand what is being said. She may also need to limit somewhat the length of what they say, mentioning perhaps that they tell only one thing. The chief emphasis in the lesson is placed on the use of the words "say" and "said." If children hesitate too long in whispering something to the next child, it doesn't serve to promote use of these particular patterns. For that reason the therapist may suggest several things at the outset from which the children can choose one to use.

183

Jack, suppose you whisper one thing to Jimmie.

Jimmie, what did Jack say?

CHILD: He said he was going to the show.

(*This may be continued until each child has had an opportunity to take part. Individual help should be given where needed on the words "say" and "said."*)

THERAPIST: Often you use "say" and "said" when you take a message for someone. For instance, I may ask one of you to go to the office and tell Miss Avery that I need the key to the speech room. I may ask you to tell your teacher I'd like to talk with her. Your message will sound something like this: "Miss Hale said she needed the key to the speech room," or "Miss Hale said she would like to talk with you."

I will send a message to each of you, and each of you will also get a chance to take a message. Before you do, let's see if you can use the "s" in "said." Listen. Watch. Try this: "Miss Hale said . . . ."

CHILDREN: Miss Hale said . . . . (*Continue until each child has demonstrated his ability to do this as well as he is able.*)

THERAPIST: Joe, you may take the first message. You will speak slowly, take it easy, and talk loudly enough for us to hear. Tell Nancy she should bring a pencil and paper with her to speech class.

CHILD: Miss Hale said you should bring a pencil and paper to speech class.

CHILD: Tell Miss Hale I will. (*Child taking the message returns to therapist.*)

THERAPIST: What did Nancy say?

CHILD: She said she would.

THERAPIST: (*Directing question to other children.*) What did you like about the way Joe took that message?

CHILDREN: (*Individually*) He talked loudly enough for Nancy to hear. He didn't hurry. He waited before he started. He smiled. He used two "s" sounds his new way.

THERAPIST: Kathie, tell Jack that I would like him to help me after school. Before you go, let's hear you use two good "s" sounds in "Miss Hale said . . . ."

CHILD: Miss Hale said . . . .

THERAPIST: Listen first: "s." Try that. Now try it in "Miss Hale said . . . ."

CHILD 1: Miss Hale said she would like you to help her after school.

CHILD 2: Tell her I can't, I have a music lesson tonight.

CHILD 1: (*Returning to therapist*) Jack said he couldn't help you tonight. He has a music lesson.

THERAPIST: Thank you.

THERAPIST: What do you like about taking messages? What speech did you particularly watch today?

These messages should be continued until each child has had an experience both in taking a message and in sending one. In each instance the message can be planned to give particular children work on sounds other than the "s." Before the child takes the message, he should repeat it and be given help in areas where it is needed. These first messages should not involve any materials, it is easier then to keep the messages centered on the speech that is being used. Also, the therapist should plan the first messages. Later, as the class members understand the procedure and are able to do so, they may send their own messages.

r

Miss Hale would like the rest of the boys and girls to come.
Miss Hale is ready for the children in speech class.
Miss Hale would like some string to wrap a package.

l

Miss Hale would like you to come to speech class.
Miss Hale wants you to look for the new chairs.
Miss Hale wants you to lay this on the office counter.

k

Miss Hale said that you are to come to speech class.
Miss Hale said that she cannot see you today.
Miss Hale said you can go to the movie today.

g

Miss Hale said for you to get the other boys and girls.
Miss Hale said for you to go on the trip with your class.

θ   ð

Miss Hale said, "Thank you for the papers."
Miss Hale said that she will be late today.
Miss Hale said the lights in the room will not turn on.

*　　*　　*　　*　　*

(A similar situation for messages may be worked out in a succeeding lesson where each child has some article for which the teacher sends.)

Unit II · Lesson 14

1. *Interpersonal Situation:* giving and accepting an apology
2. *Speaking Aspect of Situation:* stating the apology
3. *Particular Speech Patterns:*

"I'm sorry."   "You have my chair, I think."
"I'm late."   "I was just fooling you."

   "That's all right." Others as indicated in lesson

4. *Sounds Emphasized:* s l ð r θ dʒ
5. *Equipment:* none

PROCEDURES	NOTES

THERAPIST: Occasionally when you are late for something, you need to apologize for it; for example, when coming late to class after recess, being late for your music lesson, coming in late to dinner. If you turn a corner too quickly and run into someone you didn't see, you apologize. When else do you use apologies?

CHILDREN: (*Individually*) When you say something that hurts someone's feelings, when you leave a book at home you were supposed to bring back, etc.

THERAPIST: There are different ways of making an apology. One of the easiest is to say, "I'm sorry I'm late," or "I'm sorry I bumped you. I didn't see you." Practice this much first: "I'm sorry." Listen to it. Watch it. Try it.

CHILDREN: (*Individually*) I'm sorry. (*Continue until each child has had several opportunities to say this; give help where needed.*)

187

THERAPIST: Each of you think of a way of making an apology if you came late to speech class. You will need to watch the "s" in "sorry," and some of you will have other sounds on which to check yourself.

CHILDREN: (*Individually*) I'm sorry to be late. I forgot to watch the clock. I'm sorry I'm late. I was on a trip with my class. I'm sorry I'm late; we had a picture show.

THERAPIST: (*Replies to each apology.*) That's all right for today. I liked the way you gave those apologies. Each of you had a reason for being late. Giving a reason with an apology usually makes the other person feel better.

THERAPIST: Let's work on other times when you need to give an apology. Two of you show what happens when you accidentally bump into someone, perhaps making him drop a book or a package.

CHILDREN: (*Acting out this situation*) I'm sorry; I didn't see you there. That's all right. (*This can be continued until several children have given their version of a situation and the speech used in the apology.*)

THERAPIST: I've noticed that many of you have fun slipping into someone else's chair when that person isn't looking. Usually you do it for fun, but occasionally it starts trouble. When you find someone else in your chair, what can you say? How about the person who has your chair? An easy apology frequently makes things all

The value of acting out such situations has the advantage of making it more real to the children. It should be structured somewhat carefully with the emphasis on the speech that is used. Children will usually have suggestions to make both in regard to the event and the speech.

right: "You have my chair, I think."
"I'm sorry. I was just fooling you."
(*Children like to act this out. Carryover
has often been observed almost immediately
in this situation.*)

*Other situations which may be worked out
in a similar manner are as follows: 1.
Slamming a door loudly; 2. knocking over
a box, shoving some papers on the floor in-
advertently; 3. interrupting when someone
else is talking; 4. others which the children
may suggest.*

THERAPIST: What have you worked on
today? Why? Are apologies easy to
make? Why not? What can you do
about it?

Unit II · Lesson 15

1. *Interpersonal Situations:* making and accepting a suggestion
2. *Speaking Aspect of Situation:* making and accepting a suggestion
3. *Particular Speech Patterns:*

   "Let's get a toy."   "Put the . . . with the rest."
   "That's a good idea."
   "That's mine."   "What did you get?"
   "That's yours."
   "It's a . . . ."

4. *Sounds Emphasized:*   **s**   **ð**   **r**   **g**

5. *Equipment:* an assortment of small cars, boats, airplanes, etc. or other groups of articles; name cards of children

---

PROCEDURES

THERAPIST: Often when you talk, you are in a hurry and you use a shorter way of talking instead of a longer one. You may say "It's in here," instead of "It is in here." You may say "That's mine," rather than "That is mine"; or "Let's go play," not "Let us go play." Each one of the shorter ways has an "s" in it. Listen. Watch. "It's," "That's," "Let's." Listen again. Try them.

CHILDREN: It's, That's, Let's. (*Therapist gives help where needed.*)

THERAPIST: I have some toys here, but you won't come to get one alone; you will choose someone to come with you, and invite him in this way: "Let's get a toy." Try it.

CHILDREN: Let's get a toy; Let's; "s"; "Let's get a toy." (*The therapist should give help as indicated here.*)

NOTES

Because of the frequent use of contractions, several lessons can be built around these phrases.

190

THERAPIST: The person to whom you say it will answer, "That's a good idea." Try it.

CHILDREN: That's a good idea.

THERAPIST: Let's try that much. You may each choose the person you would like to go with you to get a toy.

CHILDREN: Let's get a toy.

CHILD: That's a good idea. (*Children each choose a toy from the table and return to their chairs. This should be continued until each child has either made or accepted a suggestion.*)

(*The toys may be reassembled on the table by one child working on the "r" giving the directions:* "Put the boat with the rest of the toys," *etc.*)

THERAPIST: You had fun making and accepting a suggestion. You had fun, too, picking out a toy you wanted. This time we will change it somewhat so that when you come to the table, you will see a name by each toy. You will say to your friend, "That's mine." Try it.

CHILDREN: That's mine.

THERAPIST: Then your friend may say, "What did you get?" and you will show him, "It's called a boat." You will in turn ask him what he got, and he will tell you. The whole thing will sound like this:

"Let's get a toy."

"That's a good idea."

"That's mine."

"What did you get?"

"It's a boat."

CHILD: Let's get a toy.

CHILD: That's a good idea. (*Children go to table, pick out toys labeled with their names.*)

CHILDREN: That's mine.   That's mine.

CHILD: What did you get?

CHILD: It's called a boat.   What did you get?

CHILD: It's called a train.

*   *   *   *   *

THERAPIST: Try saying each one of these words you have worked on today, because you use them often: "It's," "Let's," "That's."

Unit II · Lesson 16

1. *Interpersonal Situations:* designating possession
2. *Speaking Aspect of Situation:* asking and answering questions
3. *Particular Speech Patterns:*

"His." and "Hers."	"She . . . with it."	"Reach it."
"Please."	"He . . . with it."	"Here it is."
"Whose is it?"		
"A boy's."	"Either one."	Others as indicated
"A girl's."		in lesson

4. *Sounds Emphasized:*   z   θ   ð   r

5. *Equipment:* miscellaneous assortment of articles belonging to boys and girls: hair ribbon, pocketbook, handkerchief, hair clips, jacks, skip rope, wallet, string, marbles, key ring, etc. (Children can usually add to any collection a teacher has.)

PROCEDURES	NOTES

THERAPIST: Occasionally your caps get mixed in the coat room and the teacher has to help you get them straightened out. She may hold up one cap saying, "Whose is it?" You may answer, "It's mine," or "It's yours," or "It's his." When you play with someone's ball on the playground, you have to find out to whom it belongs when recess is over. Sometimes when I come to your room to visit, I ask your teacher, "Which picture is Ann's?" and she may point to one saying, "That's hers." Some of those answers have a new sound on which many of you will begin working today. Listen to the way these speech patterns end: "His," "hers," "yours." Listen to the part alone: "z." That sound is very similar to the "s" sound. See if you can tell the difference. I will give you two words. Tell me where the "z" sound comes — in the first word or the second?

193

caps, sweaters   hands, claps
arms, coats   shoes, walks
legs, socks

THERAPIST: I have some things here that
may be either a boy's or a girl's. If it
belongs to a girl, you may say "hers," if
to a boy, "his." Some of these things
may well belong to either a boy or girl, in
which case you may answer "either one."

*Use here is stressed before
phonetic accuracy is em-
phasized.*

THERAPIST: (*Holding up an article*) Whose
is it?

CHILDREN: His (*or appropriate responses.
This may be continued until children have
had opportunity to use these responses a
number of times. One child who is making
the "z" with a fair degree of facility may
ask the questions after the therapist has set
the pattern a number of times.*)

*The phrase "Whose is it?"
is difficult because of the two
sounds occurring so closely
together. Since some children are just acquiring the
"z" sound, the teacher will
direct that question herself.
She can make a comment as
follows: "You can hear the
new sound in the question
I'm asking, too. Listen:
'Whose is it?' Later you
will work on that, too."*

THERAPIST: Before you go on, let's see
how well you can make the "s." (*Each
child takes a turn at producing the "s"
in isolation.*) Notice that it is whispered.
The new sound has some voice: "z." Try
it in the words "his" and "hers" first.

CHILDREN: (*Individually*) His, hers.
(*Where necessary the therapist should give
the children individual help on the "z" in
isolation. Very often if the child has established an "s," the "z" is relatively simple.*)

THERAPIST: "Please" also ends with that
sound and is something you use almost as
often as "Yes" and "Thank you." Try
it.

CHILDREN: (*Individually*) Please. (*Chil-*

dren are given individual help as needed.)

THERAPIST: While Ann sits at the table where all these things are, I will ask for one this way. Listen carefully so you will know how when it is your turn.

THERAPIST: May I have something of hers, please?

CHILD: Reach it, *or* Here it is.

If the word "something" is too difficult, "one" may be substituted for it. Some children will be ready to include the "s" or "θ" in this more complex phrase.

THERAPIST: Thank you. (*This should be repeated several times, so that the children have frequent opportunities to hear the pattern.*)

THERAPIST: Before you do it, perhaps you should practice parts of it to be sure you get in your sounds.

CHILDREN: (*Individually*) Have, something of hers, please.

THERAPIST: Now put it together. (*Children take turns carrying on above group of patterns.*)

(*The following patterns may be set up in similar fashion to the preceding one and used to meet particular needs within the group.*)

z, tʃ, r
What do you want to do?
Choose one, please.
Reach one, please.
Touch one, please.

s, z, θ, v
Guess what I have.

Something of his?
Yes, I do. See.
No, guess again.

s,   z,   ð,   ʃ,   etc.

Tell me what a girl does with it?
She plays with it.
She wears it in her hair.
She jumps with it.

Tell me what a boy does with it.
He hits with it.
He shoots with it.
He carries money in it.

ʃ,   θ,   v,   z,   etc.

Show me something of hers.
Here it is.
May I have it?
Yes, you may.

*   *   *   *   *

THERAPIST: What new sound have you worked on today? In what speech responses?

CHILDREN: His, hers, boys, girls, please.

THERAPIST: Some of you began work on the "tʃ" in "reach, touch, choose"; others of you on the "ʃ" in "Show me."

Unit II · Lesson 17

1. *Interpersonal Situations:* obtaining information; guessing
2. *Speaking Aspect of Situation:* asking and answering questions
3. *Particular Speech Patterns:*

"What time is it?"	"Yes." "No."	"That's right."
"Is it . . .?"	"It's . . . ."	"Ready."
"Hide your eyes."	"Guess again."	
"Open your eyes."	"See." "Look."	
	"Breakfast."	
	"Lunch."	
	"Dinner."	

4. *Sounds Emphasized:*   z   r   s   tʃ   g
5. *Equipment:* clock with hands that can be manipulated

PROCEDURES	NOTES

THERAPIST: You often ask your teacher or your mother about the time, don't you? You ask if it's time for recess, time for dinner, time to go home, time to go to bed, etc. How do you ask?

CHILD: Is it time to eat?

It is important here to see that the "z" is blended in the pattern "izit."

THERAPIST: That's right. Do you notice that the word "is" has the sound in it that you put in "his," "hers," and "please." Try it by first practicing what you worked on the last time. Listen: "His, hers."

CHILDREN: His, hers. (*Practice continues with therapist giving individual help where needed.*)

THERAPIST: You will be using it in "is it" today. Try it.

197

CHILDREN: Is it. (*Therapist gives help as indicated.*)

THERAPIST: You usually have fun guessing. Today you are going to do it with this clock. In order to make it easier at first, you will fix the clock at one of these three places. See, I have them drawn on the board: at nine, twelve, and six — breakfast, lunch, and dinner time.

THERAPIST: (*After setting the clock and concealing its face.*) What time is it? Is it breakfast time? No, it isn't. Guess again. Is it dinner time? Yes, it is. See.

(*The therapist repeats this pattern several times so the children develop the idea of setting the clock at one of three times and of designating these times as breakfast, lunch, and dinner. Then the children should be given individual help on parts of the response, such as* "What time" *and* "is it." *The pattern will supply conversation for considerable time and offers a number of uses for the* "z" *sound. It may be expanded in the following ways: Hide your eyes. (Child sets clock.) Open your eyes. What time is it? Is it breakfast time? Yes, it is. Now it's your turn.*)

* * * * *

THERAPIST: Think of some questions you often ask about time. I will make a list of them on the board. Watch the "z" sound as you tell me.

CHILDREN: Is it time to go home? Is it time for recess? Is it time for art? Is it time for a story? Is it time for speech class? Is it time to read? Is there time

This is a way of simplifying the lesson if some children do not recognize all the numbers on a clock. If they do know the numbers, they may be given a wider choice of selection but keep the large hand at twelve so they choose only even hours. With a toy clock the large hand can be fastened with tape. A real clock usually holds more interest for children.

Limiting the children's selection makes it easier to keep the emphasis on speech, not on endless guessing. Choices may be varied on successive days when the activity is used.

During the guessing above, one child may be permitted three guesses; if he doesn't get the right answer, the leader may have another turn. As a means of keeping the group better integrated it is suggested that each child be given one turn. The one who guesses correctly may lead then. In the event that no one guesses correctly, the leader may then choose the person to follow him.

for me to finish? Is it time to go to the gym? Is it time to stop work? Etc.

THERAPIST: You see how often you use that in one day, and now you can ask it watching especially that you use the "z" sound.

Unit II · Lesson 18

1. *Interpersonal Situations:* extending a greeting; guessing; obtaining information

2. *Speaking Aspect of Situation:* asking and answering questions

3. *Particular Speech Patterns:*

"Hide your eyes."	"Where is the . . . ?"	"Reach in and get it."
"Open your eyes."	"Is it in the . . . ?"	"Show me."
"Hello . . . ."	"Yes, it is."	
"Who was it?"	"No, it isn't."	Others as indicated in
"Was it . . . ?"		the lesson
	"Who has it?"	
"It's your turn."	"Does . . . ?"	

4. *Sounds Emphasized:*   z   s   ð   r   ʃ

5. *Equipment:* small miscellaneous objects; three boxes

PROCEDURES	NOTES

THERAPIST: Because speech is part of you, your friends know you by your voice. When you talk to them on the telephone, you can usually tell who is talking. Today you will try to guess who is talking by the sound of his voice. Your eyes will be closed. I'll show you.

THERAPIST: Jimmie, hide your eyes. (*Therapist indicates one child who is to come to Jimmie saying, "Hello, Jimmie."*)

CHILD: Hello, Jimmie.

THERAPIST: Open your eyes. Who was it?

JIMMIE: Was it . . .?

THERAPIST: Yes, it was, *or* No, guess again.

THERAPIST: That will be fun to do, won't it? Before you each have a turn, let's

Procedures here include demonstration of the whole pat-

200

see if you know what sounds to watch. When you tell someone, "Hide your eyes," or "Open your eyes," what must you watch? Yes, the "z" sound that you practiced the last time in "is." Try "is" and then "eyes."

tern, practice on parts, then actual doing.

CHILDREN: Is, eyes. (*Each child has several opportunities to say this. Therapist gives individual help as needed.*) Open your eyes. Hide your eyes.

THERAPIST: "Who was it?" will be easy for you to make. Try it. (*Therapist gives individual help as needed.*) This guessing takes three people — one to give the directions, one to hide his eyes, and one to give the greeting. Let's have three people come and practice it first so you will know just how it is done when it is your turn.

CHILD 1: Mary, hide your eyes.

CHILD 2: Hello, Mary.

CHILD 1: Mary, open your eyes. Who was it?

CHILD 3 (MARY): Was it . . .?

CHILD 1: No, it wasn't. Guess again. Etc.

(*This activity provides a number of speaking experiences for the children in the role of giving a direction, extending a greeting, asking a question, answering a question, choosing the next person to have a turn. The speech response "It's your turn," can be emphasized here as well.*)

Supplementary Suggestions

THERAPIST: Ann, I have a penny here. Hide your eyes. (*Therapist places penny in one of three boxes.*) Open your eyes. Where is the penny?

CHILD: Is it in the red box?

THERAPIST: No, it isn't. Guess again. Etc.

CHILD: Is it in the blue box?

THERAPIST: Yes. Reach in and get it.

That will be fun to do, too, won't it? First you will want to work on some of the sounds there for you to watch. Let's have Jimmie and Mary try this part: "Reach in and get it." Try the "r" by itself and the "g" by itself. Now try "R . . . each," . . . now "get," . . . , and now the whole thing: "Reach in and get it." The rest of you try quickly: "Open your eyes," "Hide your eyes," and "Is it . . .?" (*When the children are handling their individual sounds, it is suggested that several practice attempts precede the actual activity, so that the children experience what is to be done, and are aware of the sounds they must check themselves on.*)

*   *   *   *   *

THERAPIST: Joe, hide your eyes. While your eyes are closed I will give the penny to someone here, instead of putting it in the box. Then you have three chances to tell me who you think has it. Open your eyes. Who has the penny?

CHILD: (*Asking person who has hidden the article*) Does Ann have it?

THERAPIST: No, she doesn't. Guess again, *or* Yes, she does. Reach over and get it.

(*Therapist may help children prepare for this activity as in the above two. Variations of these groups may extend over several lessons.*)

*   *   *   *   *

ð,   s,   z,   ʃ,   r,   k

THERAPIST: (*Showing two coins.*) Watch. I'm going to put the dime in one hand, the nickel in the other. See if you can guess where the dime is. (*Extending two closed fists*) Where is the dime?

CHILD: (*Pointing to one hand*) Is it here?

THERAPIST: Yes, it is.

CHILD: Show me.

THERAPIST: See, here it is.

* * * * *

THERAPIST: (*Extending two closed fists.*) Where is the dime?

CHILD: I think it's here.

THERAPIST: That's right. Take it *or* Pick it up *or* Keep it.

* * * * *

THERAPIST: (*Giving the dime to one child while another child is blindfolded.*) Who has the dime?

CHILD: (*Pointing to one child.*) I think she has it.

THERAPIST: No, she hasn't. Guess again.

CHILD: I think he has it.

THERAPIST: That's right, he does. It's your turn.

* * * * *

THERAPIST: Let's make a list on the board of the ways in which you have used the "z" sound today. As you tell me, watch your "z" as you talk. What other things have you watched? Let's make a list of them, too.

Chapter 7

Primary Illustrative Lessons

UNIT THREE

INCREASING FACILITY IN THE USE OF SKILLS

Unit Three contains suggestions for conversational patterns which are intended to promote further experience and wider use of newly acquired sounds, along with greater facility in use of speech as a social tool.

These suggestions will serve chiefly as a guide to the teacher in working out suitable patterns for the particular needs of the children as they progress beyond the early stages of the simpler responses contained in Units One and Two. The patterns are not intended to be inclusive, but merely representative of the kind of work that can be continued.

The teacher may choose parts from several different sequences, make one conversational unit out of them, and build an entire lesson around it. Such a lesson can be developed with two goals in mind: (1) Giving children opportunity to use speech purposefully in a situation closely resembling situations outside class where they are called upon to talk; (2) Giving children experience in using particular sounds on which they have been working.

The procedures employed will be similar to those found in Units One and Two.

The teacher may write several of these conversations on the board,

204

discuss their use, and guide the children in selection of the pattern which gives them practice they need. Each child may want to demonstrate first his ability to include certain sounds; other children may be encouraged to evaluate in such a way as, "She got the 's' sound in 'some' and 'ask' but needs to watch it more in 'store.' " A child may choose the one with whom he would like to talk. Most of the patterns are short and sufficiently simple so that after hearing them once or twice, the child can use them fairly easily.

It should be remembered that the following conversational patterns are worked out for the children who have acquired considerable automatic use of newly established sounds. These lessons are designed to give them wider use of such sounds but under conditions where the speech of the boys and girls is still somewhat controlled, and where they have opportunity to check themselves and be checked. Needless to say, an entire class will not reach this stage at the same time. The teacher will need to adapt some of this material for incorporation in lessons described previously.

A. INTERPERSONAL SITUATIONS WITH THEIR SPEAKING ASPECTS

B. SUMMARY OF ACTIVITIES

C. SPEECH PATTERNS AS INDICATED

D. EQUIPMENT. Several series of related objects

Unit III · Lesson 1

Interpersonal Situation: welcoming a friend

Speaking Aspect of Situation: exchanging greetings

Particular Speech Patterns	*Sounds Emphasized*	*Activity*
1. "Hi...."		These patterns for first and
"Hello .... Come in."	k	second graders must be kept
"Thank you."	θ	very simple. Since many
"Have a chair."	v tʃ	of them do not yet read with
		facility, most practice should
* * * * *		be on responses the therapist
		can demonstrate for them.
2. "Hi...."		
"Hi ... Come in.	k	Children like the procedure
... Sit by me."	s	of one going outside the door
"Thank you."	θ	and knocking, another an-
		swering.
* * * * *		
		The therapist may have each
3. "Hi...."		child say the responses he is
"Hi ... Come in.	k	going to use before he actually
... Meet my friends.		does it with another child.
... This is...."	ð s z	
"Hi...."		
"Have a chair."	v tʃ	
"Thank you."	θ	
* * * * *		
4. "Hi...."		
"Hi ... Come in.	k	
... I'm glad you're here.	gl	
... We are ready for	r f	
you."		

Unit III · Lesson 2

Interpersonal Situation: borrowing and lending

Speaking Aspect of Situation: asking and answering questions

Equipment: a series of related objects

Particular Speech Patterns	*Sounds Emphasized*	*Activity*
1. "May I have one of those?"	v ð z	*Children make a choice of objects, express preference, make a request.*
"Later, you may."	l	
"I'll come back. Thank you."	k θ	
* * * * *		
2. "Could you lend me that one?"	k l ð	
"Yes, right now."	s r	
"I'd like to keep it."	l k	
"See me tomorrow about it."	s	
* * * * *		
3. "May I take one of them?"	k v ð	
"Yes, which one would you like?"	s tʃ l	
"I wish I could have the blue one."	ʃ k bl ð	
"That's all right."	s r	

208

Unit III · Lesson 3

Interpersonal Situation: expressing and accepting appreciation
Speaking Aspect of Situation: giving and receiving compliments
Equipment: none

Particular Speech Patterns	Sounds Emphasized	Activity
1. "I like your . . .	l	*One child may give a compli-*
ribbons."	r z	*ment to another, the second*
dress."	d s	*child give a compliment to*
shoes."	ʃ z	*the third, etc.*
pockets."	k s	
ring."	r	*For work on a particular*
bracelet."	l	*sound the therapist may sug-*
pocketbook."	k	*gest they give the same com-*
		pliment to the boys, a different
		one to the girls. A child
sweater."	s	*working just on "l," for ex-*
shirt."	ʃ	*ample, could choose any. One*
shoes."	ʃ z	*with difficulty on "ʃ" could*
jeans."	dʒ z	*choose "shirt," "shoes," etc.*
belt."		
"Thank you. I like it		
too."	θ l	
* * * *	*	
2. "I like the way you . . .	l	
listen."	l s	
sit quietly."	s	
take your turn."	k	
watch."	tʃ	
come to class."	k kl s	
read."	r	
do numbers."	z	
draw."	dr	
sing."	s	
throw a ball."	θ	
keep your desk clean."	k sk kl	

209

Unit III · Lesson 4

Interpersonal Situation: including a stranger
Speaking Aspect of Situation: making and acknowledging introductions
Equipment: none

Particular Speech Patterns	Sounds Emphasized	Activity
1. "Ann, this is Mary. She is in the first grade." "Hi, Ann." "Hi, Mary."	ð s z ʃ z st gr	Children introduce friends to one another.
* * * * *	*	
2. "Ann, this is Mary. She is in my room at school." "Hi, Ann." "Hi, Mary."	ð s z ʃ z r sk	
* * * * *	*	
3. "My name is . . . . "I am . . . years old. "I am in the first grade. I live at . . . ."	z s z st gr l	

210

Unit III · Lesson 5

Interpersonal Situation: requesting and granting permission
Speaking Aspect of the Situation: asking and answering questions
Equipment: as designated

Particular Speech Patterns	Sounds Emphasized	Activity
1. "May I . . .		*The therapist may discuss with the children the occasions for requesting and granting permission from parents, from a teacher, from a friend.*
close the door?"	kl ð	
open the door?"	p ð	
close the window?"	kl ð	
open the window?"	p ð	
look out the window?"	l ð	
move my chair?"	v tʃ	
"Yes, I'd like you to," or	s l	*She may then have the children suggest ways in which they need to ask permission of her, and of each other. After they have practiced such speech patterns, they will have fun with each other asking and granting permission.*
"No, not right now."	r	
* * * * *	*	
2. "May I get a . . .	g	
book from the table?"	ð	
sheet of paper?"	ʃ v	
piece of chalk?"	s tʃ	
pencil?"	s	
ruler?"	r	
some crayons?"	s kr z	
some paints?"	s	
some scissors?"	s z	
a puzzle?"	z	
"Yes, you may," or	s	
"Not right now, but later."	r l	

Unit III · Lesson 6

Interpersonal Situation: going on an errand

Speaking Aspect of Situation: making a request; relaying a message

Equipment: set of related articles

Particular Speech Patterns	*Sounds Emphasized*	*Activity*
1. "Jean, tell Mary I'd like the red boat."	l ð r	*The errands and messages should be real ones children can participate in within the class; they like telling a second child what to say to a third one. Real objects make it more simple to set up such an activity.*
"Mary, Miss Hale wants the red boat."	s r	
* * * * *		
2. "Mary, tell Jim I want the blue airplane."	bl	
"Jim, Jack wants the blue airplane."	s ð	
* * * * *		
3. "Jim, tell Kathie I'd like the red car."	l r k	
"Kathie, Jack wants the red car."	s ð r k	
* * * * *		
4. "Carolyn, tell Mary I'd like to change chairs with her."	l tʃ dʒ ð	
"Mary, Carolyn would like to change chairs with you."	tʃ dʒ ð	

212

Unit III · Lesson 7

Interpersonal Situation: telephoning
Speaking Aspect of Situation: carrying on a conversation
Equipment: two toy telephones; real ones, if available

Particular Speech Patterns	*Sounds Emphasized*	*Activity*
1. "Hello."	l	*One of the primary purposes*
"Hello. This is . . . ."	s z	*in having children talk on the*
May I talk to . . .?"		*telephone in speech class is*
"This is . . . ."		*to give them some experience*
"Can you come over		*in the actual doing of it. One*
to my house and		*period might well be devoted*
play?"	k v s pl	*to giving them freedom to*
"Yes, I can. Thank		*talk casually. The therapist*
you."	s k θ	*may note speech they use*
"Goodbye."	g	*frequently, and incorporate*
"Goodbye."		*it in a pattern similar to the*
		ones presented here. A sec-
* * * * *	*	*ond period may utilize cer-*
		tain short patterns for work
2. "Hello."	l	*on particular sounds. Chil-*
"Hello. This is . . . ."	s z	*dren who are now using cer-*
"May I talk to . . .?"		*tain sounds with a fair degree*
"This is . . . ."	s z	*of skill can have more flex-*
"How are you feeling?"	f	*ibility in the speech they*
"Fine."	f	*choose to use. Others should*
"I'm sorry you've been		*be held to specific patterns.*
sick."	s v	
"I'm better now."		*Telephone conversations often*
"Goodbye."	g	*reveal interesting informa-*
"Goodbye."	g	*tion about children's facility*
		in use of speech, facility in
* * * * *	*	*shift of roles, wishes they may*
		have, etc.
"Hello."	l	
"Hello. This is	s z	
May I talk to . . .?"		
"Can you go to the show	k g ð ʃ	
with me tonight?"	ð	

213

"I'll ask my mother."   **sk ð**

"Yes, I can."   **s k**
"I'll stop by for you." **st f**
"Goodbye."   **g**
"Goodbye."   **g**

Unit III · Lesson 8

Interpersonal Situation: asking for and giving directions
Speaking Aspect of Situation: asking and answering questions
Equipment: series of related objects placed around the room

Particular Speech Patterns	*Sounds Emphasized*	*Activity*
1. "Where can I find the red stick?" "Go to the cupboard. Look on the top shelf."	k f ð r st g k l ʃ	*The children may place these objects around the room themselves. Three or four at a time is sufficient in order to keep the response controlled, give children practice on sounds.*
* * * * *	*	
2. "Where can I find the red ball?" "Go to the piano. It's on top of it."	k f ð r g s p v ð	*Usually first and second grade children can give only very general directions in regard to finding their house. It is sufficient if they know their address. For those who can give more specific information help should be given on including the sounds.*
* * * * *	*	
3. "Where can I find the wagon for the balls?" "Go to the radiator. It's underneath it."	k f ð z g ð r s	*As soon as possible children should be able to give general directions.*
* * * * *	*	
4. "How do you get to your house?" "It's number . . . on . . . street."	g s s st	
* * * * *	*	
5. "Where is the janitor's office?" "It's in the basement, next to the door."	z ð dz s s st ð	
* * * * *	*	

215

6. "Where is the principal's
      office?"   z ð s
   "It's on the first floor,   s ð st kl
      next to the clock."   fl

         *   *   *   *   *

7. "Where is the nurse's
      office?"   z s ð
   "It's on the second floor,
      right by the bulletin
      board."   ð fl r

         *   *   *   *   *

8. "Where is the gym?"   z ð dz
   "It's on the first floor,
      near the outside
      door."   s ð st fl

Unit III · Lesson 9

Interpersonal Situation: making announcements
Speaking Aspect of Situation: stating certain information
Equipment: none

Particular Speech Patterns	*Sounds Emphasized*	*Activity*
1. "It's time for class to begin."	s kl g	*Children come to front of group, give announcement.*
* * * *	*	
2. "It's time for everyone to take a rest."	s f v k r	
* * * *	*	
3. "It's time to go back to your own room."	s g r	
* * * *	*	
4. "We are going to have a paper sale next week."	g v s st	
* * * *	*	
5. "We are going to buy Christmas seals to-day."	g s z	
* * * *	*	
6. "We are bringing money for Red Cross this week."	br f r ð s	
* * * *	*	
7. "We are going to have a puppet show in our room about the Gingerbread Boy." "We'd like you to come."	g v ʃ r l k	

217

Unit III · Lesson 10

Interpersonal Situation: guessing
Speaking Aspect of Situation: asking and answering questions
Equipment: none

Particular Speaking Patterns	*Sounds Emphasized*	*Activity*
1. "I'm thinking of some-one in this room. Who is it?"	θ v s r z	*Such responses as names, grades, days in the week, numbers, all responses which children use frequently, can be utilized in this activity.*
"Is it . . .?"	z	
"That's wrong. Guess again," or	s r g	
"That's right. It's your turn."	s r	
* * * *	*	
2. "I'm thinking of a day in the week."	θ v ð	
"Is it . . .?"	z	
"That's wrong. Guess again."	s g	
"That's right. It's your turn."	s r	

218

Summary of Key Responses

RESPONSES	LESSONS		RESPONSES	LESSONS	
	Unit I	Unit II		Unit I	Unit II
k			**θ**		
Come	3, 5	3, 12, 13	Thank you	1, 2, 3,	1, 2, 3, 4,
Can . . . ?	2, 4, 5	8, 9, 10,		4, 5	5, 6, 8, 9,
(cannot)		13			11, 13
Catch		5	Both		1, 2, 3
Keep it		8, 9	Throw it		5
In my pocket		10	I'm thinking of		7
You're welcome		11			
Take		4, 8, 9			
. . . ticket		4			
g			**ð**		
May I go . . . ?		3, 12	The	2, 3, 4	6, 8, 9
. . . get		4, 8, 9,			12, 15,
		10, 12,			16, 18
		13, 15,	In the	2, 3, 4	6
		18	That one	2, 3, 4	2, 10,
. . . give		4, 12			13
Guess again		7, 8, 9,	This is	5	7
		12, 17	. . . them		1, 2, 3
I got		12	That's		14, 15
			Either one		16
f			With mine		
For you	1, 2, 3,	4, 5, 6, 8	(. . . it, the)	3, 4	1, 2, 4, 6,
	4, 5				8, 9, 15,
					16
v					
Have one	1, 2, 3, 4,	2, 3, 8			
	5				
May I have?	1, 2, 3, 4	2, 4, 5, 6, 8, 10			
What do I have?	2, 3	8, 10, 12			
. . . of		1, 2, 3, 7			

RESPONSES	LESSONS		RESPONSES	LESSONS	
	Unit I	Unit II		Unit I	Unit II
s			**ʃ**		
Yes		1, 2, 3, 4, 5, 6, 7, 8, 9, 10, 12, 17	She	16	
			Show me	18	
Hit or miss?		5	**r**		
Miss		5, 6	Reach it		2, 4, 5, 6, 8, 9, 10, 12, 16, 18
What do you miss?		6, 8			
What else?		6, 8, 9, 12	Here There		2, 3, 4, 5, 6, 8, 10, 11, 16
This		7			
Who else?		7	One more		2
Guess again		7, 8, 9, 12, 17	Right		3, 5, 7
On the house		8	Write		3, 10
On the face		9	Ready?		5, 6
A piece of		10	That's all right		14, 17
Some		11	With the rest		13, 15
Will you pass ...?		11	**l**		
May I see?		12, 17	I like. ...	4, 5	13
What did you see?		12	Lay it down		2, 4, 13
What did ... say?		13	Have a look		2, 3, 4, 5, 6, 13, 12, 17
He said		13			
I'm sorry		14	I'm late		14
That's		14, 15	Hello		18
Let's		15			
It's		15, 17			
z			**GENERAL**		
His Hers		16	Hi		
Please		16	Is your name ...?		
Whose ...?		16	What is your name?		
A boy's		16			
A girl's		16			
... is it?		16, 17, 18			
Hide your eyes		17, 18			
Open your eyes		17, 18			
Who was it?		18			
Where is the ...?		18			
Who has it?		18			
... does ...?		18			

Chapter 8

Intermediate
Illustrative Lessons

UNIT ONE

DEVELOPING THE THERAPEUTIC RELATIONSHIP

A. INTERPERSONAL SITUATIONS WITH THEIR SPEAKING ASPECTS

B. SUMMARY OF ACTIVITIES

C. SUMMARY OF SPEECH PATTERNS

Lesson 2
"The . . . ."   "May I have the . . . ?"
"On the . . . ."   "Will you give me the
                                   . . . ?"

Unit I · Lesson 1

1. *Interpersonal Situations:* getting acquainted; taking part in a discussion
2. *Speaking Aspect of Situations:* exchanging greetings; obtaining information about names; expressing an opinion
3. *Particular Speech Patterns:* none
4. *Sounds Emphasized:* none
5. *Equipment:* none

PROCEDURES

THERAPIST: Your teacher has told you that you were coming to speech class. You may be wondering why you are supposed to come. Perhaps you have an idea why you are here, but are wishing you didn't have to miss your other classes. We are going to be talking about your job here. First we need to get acquainted, to find out more about each other.

I have talked with most of you before today. Let me see if I know your names yet. "Is your name . . .?" (*Therapist asks each child, using this same pattern. If she is not certain of a name, she may ask, "What is your name?" She may extend this questioning period somewhat by asking for such information as "What grade are you in?" or "What is your home address?"*)

I have found out some things about you. I want you to know some things about me, too. My name is Miss . . . . I teach boys and girls just like your own teacher does. However, I am not so concerned about the way they read, do arithmetic, or spell, but I am interested in the ways they talk.

NOTES

Whatever responses children make are acceptable here. A child may lower his head, make a verbal response, or refuse to take a turn. He can be praised for listening, sitting quietly, learning one name. Another child, more ready, may be chosen early to set the pattern of asking each child a question. The therapist can expect and accept different degrees of participation

This experience will give the therapist an opportunity to observe the children's facility in use of speech. A few simple speech patterns may be established early if desired.

225

Some boys and girls, for instance, have a difficult time making people understand what they mean. Have you known some like that? Others can talk very well; their friends know what they say, but their speech may sound or look different from that of others so that once in a while a comment will be made such as, "He sounds funny when he says 'four,'" or "She seems to stick her tongue out more than she needs to when she talks." Other children have speech that can be understood easily, that doesn't sound or look too different from other persons', but these children may have a difficult time talking in front of a group of people, talking to someone they don't know very well, or talking loudly enough to be heard. Have you known someone like that?

I believe most of you can ask each other's name fairly easily. You may ask this way, "Is your name...?" or "What is your name?" as I did. If you know the grade of the person to whom you are speaking you may say, "You're in the fifth grade, aren't you?" If you don't know, you may ask in this way: "What grade are you in?" Listen carefully as you each have a turn. See if you can hear ways in which speech is alike, ways in which it is different from your own speech.

This part of the lesson is structured to promote participation, to encourage one child talking directly to another. Phonetic accuracy need not be emphasized. It is a way of increasing a child's confidence in his ability to use speech, of increasing perceptions of his own personal worth. Such goals will be furthered by comments of the therapist directed toward praise, by recognition of such qualities as smiling, looking at people, talking loudly enough to be heard, etc.

CHILDREN:* (*Take turns individually going around the class asking one or two questions.*) Is your name...? *or* What is your name? You're in...grade, aren't you? *or* What grade are you in?

---

* The term "children" as it is used throughout the lesson procedures designates a number of children in the group responding one at a time.

THERAPIST: (*In most groups the therapist will need to give the children a basis for the comments which follow each child's performance, such as,* "Were you able to hear Susan easily?" "Did Jean look at you when she asked her questions?" "Did George's speech seem smooth to you?" "Was it slow enough for you to understand?" *What did you like about the way Jimmie did this?*)

Let's begin making a list on the board of things you *like* about the speech of people in this class.

You have perhaps noticed that no two people ever talk exactly the same. Ann, close your eyes. Listen as each person says "O.K." (*Children do this. Others may take turns listening.*) In each instance you can about guess who it is, can't you? It's like that when someone you know calls you on the telephone. You can usually tell who is speaking if it is someone you know well and often hear talk.

While none of us talk exactly alike, most of us talk enough alike so that we don't sound too different from other people and the difference doesn't make it hard for others to understand us.

You have talked about things you like in each other's speech, about things you do well when you talk — such as talking loudly enough, smiling, going slowly enough to be understood, etc.

Most of you are here for help on one or two things that you don't do as well.

The therapist may call attention to the following characteristics, for example:

1. *Rate appropriate for the occasion.*
2. *Volume adequate for the occasion.*
3. *Quality that seems pleasant to the listener.*
4. *Rhythm and force patterns that have variety and smoothness.*
5. *Directness through eye contact, smile, etc.*
6. *Production of sounds within normal range.*
7. *Pitch that is appropriate. Notice that the first discussion of similarities and differences in speech should be built around speaking assets the children have.*

Let's see if you can discover some of these things yourself. Let's watch and listen while each of you counts to ten. See if you can notice some differences here. (*Children do this individually.*)

THERAPIST: What did you notice about Jim? Yes, his tongue came out when he made "six" and "seven." You are lucky, Jim, in that no one has trouble knowing what you say, but you look somewhat different from other people when you say those two words. Watch me. Can you tell the difference? (*Therapist makes the two words — one with lingual protrusion "s," the other with an "s" that is within normal range.*) You are also lucky, Jim, in that usually that sound is easy to improve. Try it right now. Just keep your teeth together and say "s." The words "six" and "seven" are not as easy as some others. Try that sound with your teeth together in the word "Yes." Show the other children. Isn't that better already?

What did you notice different about Jean? Yes, her words "three" and "four" sound different. What particular sound is difficult for her? Yes, the "r." That sound has to be made by moving the tongue more than she may be moving it. Make it for her. (*Children do this individually.*) Now try it yourself, Jean. You will need more help on that, but you are already moving your tongue more and that means the sound will improve.

(*The therapist may go on in this fashion pointing out differences, letting the children*

Much of the importance of this lesson lies in the therapist being casual, objective, but encouraging about the particular speech problem each child has. Approaching it first through assets that he has in speech, then discussing the fact that all speech is different in many respects, then going on to point out one or two differences that are great enough to "make a difference," and concluding with some brief demonstration of what can be done about the "difference" will give the child some insight and reassurance regarding his coming to speech class.

The extent to which the therapist explores this area of speech-needs on the first day of class will depend somewhat on the group. For some children it is highly essential that they know from the beginning the reasons for their being in speech class. For others, a general discussion of speaking assets will be sufficient for the first meeting. The speech problems may be considered at greater length than on subsequent meetings. It is believed that the therapist will get better results over a long period of time if she proceeds slowly in the first lessons, helping the children develop awareness of similar-

evaluate *particular sounds, showing them how certain sounds are made, getting various members in the group to set the patterns for other children, etc.)*

Before you go back to your room, let's see what you have learned about speech today. Is all speech alike? In what ways is it different? What did the other people here like about your speech today? What can you do to improve your speech? In what ways is it important for you to improve your speech? We will be talking more about that next time.

ities and differences in speech and giving them experience in using speech. Much of this can be done through the medium of the following lessons rather than just discussions.

Supplementary Suggestions

The therapist will want to begin patterning the needs of children in these early lessons: i.e., predominance of a need for belongingness, recognition, participation, permissiveness, success, etc. She needs to establish the feeling in each child that he is *liked* by the therapist, that there are many things he can do well, and that she * is there to help him.

The situations which are suggested in this first lesson may serve as the basis for meeting various individual needs such as those mentioned above. Children who have particular speech needs other than those indicated in this lesson do not necessarily have to begin working on sounds immediately since their first classes are conceived of as a readiness period for such work, a time in which they become aware of their abilities in speech, as well as a time for developing a sense of satisfaction through participating in the experiences provided.

It is understood that a child may come into speech class with some anxieties and insecurities concerning this new experience, some resentment at being singled out as "different" from his other class members. The therapist needs to recognize and accept behavior indicating such feelings. The child will need warmth and support, reassurance, emphasis on assets, not stressing of liabilities. If he doesn't volunteer to enter into these first lessons, he should not be forced or penalized,

---

* For purposes of simplicity and clarity in language structure the therapist is designated by the pronoun "she," the child by the pronoun "he."

but given time until he is ready to take part. She may take his turn with him for a time, or let another child help him.

One child may come with excessively high levels of aspiration determined to do everything "perfectly" and be easily upset when he doesn't live up to his own standards. The dynamics of this behavior are undoubtedly related to deep-seated feelings of inferiority and a need for winning approval. The therapist will want to guide him in achieving satisfaction by helping him to do better than he was, and by encouraging him to give a response more adequately than he did previously. She will want to praise him for willingness to take his turn, to listen to others, etc. She may help him understand that everyone in the class needs assistance from time to time, that everyone has some things he can do more capably than others, and thereby allow him to accept for himself a less high standard of performance.

Another child with an excessively low level of aspiration is undoubtedly struggling with feelings of inadequacy and inferiority, feelings that there is no use in trying, that he is not liked, not wanted, etc. Here the therapist can begin by noticing areas in which he merits praise, even for such a simple task as arranging the chairs, helping her carry materials. She may see that he receives recognition from the group for taking part in any limited way that is possible for him at this stage of his development. She may structure his turn so he is able to succeed and from that guide him in increasing perceptions of his own personal worth.

Unit I · Lesson 2

1. *Interpersonal Situations:* borrowing and lending

2. *Speaking Aspect of Situations:* asking and answering questions

3. *Particular Speech Patterns:*

"The . . . ."	"May I have the . . . ?"
"On the . . . ."	"Will you give me the . . . ?"

"Thank you." "Yes." "No."

4. *Sounds Emphasized:* ð θ v s

5. *Equipment:* desk articles used at school, such as pencil, pen, ink, paper clips, thumbtacks, ruler, crayons

---

PROCEDURES

THERAPIST: You use speech in many ways during a day. Can you give some examples? I'll write them on the board. For instance, I use speech on my way to school in the morning when I say "Hi," to someone I know. For what different purposes and different times do you use it?

CHILDREN: (*Responding individually*) When you ask or answer a question, tell your mother something you want to eat, ask what time it is, talk on the telephone, invite someone to a party, give a book report, give an apology, ask permission to go to the show, ask a direction, etc.

THERAPIST: There are very few times when you don't need speech. If you are playing ball, the playing counts more than the speech, but you need to talk sometimes, too, about choosing sides, following the rules, talking over a decision the umpire made, etc. You may not need very much speech when you go

NOTES

Use of this activity encourages both participation and functional speech. Phonetic accuracy, where children are ready for it, can be promoted also. A child with delayed speech or very distorted speech may be encouraged to get proper over-all syllabification if he is ready. Sounds may be stressed later for him.

This illustrates procedure from whole to parts: discussion of the situation first, then the speech involved and, lastly, the sounds included.

231

to the library to look for a book to read. However, if you can't find one, or a certain one for which you are looking, you will need to ask the librarian for help and then thank her for it. In this class you will be working on different uses of speech as well as better ways of speaking.

Today, for example, you are going to be working on speech that you often use. What does mother do if she is cooking dinner, finds out that she is out of salt, and the store is closed? What does your dad do if he is working on the car and needs a special tool he doesn't have? What do you do at school if you have no pencil, or your pen is dry, or you are working on a history notebook and run out of paper? That's right, you ask to borrow.

How do you ask when you want to borrow something?

CHILDREN: (*Individually*) I need some paper. May I use your pencil? May I borrow some ink? How about lending me your ruler?

THERAPIST: There are many ways to ask. You are going to work on one way today that is easy for you. In the box I have some things you keep in your desk or use at school. Listen and watch as I take out one object at a time and put it on the table. "The pen," "The paper," "The crayon," etc. Notice that I put the "ð" sound in each time I named one thing. That is an easy sound for some of you. Four of you often say it incor-

The therapist should place the object on the table, allow time for the children to look at it, then name the object as the children's attention is focused on what she is saying, not on the object.

As the children make these simple responses, the therapist should mention some positive asset of each child, thus promoting his sense of

rectly or leave it out. Each of you try it in the word "the."

personal worth, ability to perform certain tasks, etc.

CHILDREN: (*Individually*) The.

THERAPIST: As I point to one of the materials, see if you can tell me what it is called. As you do, watch to see that you are including the sound "ð" in "the."

THERAPIST: What do you call it?

CHILDREN: The . . . , etc. (*Continue until each child has had a turn.*)

THERAPIST: You may choose one thing you'd like to have. If you watch the "ð" very carefully, I will give it to you. The article you want may be on the table, or another child may be holding it.

Eventually the children will be able to make comments about each other's speech. This serves to keep group members a part of each activity and gives individual children recognition from their peers, promoting group belongingness, feelings of success.

THERAPIST: Jean, what do you want?

CHILDREN: (*Individually*) The . . . . (*Continue until each child has had a turn, received an article.*)

THERAPIST: Now that most of you have something, I will show you how I go about borrowing.

THERAPIST: May I have the pen? (*Addressing each child*)

CHILDREN: (*Individually*) Yes.

THERAPIST: Thank you. (*Continue until therapist has re-collected items.*)

THERAPIST: Each of you ask for this one thing for practice now. Check yourself

Therapist continues this procedure until articles are again on the table. In this manner she presents the whole pattern, "May I have the . . . ," so that the children hear it a number of times. As she does it, she may pause occasionally to point out use of "ð" and "θ" in "The . . ." and "Thank you."

on saying "have the." If you do it as well as you can today, then you may actually begin borrowing what you want.

CHILDREN: (*Individually*) May I have the pen? (*Continue until each child has had a turn, therapist giving help where needed.*)

THERAPIST: You are ready to begin borrowing. Usually when someone asks to borrow something, you are willing to lend it. There are some exceptions, some times when you will say "No." You may feel free to say "No" occasionally today, although in order for each of you to have the practice you need, you will need to say "Yes" to the request most of the time.

If the response "May I have the . . . ?" is too difficult for a child needing work on both the "ð" and "v," "May I have a . . . ?" or "May I have it?" can be substituted.

Children need permissiveness to refuse a request occasionally. If a child is reluctant to relinquish his object, or makes little attempt to use the pattern as it has been suggested, the therapist will be guided by her understanding of the child's dynamics in handling such a situation. He may have been held to rigid standards of performance and have a great need at the moment for permissiveness to "do it wrong." He may feel insecure, wanting the therapist to like him, and not sure she does; he may be testing her to see if he can keep her love even though doing something of which she will not approve. Likewise he may be testing his relations with one or several members in the group.

Whether the therapist chooses to ignore the behavior, accept it, or suggest the child's doing differently, she will be careful not to reject him, label his behavior "bad" or punish him.

As the child grows in his feelings of security and belongingness, he will be more ready to be guided in acceptable forms of behavior and will learn to act in terms of consequences for himself and the group.

CHILD: May I have the scotch tape?

THERAPIST: Yes.

CHILD: Thank you. (*Continue until two or three children have items.*)

THERAPIST: You are finding the "v" and "ð" sounds easy, aren't you? Notice that you use a "θ" sound which is

There may be occasion to refer to production of the "s" sound in "yes" here. The therapist should be guided by the needs of the group. A child with multiple sound substitutions ought to have emphasis placed only on the sounds mentioned previously, the "v" and "ð." The therapist may choose to look upon these first periods as a

similar in the word "Thank you." Try it.

CHILDREN: (*Individually*) Thank you. (*Therapist gives help on "θ" as needed.*)

THERAPIST: You may go on with your borrowing now, so that each of you has several chances to borrow what you would like.

CHILD: May I have the . . .?

CHILD: Yes.

CHILD: Thank you.

THERAPIST: What did you like about the way Jim asked for the ink? Yes, he smiled, looked at the person to whom he was talking, and talked loudly enough to be heard.

You have practiced borrowing and lending today. Mother often asks, "Where did you hang your coat?" and you reply, "In the closet." Or Dad says, "Have you seen the wrench I like?" and you answer, "It's in the garage." Notice that the word "the" occurs over and over. That is one reason you need to work on it. You may place the article which you have borrowed "on *the* table" now. Do you hear the sound "ð" in that phrase? Watch it. It will be harder for some of you. Try it.

CHILDREN: (*Individually*) On the table. (*Therapist gives help where needed.*)

THERAPIST: Where will you put the paper clips?

time for encouraging children to participate, building up an awareness of their assets, and not a time to focus on the more difficult sounds.

The therapist should guide and encourage the children in their evaluation of each other's speech, gearing it positively as much as possible. Some mention may be made of the voiced and voiceless "th" ("ð" and "θ"). Usually children differentiate these sounds fairly easily, producing them through imitation.

Here the therapist will accept from each child the response he is capable of and ready to make. One child may merit praise for merely taking his

CHILDREN: (*Individually*) On the table.

THERAPIST: Thank you. (*Continue until all the items have been re-collected.*)

THERAPIST: What have you worked on saying better? Let's see. All of you said "May I have the ...?" several times, and "Thank you." Some of you are using the "ð" sound now in it. Each of you used "the" in two ways, some of you with the "ð" sound.

In addition I noticed that Mary offered to take several turns herself today, Roger sat in his chair without annoying the person next to him, John came with a happier look on his face, Ann talked loudly enough for us to hear her, Kenny didn't mind so much saying the one answer wrong because he knows now he can do it better. Bill didn't feel like borrowing and lending things today so he watched while you did it. I noticed that he kept track of who hadn't had a turn, and that was a help to me.

turn in placing the object on the table, another for using four syllables, another for smiling, a fourth for including the "ð" sound.

The therapist needs to begin developing in the child awareness of his job in speech class regarding both what speech responses he uses adequately under guidance and the responses on which he requires help and practice. At first she will point this out rather specifically at the conclusion of each lesson; later on the children will do more of it themselves.

Unit I · Lesson 3

1. *Interpersonal Situation:* borrowing and lending
2. *Speaking Aspect of Situation:* asking and answering questions
3. *Particular Speech Patterns:*

"The . . . key."   "May I have the . . . ?"
"On the . . . ."   "Will you give me the . . . ?"

"Thank you."   "Yes." "No."
"I'm thinking of a . . . ."

Additional patterns included at the end of this lesson:

"Hello."   "Will you give me . . . ."
"Lay it . . . ."   "Get me . . . ."
"May I look?"
    "Choose one."
"Reach one . . . ."   "How much?"
"Put it right in . . . ."   "Change . . . ."
"Put it in here . . . ."   "Join . . . ."
    "Show me . . . ."
    "I wish . . . .
    "I'll trade."

4. *Sounds Emphasized:* θ ð f v g
   Additional sounds emphasized: l ɾ g tʃ dʒ ʃ

5. *Equipment:* blackboard and chalk, keys and blank key tags

---

PROCEDURES	NOTES

THERAPIST: The last time you were here you talked about articles which you often have to borrow in school. What were they? Did you borrow anything after class? Did you hear any of your friends borrowing? What speech did they use? What speech did you use? There are many ways of asking. What way did you work on? Why? Yes, it is one people can understand easily, one others use often, one some of you need help in saying.

What are some things your mother bor-   *Giving children a moment to*

237

rows? Your father? Do you ever have to ask for a key? When? There are many kinds of keys which you have chances to use at various times. Let's make a list on the board. I'll give you a minute to think of two kinds. Get ready to tell me and check yourself on using "ð" in "the," which you worked on. I'll begin: "The door key."

THERAPIST: Jean, tell me one kind.

CHILDREN: The car key. (*Each child has a turn to supply name of one key. Therapist lists on board.*)

THERAPIST: I will mark the key tags on these real keys according to your suggestions on the board. I will leave the list there, so that you may use it if you need it.

THERAPIST: Jack, which key do you want? Before you answer, what sound will you need to check yourself on? That's right, you will need to watch "ð" when you answer.

CHILD: The car key.

THERAPIST: Here it is, *or* Reach it.

CHILD: Thank you. (*Each child takes a turn, receives a key.*)

THERAPIST: Ann, you are using the "ð" sound much better than you were. You may collect the keys now. What will you ask?

CHILD: May I have the key?

think of one or two kinds of keys keeps the emphasis on the speech. The therapist should also be ready with suggestions. Time should not be consumed waiting for children to supply names of keys.

For the child who may substitute the "t" for "k," the therapist may call his attention to the way the word "key" is said. Since this word does not occur frequently in a child's vocabulary, it probably should not be stressed here unless the child is able to produce the sound and include it with a fair degree of ease.

The children will be able to suggest a number of different keys. It is suggested that they be limited on the board list to seven or eight. The children are not to be held responsible for sounds in the various items as trunk, floor, suitcase, store, etc., but only for "ð" in "the . . . ." The therapist may call attention to a particular sound, make some comment about it, repeat the pattern within normal range, and indicate that the child will receive help with it later.

CHILDREN: (*Individually*) Yes.

CHILD: Thank you.

THERAPIST: Ann, you did that well, remembering the "ð." Joan, listen as she does it for you again. She is using the "v" sound in "have," too. That is one you must watch. Now you try it. That is much better. Try it again. See if you can get these keys away from me by asking the way Ann did, but checking yourself on the "v."

CHILD: May I have the . . . key?

THERAPIST: Yes.

CHILD: Thank you.

THERAPIST: I believe you are all ready now to borrow a particular key you want. Jimmie, what will you need to watch when you ask? Ann? Jean? Now you may ask for any key that is here. I will check off the keys on the list here on the board as you call for them. You may not ask for a key that someone else has until later. Jim, you may ask first.

CHILD: May I have the store key?

THERAPIST: Yes.

CHILD: Thank you.

THERAPIST: Jimmie, that is easy for you. Let's see if you can still make that new sound "s" in "yes" with your teeth together and your tongue behind. Try it.

CHILD: "s"

Legitimate, sincere praise should constitute an integral part of each lesson. It contributes to developing a child's sense of confidence and belongingness, makes him better able to profit from help,

THERAPIST: I liked that. Now try it in the word "Yes."

and gives him status in the group.

CHILD: Yes.

THERAPIST: That is much better than your old one. You may take my place here, and as the children request a key, you may give them one. It will give you practice on the "Yes." (*All children but one or two have a turn.*)

THERAPIST: Mary and George don't have keys yet. There are none left on the table. Hold your key in your hand where they can see which one you have. Mary, you may choose any one and request it in the same way. If she gets your key (*turning to other children*), then you will have the next turn.

The children should be permitted freedom to refuse a request. The therapist may place some limits on it, such as refusing once, etc.

CHILD: May I have the . . .?

CHILDREN: (*Individually*) Yes, *or* No.

CHILD: Thank you.

THERAPIST: What have you worked on today?

Supplementary Suggestions

For the therapist who finds certain children ready for work on specific sounds, or who feels compelled by time limits to begin work immediately, the following suggestions may prove helpful. For most satisfactory results the same responses should be incorporated in a number of lessons.

A child who has difficulty only with "l" can being working on it in "Hello," greeting members of the group at the beginning of each class period. He may direct the children at the conclusion of the activity with keys or desk materials to "Lay it on the table." He may ask, "May I look at your key?" or "May I look at what you have?"

A child who has difficulty only with "r" and for various reasons is believed ready for work on it may have to work on it for some time. If this is true, as the therapist has other children working on the "v" or "ð," she should point out these latter sounds are easy for him, and he can help the others since he makes them so well. She may go on to begin showing him movement and direction for one key response which she selects. For example, the child may hold out a box, saying, "Put it in here." He may pass out the keys saying to each child, "Reach one." He may collect the keys, directing each child to "Put it right in the box."

If a child has difficulty only with an "s," it is suggested that he be given recognition for the simpler sounds which he makes easier and be called on frequently to set the patterns for some of the other children. When the therapist feels it wise to begin working on this sound, she may give him various directions which guide him to produce the sound within normal range. As soon as the sound is going in the direction of normal, he should be given help incorporating it in one response such as "Yes," which can be utilized in a number of ways in the previous lessons, as already indicated.

If a child has difficulty with the "k" and "g" sounds, he also can first receive recognition for the sounds he makes well. He then may be helped to make the difficult sounds through imitation and incorporate them in one key response, such as "Will you give me the ...?" or "Will you get me the ...?" or "Come, put it on the table."

If a child has difficulty only with one or two consonant combinations, such as "tʃ," "dʒ," "ʃ," "tr," some key responses, such as "Choose one," "Which one ...?" "How much," "Change this one for that one," "Join yours with mine," "Show me the ...," "I wish I had a ...," "I'll trade you ...," etc., may be used.

Children who have considerable difficulty with the first sounds introduced, the "θ," "ð," and "v," should just be held responsible for the patterns already suggested until they can use them almost automatically in a variety of situations. Other children who acquire facility in using these sounds more rapidly may be encouraged to use some of the following key responses in activities.

THERAPIST: What will you put in?

CHILD: One of the ....

*   *   *   *   *

THERAPIST: How many will you put in?

CHILD: . . . of them.

*   *   *   *   *

THERAPIST: How many do I have?

CHILD: Three.   Four.   Five.   Seven.   etc.

*   *   *   *   *

THERAPIST: Which ones do you want?

CHILD: Both.

THERAPIST: Where will you put them?

CHILD: With mine.

*   *   *   *   *

CHILD: (*Distributing articles*)   They (or these) are for you.

*   *   *   *   *

CHILD: I'm thinking of a key.   Guess.

CHILD: The front door key? *or* The scotch tape?

CHILD: Yes *or* No.   (*The element of guessing adds a great deal of interest and can be used a number of times.*)

Unit I · Lesson 4

1. *Interpersonal Situations:* making and fulfilling a request

2. *Speaking Aspect of Situation:* asking and answering questions

3. *Particular Speech Patterns:*

"The ...."	"May I have the ... ?"	"Some money."
"On the ...."	"Will you give me the ... ?"	"How much?"
"With mine"		"Give me the ...."
"That one."	"Yes." "No."	"Where will you put it?"
"Thank you."	"Reach a ...."	"Take it."
"I'm thinking of one."	"It's right on ...."	

4. *Sound Emphasized:* ð θ v r s and others

5. *Equipment:* several coins, such as pennies, nickels, dimes

---

PROCEDURES	NOTES

THERAPIST: On the first day that you came to speech class we talked about differences in people's speech. Can you name some of those differences?

CHILDREN: (*Individually*) Rate, volume, directness, quality, smoothness, pitch, and sounds.

THERAPIST: What is there about your own speech which other children in the group liked?

CHILDREN: (*Respond according to previous comments made. Therapist may add to these using specific examples she has noted in the three lessons.*)

THERAPIST: What is there about your speech which you are working to improve?

This constitutes an example of helping children learn to share attitudes (Chapter 3). Ability to communicate feelings verbally is important to the child in several ways. As an expression of feeling it can serve to dissipate some of the force of that feeling; for example, to be able to say, "Somebody laughed at me and made me mad," can constitute a way of facing that ridicule, especially when it leads to the discovery that other children have experienced a similar situation.

This discussion makes it possible to talk over such happenings and through it to arrive at more rational handling of the situation. Perhaps the most important aspect of sharing attitudes

243

CHILDREN: (*By now each child should have developed some awareness of one or two aspects of his speech he is working to improve.*)

THERAPIST: In what ways does your speech sometimes interfere with what you want to say or make you feel conscious of it? Can you give one example?

CHILDREN: (*Frequently children will cite examples of not being understood, of having other children make fun of them, etc. Some children will have been unaware of any difference in their speech and will say so quite frankly.*)

THERAPIST: What can you do if someone makes fun of your speech? Yes, you can get angry, walk away, or try to forget it. There are some other ways of working it out, too. Your speech is only a part of you, and while you do have some trouble with it, what other things do you do very well without much trouble?

CHILDREN: (*Will often make a variety of responses to this question, such as swim, play football, help mother, read, do arithmetic, spell, etc.*)

THERAPIST: Do you know anyone who is equally good in all things? We all do some things better than others. In the first place, when someone comments about your speech, then you can remember that there are other things you do better. The very person who makes the remark can't do everything well either. Secondly, you can remember that you are working to

involves bringing one's own private feelings more into line with those of others; discovering that many "private" problems are in reality not private but rather common human problems; correcting distortions that otherwise might not be recognized as distortions; understanding that one may indeed have conflicting feelings of being angry at a person, but liking him also.*

Pointing out abilities is a way of developing in the child strong perceptions of his own personal worth, realization that "poor speech" does not make him a "poor person," but that in reality he possesses a great many assets and capabilities. As perceptions of the child's worth increase, he becomes freed from many feelings of inadequacy and becomes better able to profit from speech training.

* See Chapter 3, pp. 28–29.

improve your speech. Each one of you in here will eventually show much improvement as you work, practice on speech that you use often, and even work outside of speech class on making your speech better. Let's make a list on the board of one thing each of you is doing better right now. (*This may serve as the basis for a brief review of speech patterns introduced at this stage.*)

THERAPIST: You have practiced the speech you use in borrowing materials which you need, or some object like a key. Another thing for which you often need to ask is money, isn't it? What are some ways in which you use money?

CHILDREN: (*Individually*) To go to a show, buy a tablet, get a new pencil, bring money for the Red Cross, pay Girl Scout dues, put in my bank, etc.

THERAPIST: What ways have you worked on to ask for such things? Try "May I have the . . .?" for practice to be sure you are getting in the "v" and the "ð."

CHILDREN: (*Individually*) May I have the . . .? (*Therapist gives help as needed.*)

THERAPIST: Watch and tell what I have here. I'll begin: "The penny," etc.

CHILDREN: (*Individually*) The penny. The dime, etc. (*Each child enumerates a coin as it is laid on the table.*)

THERAPIST: When you ask for money, you may ask for exactly a nickel or a dime, or you may ask for "some money." That

Genuine money has more interest for this older age group than play money. Unless it creates particular problems, it can be used more successfully.

The therapist may judge the

has a sound in it which is not as easy for five of you. Do you hear it? "S . . . some money." You have begun work on it in "yes," but most of you are not ready to use it yet in "some." You will get to it later on. You may use it the best you can when you ask, "May I have some money?" Try it. Watch the "v" in "have."

CHILDREN: May I have some money? (*Each child practices it, the therapist giving help where needed.*)

THERAPIST: You are ready to ask for it now. When I ask you "How much?" you may tell me "the dime" or "the penny," or whatever you see here that you want. What sound will you need to check yourself on?

CHILDREN: (*Individually*) The . . . .

CHILD: May I have some money?

THERAPIST: How much?

CHILD: The penny.

THERAPIST: It's right on the table.

CHILD: (*Taking it.*) Thank you. (*Continue until each child has had a turn.*)

THERAPIST: When someone asks you a question as I did, you often answer with a very short answer. Often you use a longer answer, too. You could answer my question "How much?" with "Oh, give me the half-dollar." I'll do it now.

extent to which the "s" sound should be stressed in "some money." Some children will be ready for help in it here. Others should not attempt this yet.

A child who needs work on the "ð" sound may lead this activity, or one who is beginning to incorporate an "r" sound.

The therapist may take time out as this speech pattern is being established to work with the entire group on a sound as it is needed, in this case the "tʃ" or the "r." Attention should be called to the children who make one

THERAPIST: *(To one child)* May I have some money?

of the sounds easily, even though they have difficulty with another sound.

CHILD: How much?

THERAPIST: Oh, give me the nickel.

CHILD: It's right on the table.

THERAPIST: Thank you.

*   *   *   *   *

Other speech patterns which may be used with a similar exchange of coins are as follows:

THERAPIST: I have a penny for you.

CHILD: Thank you.

THERAPIST: Where will you put it?

CHILD: *(Already holding one coin)* With mine.

Note that these responses represent ones which the child has frequent occasion to use in his classroom and at home; however, use is made of it in the immediate present in a situation real to the child.

THERAPIST: Let's practice parts of that. Try "thank you." Now "with mine." They each have a similar sound. Try each one again. Let's ask Ronnie to pass out the coins. He says "have a" easily, but has trouble with "you." Try it alone, Ronnie. Now the whole thing: "I have a penny for you" and "Where will you put it?"

*   *   *   *   *

CHILDREN: *(Individually)* *(To one child holding a number of coins who is using the "s" in "Yes.")* May I have some money?

These patterns may be shifted to meet the needs of the group. They can best be established by actually going through one set of patterns several times in order for the children to

CHILD: Yes. How much?

CHILDREN: (*Individually*) The dime.

CHILD: Take it, *or* You may have it.

CHILDREN(*Individually*) Thank you.

*   *   *   *   *

CHILD: May I have your money?

THERAPIST: (*To this child with a small box who is beginning to incorporate the "r" in "right"*) Where will you put it?

CHILD: Right in the box.

THERAPIST: (*Individually*) Take it, *or* You may have it.

CHILD: Thank you. (*Continue*)

*   *   *   *   *

CHILD (*looking at four coins on table*) I'm thinking of one.

CHILDREN: (*Individually*) That one? (*pointing to a coin*) *or* The penny?

CHILD: Yes, *or* No. (*Continue*)

THERAPIST: You had fun today borrowing money. What speech patterns do you feel are getting easier for you now that you have worked on them? Is there something you can do now, too, when someone makes a comment about your speech the next time?

see and hear the whole pattern. The therapist may then call attention to particular elements on which the children need help or to particular sounds which various children need to watch. The patterns can also be established by writing them out on the board, going through them, isolating some elements for work, then gradually putting the parts together, and then erasing the board, since practice should not be a reading but a speaking activity.

Unit I · Lesson 5

1. *Interpersonal Situations:* expressing and accepting appreciation; expressing an opinion; guessing

2. *Speaking Aspect of Situation:* giving and receiving compliments; indicating a preference; asking and answering questions

3. *Particular Speech Patterns:*

   "The ...."   "This one right here."
   "That one."
                       "I like the ...."
   "Thank you."
   "I'm thinking of ...."   "Which car would you like to have?"
                            "Can you think of a car?"
   "Yes." "No."   "Show me the name of a car you like."
                       "This one right here."

4. *Sounds Emphasized:*   ð   θ   v   r   s   l   k   tʃ   ʃ

5. *Equipment:* blackboard and chalk

PROCEDURES	NOTES

THERAPIST: It is usually rather easy to remember to say "Thank you" when someone gives you something, such as some money, a piece of cake, a marble that you like, etc. George, Ann, Mary, and Bill, you are saying "Thank you" better too. Show us how you do it, watching that your tongue comes forward slightly as you say it.

Compliments serve as a valuable means-end in speech therapy, helping the child modify perceptions of self when someone notices his jeans, his shoes, his smile; helping him modify perceptions of his environment, as "I guess they like me if they like my belt"; satisfying needs for being noticed, liked, recognized; promoting interrelatedness as he in turn compliments others.

CHILDREN: (*Individually*) Thank you.

THERAPIST: There is another time when you use "Thank you." Sometimes Mother tells you she likes the way you hung up your coat or helped with the dishes. Your teacher may tell you she likes your neat paper in arithmetic, or the way you washed the boards for her, or the idea you had for the play your room is giving. Each time someone tells you something that you like, what do you usually say? That's right, "Thank you." You like getting a compliment. It makes you feel good. You like to give compliments, too.

Think of some compliments you might give your mother, your father, your teacher.

CHILDREN: (*Exchange ideas*)

THERAPIST: Think of some compliments you might give each other. They may concern something the person is wearing, something you know he does well in the room or on the playground, something he is saying better. See if each of you can think of compliments to give two people in the group. When you get a compliment, what will you say?

CHILDREN: (*Individually*) Thank you.

CHILD: I like the way you bat a ball.

CHILD: Thank you. (*Continue until each child has given two compliments.*)

*   *   *   *   *

THERAPIST: You are using the "θ" sound and the "v" sound fairly easily now. Today you are going to work on those, and some of you will get practice on other sounds you need help with, such as the "r," "s," "tʃ," "k," "ʃ," and "l." Can you think of a car? (*Therapist waits a moment.*) How many of you like cars, like to ride in them? There are many cars that are just new. They look different from the old ones, don't they?

This lesson is designed chiefly to help bring about these changes in personality structure. It also is a way of developing social skill both in giving and accepting the compliments. Phonetic accuracy can be stressed only as certain children show a readiness for help in this direction.

Chief emphasis here can be centered on the "θ" "ð". If a child is having difficulty with the "l," the therapist may work with him on including it in the word "like."

Children will need some individual practice on these sounds, but it is better if such practice is done in context with a particular speech pattern which is being used in the class activity. It is suggested that the therapist establish carefully and slowly a group of speech patterns which is to be used, giving adequate help as she does it. She might take out the phrase "Which one," for instance, having several chil-

In what ways? Do you think together you can make a list of ten cars? More than ten? Let's try. I will expect each of you to watch the "ð" sound in your answer, as "the Ford." Take a minute to think of one car or maybe two. Listen to my question again. Can you think of a car? I'll write it on the board. Ann, draw a line under the sounds you must watch. Try it all. Each of you try it once. Check yourself on the part that may be hard for you.

dren say it who do not have difficulty with it, helping one child with the sound in isolation, and then having him combine it in this phrase.

CHILDREN: (*Individually*) Can you think of a car? (*Therapist gives help as indicated. Special emphasis should be placed on the "θ" and "v." For some children the "k" in "can" and "car" may be emphasized.*)

Notice that practice proceeds from hearing the entire pattern, to saying it, to work on individual parts, back to the whole pattern again, and then use of it in the activity.

THERAPIST: Bill, I understand from the compliments you received that you spell well. You write out the list on the board as the children give you suggestions. I'll begin.

THERAPIST: Can you think of a car?

CHILD: Yes.

THERAPIST: Which one?

CHILD: The Pontiac. (*As each child answers, he asks the same question of another child. The therapist may stop the question and answer period to give particular help on the "s" in "Yes" and the "tʃ" in "Which one" where needed.*)

THERAPIST: That's quite a list of cars you have now. Let's not make it any

The production and use of the "s" have been centered chiefly on the one response "Yes." More lessons will be constructed with this sound as the chief area of emphasis. In the meantime, since the sound is often defective and requires a great deal of help, work may be started on it within the framework of these first lessons. A child feels less anxiety if he is held responsible for a newly acquired sound that may still be difficult for him in only one phrase at first. As he learns

longer but talk about it. Which car would you like to have? No, don't answer right away; think about it, and think about the reasons you would like to have that particular one. Watch me. Which car would I like to have? This one right here because it doesn't cost so much to run. Have you thought of the one you'd like, and the reason? Now think about the speech you will use, because you are talking about cars in order to get some special practice on your speech. I'll write the question and part of the answer on the board.

this one pattern "Yes" with a fair degree of ease, his classroom teacher and parents can encourage him in its use.

"Which car would you like to have?"
"This one right here because . . . ."

The pattern "Which car do you want?" is more simple phonetically and may be substituted.

What part will you have to watch? Let's work on the "l" in "like" because two of you need that.

CHILDREN: Like. Which car would you like to have? (*Therapist gives each child practice on this phrase, emphasizing the "l," "tʃ," "k," and "v" as needed. The answer is designed to give practice on use of the "r." The therapist may emphasize the sound only in "right" or only in "here," depending on usage of the "r" in the particular area in which the child resides. The child should not be held for the "r" in both responses at this stage.*)

THERAPIST: I believe you are ready now to tell the car each of you would like. Check yourself carefully on your sounds as you have fun talking about the cars.

CHILD: Which car would you like to have?

Note that the child is to be held responsible only for key

CHILD: (*Pointing to one on the board.*) This one right here because . . . . (*After answering the question, this child asks another child. This may be continued until each child has had a turn.*)

This above pattern may be varied for a child needing work on the "ʃ" to "Show me the name of a car you like," to which the children make a response similar to the one above.

responses in the phrase, not for the entire array of sounds.

*　*　*　*　*

THERAPIST: I'm thinking of a car.

CHILD: The Ford?

THERAPIST: No, guess again, *or* Yes. It's your turn now.

THERAPIST: You have worked on giving compliments today, expressing your ideas about cars, and guessing. What speech are you using better since you have worked on it today?

One child may have three guesses. If he doesn't guess, the first child may tell the car he had in mind and choose the next child for the activity. Another possibility is to give three individual children a guess. If the car is not guessed by then, the child leading the activity may choose another one to lead it. A child who does guess correctly may get the next turn.

Unit I · Lesson 6

1. *Interpersonal Situation:* giving a party
2. *Speaking Aspect of Situation:* exchanging greetings; making introductions; issuing invitations; passing and accepting refreshments; leave-taking
3. *Particular Speech Patterns:*

"Hi. . . ."	"Have a chair."
"Come in."	"Sit by me."
"Thank you."	"Have one."
"Meet my friends."	"May I have a . . . ?"
"I'd like to."	
"This is . . . ."	"For you."

4. *Sounds Emphasized:*   θ   ð   f   v   l   s   tʃ   j
5. *Equipment:* straws, napkins, paper cups, fruit juice; dixie cups, napkins, spoons; pop, straws, napkins, cookies; tray

---

PROCEDURES

THERAPIST: You often use speech in many ways when you go to a party, either when you give the party yourself or are invited to a party. A party in speech class will give you many different opportunities to work on speech that you need. Before you can give a party, what do you have to do? Yes, you must decide what guests you will invite, when it is to be, and what you will do at the party. In addition, you must plan the invitations and be ready to introduce the people to each other. Let's talk about some of those things.

Let's work today on two parts of the party, the speech you will use in inviting your guests and the speech you will use in welcoming them when they come. Think of different things you may say in issuing an invitation.

NOTES

A party provides opportunity for learning simple social patterns; for winning acceptance and support from those invited; for a shift in roles, such as preparing refreshments, answering the door, giving invitations; for modifying certain unsocial adjustive techniques into behavior acceptable at a party.

The party serves as an opportunity for various uses of speech. It needs to be planned around the speech of the children, planned for in some detail. Practice on the speech patterns may take several lessons previous to the actual party. The children may decide to have their mothers as guests, a friend from their own room, a brother or sister. They may

254

CHILDREN: (*Individually*) Will you come to our party? I'd like to have you come to a party we are having. We are having a party in speech class. Can you come?

THERAPIST: I have written your suggestions on the board. Let's go over them one at a time. How many of you see a sound you have been working on that you will need to check yourself on? (*The therapist may give the children a choice of the pattern they are to use, or she may suggest that they all work on one way of doing it. This will depend on the abilities of the group.*)

THERAPIST: Each of you try this way: "Will you come to our party?"

CHILDREN: (*Work on this individually, therapist giving help as indicated.*)

THERAPIST: What else should an invitation include? Yes, the time, the place, and the day. I'll write that on the board, too. Check the sounds you will need to watch. "It's going to be on Thursday, at two o'clock." "It will be in the lunch room."

(*Proceed with work on this as suggested above. Children should then try the entire invitation, giving it to each other or to the therapist.*)

*   *   *   *   *

THERAPIST: Let's work now on the way you will greet the person who comes to the party. Let's take our chairs over where we can face the door and hear a knock when it comes. Usually when

decide to hold the party after school and invite their teachers.

The speech therapist will want to make some previous arrangements before this project is undertaken, talking it over with the classroom teacher first so that the plans can be worked in with the regular school program.

These speech patterns should be set up carefully, patterned very simply with more emphasis on their use than on phonetic accuracy, although the latter should be encouraged whenever the children are ready for it. Two lessons, three at the most, may be thought of as preparation for the party. If there is more than this, the children are apt to lose interest and a sense of relationship between what they are working on and its application.

The ideal "follow-through" on the invitations would be for every member of the class to go to the various people to be invited and individually extend his invitation. If each member of the group is inviting a friend, the friends may be brought down to speech class at the conclusion of this class and be given their invitations.

Some mention should be made of ways to accept an invitation.

The goals of this party situation are conceived of as re-

someone knocks at the door, you go to the door, open it, and greet the person who is standing there. If you are having a party, the people who knock will be coming to your party as a rule, and you will invite them in. Jimmie, you go outside the door, knock, and I will show you how it is done. Listen to the speech that I use.

CHILD: (*Goes outside the door, and knocks.*)

THERAPIST: (*Walking to the door and opening it*) Hi, Jimmie.

CHILD: Hi, Miss . . . .

THERAPIST: Come in.

CHILD: Thank you.

THERAPIST: Each of us said two things. What were they? Yes, we each said "Hi." I said "Come in," and Jimmie said "Thank you." Let's practice these for a moment, and then you may each have a turn, both going outside the door and knocking, and greeting someone at the door.

CHILDREN: (*Individually*) Come in, *and* Thank you. (*Therapist gives help as indicated.*)

THERAPIST: "Thank you" is fairly easy for you now. Jack, what do you have to watch when you say it? Each of you say it for Jack. "Come in" is one Mary has done some work on. Most of you say it very well. Show her how you do it. Say "Come in" for Mary. Now you try

duction of anxiety, building self-confidence, increasing group belongingness, participation in using speech to the best of the child's ability at this time. They are concerned with details of speech production only as individual children show a readiness for it.

In this way the child is not only changing in broad fundamental ways necessary for learning, but also is experiencing the very situation for which he will develop a need for more accurate production of speech. If experiencing success makes the child more eager and able to go on succeeding at harder tasks, the party gives him the possibility of succeeding right from the first (for example, answering the door even though he does not then use speech); of using speech in that act even though he cannot yet say the pattern correctly; and finally of solving the problem of transfer of training from production to use by teaching him to use the pattern correctly in such a situation.

it, Mary. See if you can say it carefully three times so that it sounds all right to us.

Now you will practice knocking at the door and being greeted. (*This should be done until each child has had several turns.*)

After your friend comes to your party, you will want to see that he meets your other friends. I will show you first how to make an introduction.

(*To child after he has knocked at the door and been greeted.*) Meet my friends, This is . . . . (*Continue until he has been introduced to each child.*)

This will be fun to do because you know each other's names so well. But if you do forget someone's name, what can you do? Yes, you can ask, "What is your name?"

CHILD (*Goes outside the door, and knocks*)

CHILD: (*Answers the door*) Hi, Ann.

CHILD: Hi, Jimmie.

CHILD: Come in.

CHILD: Thank you.

CHILD: Meet my friends. This is . . . .

CHILDREN: (*Being introduced*) Hi.

THERAPIST: I like the way Ann looked at each person she was introducing. I

While these lessons are planned as preparation for the party, the actual speaking situations are ones which the child has occasion to use frequently, and they are worked out as real events even during practice.

Giving invitations, welcoming at the door, making introductions, and inviting the person to have a chair are all that should be undertaken in one lesson. The second lesson could include the actual giving of the invitations; the third could be centered around review of welcoming at the door, etc., and work on speech used in passing refreshments.

liked the way you looked so pleased to meet Jimmie, as if you were glad he came to the party. I noticed that Jimmie got his "θ" sound in "Thank you." I was surprised to notice that Nancy got the "ð" sound in twice when she used "This," and she hasn't worked on that yet.

*   *   *   *   *

After you have welcomed your guest, and introduced him, you may want to invite him to sit down so that you can talk with him later. What could you say?

CHILDREN: (*Individually*) Sit by me, *or* Have a chair.

THERAPIST: Since you have been working on the word "have," practice saying "Have a chair."

CHILDREN: Have a chair. (*Continue until each child has had a turn, therapist giving help where indicated.*)

THERAPIST: Let's put the whole thing together now — greeting at the door, introduction, and invitation to sit down. (*Children continue to practice this.*)

*   *   *   *   *

THERAPIST: When you pass refreshments, such as cookies, at the party, what can you say that you have worked on? Yes, "Have a cookie." What will you watch especially? You might also say "For you." Then what will you watch? If someone forgets to pass you a napkin, what could you say? Yes, "May I have a napkin?" And, of course, when someone gives you something, you will know about thanking them, won't you?

(Give individual practice on each response as needed. A tray with napkins, empty dixie cups, straws, wooden spoons, etc. will be useful in making the work real.

Leave-taking can be pointed up next, and practice given on such patterns as "Thank you for the party," "I liked the cookies," "I had fun at your party. Thank you for inviting me, *etc.)*

Why do you suppose you are having a party in speech class in two days? Yes, to have fun, and to eat cookies, and to invite a friend. Most important of all, the party is a chance for you to *do* things as they are done at a party — welcoming someone, introducing him, passing refreshments, and using speech in different ways.

CONTINUED

Intermediate
Illustrative Lessons

UNIT TWO

ACQUIRING SPEAKING SKILLS

A. INTERPERSONAL SITUATIONS WITH THEIR SPEAKING ASPECTS

B. SUMMARY OF ACTIVITIES

C. SUMMARY OF SPEECH PATTERNS

Lesson 1

"Yes." "No."

"Both."
"Both of them."
"Thank you."

"With mine."

"Reach it."
"Here." "There."

"Where will you get a card?"
"Lay it down."
"Have a look."

"May I have one?"
"Do you want one?"

"Keep it." 270

Lesson 2

"Yes." "No."

"Both."
"Both of them."
"Thank you."

"With mine."
"That one."
"The . . . ."

"Lay it down."

"May I have a . . . ?"
"Do you want one?"

"Can you . . . ?"

"Keep it . . . ."

"Who else?"
"Guess again."

Lesson 9

"A piece of . . . ."
"What do you miss?"

"What do you have?"
"May I have . . .?"

"That one."

"Can you . . .?"
"Yes, I can."

"Reach it."
"Write . . . ."

"In my pocket."

"Here."
"Ready?"
"That's right."
"That's wrong."

"Get it . . . ."
"Will you give me . . .?"

"Which one . . .?"
"Show me . . . ." 315

Lesson 10

"A piece of . . . ."
"Miss . . . ."

"Take this piece."
"Will you get me . . .?"

"To wrap a package."
"Here you are."
"Right here."

"Just one piece . . . ."
". . . of red chalk"

"Miss Hale would like . . . ."

"Will you ask . . .?" . . . 322

Lesson 11

"May I see what you
    have?"
"Yes, you may."
"What did you see?"
"What else?"
"Guess again."
"Guess what I saw?"

"Reach in and . . . ."
"Get me the . . . ."
"Will you give me . . .?"
"I got the . . . ."
"Go to the . . . ."

"Come back."

"Look out." 325

Lesson 12

"What did Jack say?"
"He said . . . ."

"You should bring . . . ."
"She would like . . . ."

Lesson 17

"Hide your eyes."	"Where is the . . .?"
"Open your eyes."	"Is it the . . .?"
"Who was it?"	
"Was it . . .?"	"That's right."
"Who has it?"	"That's wrong."
"Does . . .?"	"Reach in and get it."
	"Show me . . . ." 345
"It's your turn."	

D. SUMMARY OF EQUIPMENT

Unit II · Lesson 1

1. *Interpersonal Situations:* exchanging materials; expressing an opinion

2. *Speaking Aspect of Situation:* asking and answering questions; expressing an opinion; indicating a preference

3. *Particular Speech Patterns:*

"Yes."　"No." *　　"Reach it."　　　　　　　"Keep it."
　　　　　　　　　　"Here."　"There."
"Both."　　　　　　"Where will you get a card?"
"Both of them."
"Thank you."　　　"Lay it down."
　　　　　　　　　　"Have a look."
"With mine."
　　　　　　　　　"Do you want one?"
　　　　　　　　　"May I have one?"

4. *Sounds Emphasized:*　　s　θ　ð　r　l　k　g　v

5. *Equipment:* a pack of trading cards

PROCEDURES

THERAPIST: If your mother says to you, "Do you want a piece of cake?" you will probably say "Yes." Your teacher may point to a book saying, "Do you like this book?" to which you will often answer "Yes," *or* "No," or perhaps "I liked one of the stories in it." When mother asks if you will go to the store, your answer may be "Yes." You use "Yes" in many ways. Can you think of some?

CHILDREN: (*Individually*) When my dad asks if I want to go to the baseball game with him; when my mother asks if I'd like to go to the show with her; when someone asks me to come out and go bike riding, etc.

NOTES

The "s" which is apt to be difficult for many in the class, requiring considerable care and time in teaching, will give opportunities for success and recognition of the child who may have different problems, such as with an "r," "ʃ," etc. It cannot be emphasized too strongly that continuously giving children the feeling that they have assets in certain directions makes them more ready to learn in an area which poses some difficulty for them.

Some children make the sound "s" through imitation fairly easily. These children

---

* The speech response "Yes" may be replaced by "Sure," "O.K.," or "All right," if individual children need work chiefly on "ʃ," "k," or "r," rather than "s."

270

THERAPIST: I have a pack of trading cards which Bill brought. They are a part of his collection. There are enough of them for you to make a collection, too, during class, although Bill will want these back. If you want one now, I will give it to you. However, I have a special reason for giving one to each of you. I want you to hear each other make the new word "Yes," since that is something many of you will be working on. Watch as each person has a turn, see if everyone's word sounds the same, or if you see and hear some differences.

THERAPIST: George, do you want a card?

CHILD: Yes.

THERAPIST: (*May give each child one turn or two without commenting on production of the "s." She may give the children each another turn making such comments as the following:*)

Jimmie keeps his teeth together when he says "Yes." That keeps his tongue back.

Ann's tongue comes forward when she says "Yes."

Bill says "Yeah" without a "s" sound in it. Some people do it that way. You are remembering that no one talks exactly like everyone else.

Kathie's "s" has a "bubbly" sound, which means the air is coming out a different place from Ann's and Jimmie's.

It should be noted here that first comments

should, under careful guidance, begin immediately incorporating it in the response "Yes."

Others will be able to produce it partially better; that is, a child who has a marked lingual protrusion may make an "s" in which his tongue is back, although the sound is not yet sharp. If the sound is going in the direction of normal, he, too, can be given assistance in including it in the one response. Each time the child makes the response, the therapist should comment on what ways it is better than his former sound and in what ways it needs more work. For the child who may have to work on the sound in isolation for some time before he gets a semblance of a normal sound — for example, some children with cleft palate, one with a markedly lateral lisp, etc., — there are a number of alternatives. The therapist should be sure that along the way this child receives recognition for other sounds he makes easily. He should also be given the opportunity to use the response "Yes" in an activity, since his awareness of where the "s" should be included will begin to develop in that way as well as through hearing the other children use it.

It may be advisable to separate the pattern first, as in "Ye . . . s," in order to prevent recurrence of a former defective pattern. This practice should be kept to a

do not include an evaluation of "right" or "wrong," but simply call attention to differences.)

THERAPIST: Let's try making it this way now. Listen. Watch. "Ye . . . s" Listen to just this part — "s." Try it.

CHILDREN: "s" (*Each child has several turns.*)

THERAPIST: (*Wherever possible, it is desirable for these children to learn the "s" through imitation rather than through direction pertaining to tongue movement. In some cases giving some special direction proves to be helpful, however. Comments such as the following are useful:*)

Jimmie makes the sound as most people do. It is easy for him. Jimmie, go to each boy and girl and show him how you do it.

Ann, if you keep your teeth together, that will help you put your tongue back further. Don't push too hard.

Bill, listen first. Now try it. That's just right.

Kathie, begin saying "he" out loud, now whisper it, now put your teeth together and whisper it. Now go from "he" to "s" like this. (*This is one way of directing the air stream centrally; other techniques which the therapist finds useful may be valuable here.*)

THERAPIST: More of you are making the "s" alike now. Most of you are making

minimum. Care should be taken, too, to prevent too much force on a newly acquired sound.

There are other speech patterns included here which give children requiring work on sounds other than "s" opportunities for speech in the same activity. A child who has numerous defective sounds should be held responsible only for the "s" a first.

it well enough to use it in one easy word, "Ye . . . s." Try it first. Listen to me.

CHILDREN: (*Individually*) Ye . . . s. (*Where needed the therapist may give a direction first before the child says "Yes," such as "Ann, watch me; see my teeth are to-gether at the end," etc.*)

THERAPIST: You may have a card now, if you want one, providing you watch how you use the "s" in "Yes."

THERAPIST: Do you want one?

CHILDREN (*Individually*) Ye . . . s.

THERAPIST: (*To one child not yet making the "s" well enough to include it in the response*) That "Yes" is still hard for you. Try just "s." (*Child makes "s" a number of times in isolation as the therapist gives directions which enable him to begin establishing proper movement and direction for the sound. As soon as the sound is going in the direction of normal, the child should begin incorporating it in a response. In the meantime, the therapist may encourage the child as follows:*) You have learned to use "Thank you" so well, suppose you tell me "Thank you" when I give you a card. Here is a card for you.

CHILD: Thank you.

THERAPIST: Jimmie, that "Yes" is easy for you. You need to practice on the "r." Try it. Listen to me first. Remember that your tongue must come up.

CHILD: "r"

THERAPIST: I liked that because your tongue did come up when you made it. Try it again. See if you can make it four times just that way. The word you are going to use is "R . . . each it." Try it.

CHILD: R . . . each it.

THERAPIST: Ann and Jean, this sound is easy for you. Show Jimmie how you say it. "R . . . each it." Now, Jimmie, you may take some of these cards by answering my question with the best "r" you can make. See how many cards you can get. What will you do to get a card?

For a child who has difficulty with both "r" and "tʃ," "Reach it" is too complex. Another response should be substituted, such as "It's all right for you to have a card."

CHILD: R . . . each it. (*Continue until this one child has acquired several cards.*)

THERAPIST: You have many cards now. You may give one to each boy and girl by telling him "R . . . each it."

CHILD: (*Distributes cards one at a time by giving the direction "Reach one." Therapist checks him carefully on production of "r" in the response. Children reach out and choose a card.*)

THERAPIST: Let's go ahead now, giving more of you practice on "s" as you add another card to your collection. Do you want one?

CHILDREN: Yes. (*Continue until each child has had a turn.*)

(*Another child who is able to include an "r" sound more easily in the responses "Here"*

Those responses are appr priate for use only in certai

and "There" may answer the question "Where will you get a card?" by replying "Here" or "There" as he points to a card on the table. He may then give the direction, "Take a card here" or "Take a card there" to the other children.)

(The child working on "l" may use the response "Lay one on the table," giving the direction a number of times to various children as a means of getting the cards together again.)

THERAPIST: Each of you has two cards left. I have two cards, too. Watch where I put the next card I get: "With mine." Watch where I put the next one: "With mine." In a short time you will get another card, too. Where will you put it?

CHILDREN: (*Individually*) With mine.

THERAPIST: What sound do you have to watch?

CHILDREN: (*Individually*) "ð"

THERAPIST: Let's see if you can each say it right. Then you will have a turn to get a card.

CHILDREN: (*Individually*) With mine. *Continue until each child has said it once or more depending on the need for practice.)*

THERAPIST: Where will you put it?

CHILD: With mine. (*Continue until each child has had a turn.*)

THERAPIST: I have two cards here.

sections of the country.

The response "Both of them"

This time you may choose two cards.
Watch me. I'll take "Both." Listen
again: "Both." What sound do you
need to watch?

*may be used here if children
are ready for work on three
difficult sounds within one
phrase.*

CHILDREN: "θ"

THERAPIST: (*Holding out two cards*) What
one do you want?

CHILDREN: Both. (*Continue until each
child obtains two cards.*)

THERAPIST: Each of you has had special
help today, some with "s," some with
"θ" and "$\eth$," some with "r" and "l."
Susan, these sounds were easy for you.
What one is it you need some help on?
Yes, the "k." Try it by itself. Do it
four times. Listen to me first. Take it
easy, don't push too hard: "k."

CHILD: "k"

THERAPIST: Try it in "Keep it." Listen.
Going slowly will make it easier. Dividing it will keep the old sound from creeping in. "K . . . eep it."

CHILD: K . . . eep it. (*Practice several
times.*)

THERAPIST: I liked that because you are
taking it slowly and thinking first of your
sound. You rest for a minute and let the
other boys and girls show you how they
do it. Ann, Bill, and Kathie, who have
had to work very hard on the "s" sound,
make this one easily. (*These children
demonstrate this sound.*)

THERAPIST: This time you may pass out the cards, Susan, telling each boy and girl to "Keep it." Try it once more.

CHILD: (*Distributing cards, saying* "Keep it.")

CHILDREN: (*Acknowledging cards individually*) Thank you.

THERAPIST: George, what can you say in collecting the cards? You may take all the cards from each person since our time is getting short.

If children respond "No" to this question, the therapist may permit them to keep the cards until they have left class, or she may give them the privilege of refusing once, but require them to give up their cards the next time they are asked.

CHILD: May I have your cards?

CHILDREN: (*Individually*) Yes. (*Therapist calls attention to production of "s" here.*)

CHILD: Thank you.

THERAPIST: Now all the cards are back on the table. What do you tell Bill for letting us use them today? What speech have you worked on while you were having fun with the cards?

CHILDREN: Yes, Reach one, Both, Thank you, Lay it on the table, Keep it, With mine, etc.

THERAPIST: That's right. You have worked especially on the "s" sound in Yes." You will be using that some more in class. Listen when other people say it. See how many differences you can hear.

Unit II · Lesson 2

1. *Interpersonal Situations:* exchanging materials; expressing an opinion
2. *Speaking Aspects of Situation:* asking and answering questions; indicating a preference
3. *Particular Speech Patterns:*

"Yes." "No."	"Reach it."	"Can you . . . ?"
	"Where will you	"Keep it."
"Both."	put it?"	
"Both of them."		
"Thank you."	"Lay it down."	
		"Choose the one . . . ."
"With mine."	"May I have a . . . ."	"Which one?"
"That one."	"Do you want it?"	"How much?"
"The . . . ."		
"On the . . . ."		"Show me."
"What will you do with it?"		
		"Just any one."

4. *Sounds Emphasized:*   s   θ   ð   r   l   k   tʃ   ʃ   dʒ
5. *Equipment:* coins or colored pencils

PROCEDURES

NOTES

THERAPIST: The last time you were here, you worked especially on the "s" sound in "Yes." You got trading cards by replying "Yes" when I asked you if you wanted one. Have you noticed how differently people say "Yes"? Sometimes they simply nod their heads meaning "Yes" without saying anything. Sometimes they use "uh-huh" or "yeah." If you say "Yes" when you will do something your mother asks, but don't want to very much, it will sound different from saying it when you want to do it very much. But for the most part when people say "Yes," the last sound in it is rather alike, regardless of who says it. Many of you are going to be working on making your "s" sound more like other people's.

278

Listen to me now, and see if you can tell which "Yes" that I make is better, the first or the second one? Can you tell why?

THERAPIST: (*Gives several series of the word "Yes" in sets of two, one of them made with a lingual, lateral, or whistling "s" or with it omitted altogether, the other within normal range. Children differentiate between the sounds. Therapist helps them both see and hear differences.*)

Instead of making a collection of trading cards today, you are going to make a collection of these colored pencils I have here. You will get them by making the best "s" you can in the word "Yes." Try it first.

CHILDREN: (*Individually*) "Yes," "s". (*Therapist gives each child several opportunities to make this, giving help where needed.*)

THERAPIST: Do you want a pencil?

CHILD: Yes.   (*Continue until each child has had a turn. The therapist should make appropriate comments along the way, as suggested in the previous lesson.*)

THERAPIST: I have enough pencils here for each of you to have two more. Mary, you may pass them out, asking two questions: first, "Do you want it?" and secondly, "Where will you put it?" Try these two questions

CHILD: Do you want it? Where will you put it? (*Therapist gives help as needed. If the child she selects has some stuttering*

This suggestion for "ear-training" can be utilized as needed in context with the various speech patterns used. As soon as possible it should be developed in such a way that the child evaluates his own sound as well as those of others. Such questions as "How did that sound to you?" "Where was your tongue?" "Did the air come through your mouth or nose?" "Did the air come through the center or sides?" serve to guide a child in self-evaluation.

If the therapist is maintaining a relatively slow tempo in the class, it is easy to sug-

symptoms, she may suggest that he wait a moment before beginning, ask the questions slowly and easily, without pushing too hard, etc.)

CHILD: *(Extending a pencil)* Do you want it?

CHILDREN: *(Individually)* Yes *or* No.

CHILD: Where will you put it?

CHILDREN: *(Individually)* With mine.

(The pencils may be collected and redistributed for additional work on the speech patterns suggested below. The therapist may need to call attention to the fact that collecting the pencils is a way of getting practice on speech.)

gest that the child pause a moment before making a reply in order to consciously include the newer sound. This will reduce the number of times a child makes an incorrect response and has to repeat it. Praise should be given for a response which is within normal range on the first attempt, although a child need not be penalized for failing to succeed the first time, but rather should be helped to do it better the next time.

Supplementary Suggestions

CHILD: Do you want a pencil?

CHILDREN: *(Individually)* Yes.

CHILD: Reach it.

CHILDREN: *(Individually)* Thank you.

*   *   *   *   *

CHILD: May I have a pencil?

CHILD: Yes.

CHILD: Thank you.

*   *   *   *   *

CHILD: Do you want a pencil?

In stressing the "s" in "Yes," the therapist should be careful to accept "No" as an appropriate response, too. Children need not reply parrotlike with "Yes" each time a question is asked or an article is extended to them. Permissiveness to express dislike or respond negatively should be granted them. On the other hand, the therapist can structure the lesson so that most of the time the children will want to respond positively.

CHILD: Yes.

CHILD: What will you do with it?

CHILD: Keep it.

    *   *   *   *   *

CHILD: Do you want a pencil?

CHILD: Yes.

CHILD: Where will you put it?

CHILD: With mine.

    *   *   *   *   *

CHILD: (*Extending two pencils*) Which do you want?

CHILD: Both *or* Both of them. Thank you.

CHILD: Where will you put it?

CHILD: On the table.

    *   *   *   *   *

CHILD: Which one do you want?

CHILD: That one, thank you.

    *   *   *   *   *

CHILD: Choose the one you want.

CHILD: Just any one, thank you.

    *   *   *   *   *

CHILD: Lay one pencil down.

CHILD: Where?

CHILD: On the table.

*   *   *   *   *

CHILD: Show me the pencil you like best.

CHILD: That one.

*   *   *   *   *

CHILD: (*Collecting pencils*) Will you put yours with mine?

CHILD: Yes.

CHILD: Thank you.

Unit II · Lesson 3

1. *Interpersonal Situation:* obtaining and giving information

2. *Speaking Aspects of Situation:* asking and answering questions

3. *Particular Speech Patterns:*

"Yes." "No."	"Right here."
"Guess again."	"Is this right?"

Street addresses	"Can you find my birthday?"
Age	
Birthdate	"I'm thinking of a birthday."
Telephone number	"When is your birthday?"
	"Is that your birthday?"
	"Where is your birthday?"
	"Show me your birthday?"

4. *Sounds Emphasized:*   s   θ   ʃ   r   ð   k

5. *Equipment:* blackboard and chalk

PROCEDURES	NOTES

THERAPIST: If you go to the doctor or the dentist, or enroll in a new school, or ask for a package to be sent, what are some questions you are usually asked?

CHILDREN: (*Individually*) They ask your name, your address, how old you are, when your birthday is, and sometimes what your telephone number is.

The speech therapist will usually have this data available in her records. She should have it accessible in this lesson in case a child needs help.

THERAPIST: Today you are going to be working on speech you use in getting information about other people, or giving information about yourself, particularly birthdays. Try the word "birthday." It has a "θ" sound in it like "thank you" and "think."

The word "birthday" (containing "r" and "θ") is more difficult phonetically for some children and should be stressed only with children able to handle it, but can be used by all.

CHILDREN: (*Individually*) "Birthday."

283

(Therapist gives help where it is indicated.)

THERAPIST: Do you like having a birthday? I'm going to ask you some questions about birthdays. Some of the questions will require "Yes" for an answer, some of them "No." Let's see how well you can make the word "Yes" today. It is getting easier for some of you.

The therapist may ask questions similar to those suggested. In many groups the children will be able to do the asking. A few leading words on the board as cake, spanking, presents, party, may give them ideas around which to construct their questions.

CHILDREN: *(Individually)* Yes. *(The therapist may require their giving this response fairly rapidly, singling out those who need help.)*

THERAPIST: As I ask these questions, you may think of some questions to ask, too. "Do you *sometimes* have ice cream on your birthday?"

The word sometimes *is essential in phrasing the questions.*

CHILD: Yes.

THERAPIST: Do you sometimes have cake on your birthday?

CHILD: Yes. *(May continue by asking the next question.)*

(Other suggestions: Do you sometimes have presents, a spanking, a party, a surprise, a picnic, birthday cards, special fun, etc. on your birthday? Do you sometimes eat the cake, open the presents, hurt from the spanking, see friends at the party, get surprised, have fun, cut the cake, blow out the candles, read the birthday cards on your birthday?)

The therapist should guide this question and answer period so that chief emphasis is placed on the response "Yes." She may do it by stopping the conversation for a moment and asking, "Why are you asking each other questions? Yes, to get practice on the words 'Yes' and 'birthday.' Keep that in mind as you go along."

THERAPIST: Let's find out when your birthdays are. That is a question you often ask a new friend. Listen: "When is

The response "your" may be utilized for work on the "r" if it is appropriate for

your birthday?" Try asking it, watching the "θ" especially.

the area in which the child lives.

CHILDREN: (*Individually*) When is your birthday?

THERAPIST: As you give us information about your birthday, I will write it with your name on the board. I'm going to suggest that we begin on this side of the circle and go straight around. It will be easier to keep the dates straight that way. I will ask the first question; you can go on from there.

The ordinals are somewhat difficult for children who have defective sounds. It is suggested that the therapist help individual children as they show a need for it, but not go on giving particular work on it at this time.

THERAPIST: When is your birthday?

CHILD: On August seventh. (*Continues with questioning.*)

THERAPIST: Take a look at each of the birthdays that are listed here. I'm going to erase the names soon, and see if you remember whose birthday comes at each date. If you have difficulty, you can count around the group and figure it out that way. (*Erases names after children have studied list.*)

THERAPIST: Can you find my birthday?

CHILD: Yes. Is this right? *or* Right here?

THERAPIST: Yes.

THERAPIST: Before we go on, let's give the people who are having difficulty with "r" some work on the speech response "Is this right?" or "Right here?" (*Gives help as indicated.*)

(Continue with above pattern guiding the children to check themselves on the "ð," "s," "r.")

(Other patterns which may be worked out in connection with the list on the board:)

CHILD: Show me your birthday.

CHILD: That one.   *(Continue)*

*   *   *   *   *

CHILD: Ann, is that your birthday?

CHILD: Yes.   *(Continue)*

*   *   *   *   *

CHILD: I'm thinking of a birthday.

CHILD: That one?

CHILD: No. Guess again.

CHILD: That one?

CHILD: Yes.   *(Continue)*

*   *   *   *   *

THERAPIST: Can you erase your birthday?

CHILD: Yes.

CHILD: Should I erase my birthday?

CHILD: I think so.

*   *   *   *   *

THERAPIST: What have you worked on saying better today? Why?

A similar lesson can be worked out dealing with street addresses and telephone numbers. Such lessons can be utilized to help children with the ways in which they say numbers, important in various phases of school work as well as in furnishing the above information.

Unit II · Lesson 4

1. *Interpersonal Situation:* obtaining and giving information; expressing an opinion

2. *Speaking Aspects of Situation:* asking and answering questions; indicating a preference

3. *Particular Speech Patterns:*

"Yes." "No."	"Is this right?"
"Sometimes."	"Right here."
"Guess again."	"This one right here."
Names of favorite sports	"What is your favorite sport?"
	"Is that your favorite sport?"
	"Show me your favorite sport?"
"I think so."	"Can you find my favorite sport?"
"I'm thinking of a sport."	"What sport do you like best?"
	"Should I choose my favorite sport?"

4. *Sounds Emphasized:*   s   θ   ð   r   l   ʃ   k   tʃ

5. *Equipment:* blackboard and chalk

PROCEDURES	NOTES

THERAPIST: In what ways do you use speech when you are taking part in a sport, playing a game?

CHILDREN: (*Individually*) When you choose sides, call out the score, tell someone whose turn it is, talk over the decision of the umpire, give signals, etc.

THERAPIST: Sometimes when you aren't playing you talk over sports, too, don't you? Maybe you talk about the team you're going to form when spring comes, or the basketball game you saw last Friday night, or the place you'd like on the team, or your favorite sport. Today you are going to get practice on certain things in speech as you talk about your favorite sports.

287

First I will give you some practice on using the "s" in "Yes" as I ask you some questions. I don't know so much about what you do in sports; perhaps I'll get more "No" answers than "Yes." Let's see how well you are making the "s" today. Try it in "Yes."

CHILDREN: Yes. (*Teacher gives individual help where needed on the sound "s."*)

THERAPIST: (*Asks questions such as the following with the idea of giving the children opportunity to use "Yes."*) Do you like football? (. . . baseball, kickball, volley ball, handball, softball, tennis, bowling, car racing, hill climbs, basketball, roller skating, swimming, skiing, ice-skating, marbles, jump rope, etc.)

CHILDREN: Yes, *or* No, *or* Sometimes.

THERAPIST: I liked the way you are getting the very best "s" you can make in that word "Yes." Four of you are making it easily enough to include it in a longer answer. Try "Yes I do." Try this. Listen: "Yes, I do."

CHILDREN: Yes, I do. (*Teacher gives help as indicated.*)

THERAPIST: Three of you are showing fine improvement on your "s." It is much better than it was, but you still must watch it carefully, so keep it in the shorter answer. That will make it easier for you.

Can you sometimes kick a ball? (. . . bat a ball, run with a ball, throw a ball,

Care should be taken that the children use a blended pattern here when including the "s" in the pattern "Yes, I do."

Children easily accept different standards of speech according to the rate and ease with which they acquire a sound. Such different standards should be set up according to each child's particular need.

catch a ball, make a touchdown, make a basket, make a goal, float, turn around on skates, run fast, make an out, call signals, catch a fly, bat a home run, etc.)

CHILDREN: Yes, Yes, I can, No, *or* Sometimes.

THERAPIST: Can you think of a sport? We have already talked of many different ones. Do you think together you can make a list of ten sports? More than ten? Try it. Listen to my question again.

Phonetic emphasis here centers around the speech that is used as the list is compiled, not on the specific names of sports. Children will enjoy seeing how quickly they can make a list.

"Can you think of a sport?" I'll write it on the board. George, draw a line under the sounds you must watch. Try all of it. Each of you try it once. Check yourself on the part that may be hard for you.

CHILDREN: (*Individually*) Can you think of a sport? (*Teacher gives help as needed.*)

THERAPIST: Harry, you may write out the list as the children make it. I wonder if they will really have ten suggestions for you. I'll begin the questions; then you can carry on.

Children just acquiring use of an "s" within normal range should not be required to include it in the word "sport." One exception to this might be the child who omits an "s" but can make it very easily. He will be able to say the word through imitation.

THERAPIST: Can you think of a sport?

CHILD: Yes, I can, *or* Yes.

THERAPIST: Which one?

CHILD: Baseball. (*As each child answers, he asks the next question of another child.*)

THERAPIST: That's quite a list of sports you have now. Let's not make it any longer, but talk about it. What is your favorite sport? No, don't answer right away, think about it, and think about the reasons you would choose that as your favorite sport. Now think about the speech you will use, because you are talking about sports in order to get some special practice on your speech. I'll write the question and part of the answer on the board.

"What is your favorite sport?" *or* "What sport do you like best?"

THERAPIST: Two of you need work on the "l" in "like," so let's each one work on the question "What sport do you like best?" (*Children practice this, teacher giving help where needed.*)

The children should not be held responsible for all the sounds in this speaking sequence, but the therapist will use her judgment about the area of emphasis. It is largely designed for practice on the "s," "k," "l," and "ð," in key responses.

If you go to the board and show the person who asks you the question the name of your favorite sport, it will give all of you a chance to use the "r" in "This one right here." Work on it first.

THERAPIST: Now you are ready to begin. Why are we talking about sports? What will you need to watch? What sport do you like best?

CHILD: (*Going to board*) This one right here. (*Continues with question, asking it of another child.*)

Supplementary Suggestions

CHILD: Can you find the sport I like best? (least)

CHILD: Yes. Tell me the name.

CHILD: Football.

CHILD: (*Pointing to list on board*) It's right here.

* * * * *

CHILD: Show me which sport you like.

CHILD: (*Pointing to board*) That one.

* * * * *

CHILD: I'm thinking of a sport.

CHILD: That one?

CHILD: Yes, *or* No, guess again.

* * * * *

THERAPIST: Can you erase the name of one sport?

CHILD: Yes, I can.

* * * * *

THERAPIST: What did you talk about today? What speech did you work on?

Unit II · Lesson 5

1. *Interpersonal Situation:* requesting and granting permission
2. *Speaking Aspect of Situation:* asking and answering questions
3. *Particular Speech Patterns:*

"Yes." "No."   "May I *write* my name on the board?"

"No, I'm sorry."   "May I *get* one *thing* from the table?"

    "May I borrow a *sheet of* paper?"

"Thank you."   "Will you *let* me *get* a drink?"

"You're welcome."

    "O.K."

    "All right."

    "Surely."

4. *Sounds Emphasized:*   s   r   θ   ð   ʃ   l

5. *Equipment:* none

PROCEDURES	NOTES

THERAPIST: There are many times when you need to ask permission of your mother, your dad, or your teacher to do something special: — you ask permission to bring a friend home from school, to go to someone else's house on Saturday, to be excused from school early to go to the dentist, to go to the show on Friday night.

Sometimes you don't like to ask permission because you are afraid that you may not get to do what you want to. That happens to all of us. One time I wanted to be excused a day early from school to start on a long trip. I thought I might not be permitted to go. You need to expect when you ask that sometimes there are reasons why you cannot be given permission. Then you won't be upset if you cannot do as you ask.

In discussing various uses of speech the therapist should contribute examples from her own life. It will serve to promote interaction as well as make the need of working on certain phases more real to the children of this age.

292

Today you are going to work on speech you use in asking permission. You will have fun doing it because part of the time you will ask for permission, and part of the time you will give the permission.

You may ask any of these four things. Listen carefully. You may be able to do several of them. I will tell you and then write them on the board.
"May I write my name on the board?"
"May I get one thing from the table?"
"Will you let me get a drink?"
"May I borrow a sheet of paper?"

The therapist may choose any four items which can be built around the particular speech needs of individuals in her group. She does not need to require the children to include all the sounds that are difficult, but only the one or two on which they have been working.

Later on you may make up some things to ask, but I have chosen these because they will give you practice on sounds on which you are working. They also represent the sort of thing you often do have to ask.

The first examples are suggested by the therapist. Later examples may be suggested by the children themselves.

THERAPIST: Let's practice each one first; then you may choose the one which will give you the work you need. Look at the first one. Listen. "May I write my name on the board?" Jimmie, underline the one special sound you must watch there. Try it by itself. Now in the word "write." There are three of you who need to watch that. All of you try the word "write" including the "r."

CHILDREN: "Write," "r," "May I write my name on the board?"

(Therapist gives individual help as needed, and calls attention to the "ð" sound also. A somewhat slower rate should be empha-

sized here, and phrasing: — "May I write . . . my name . . . on the board?"

The second question, "May I get one thing from the table?" should have similar practice with attention placed on the "g," "θ," and "ð." The third question, "Will you let me get a drink?" provides for emphasis on the "l" and "g"; the fourth one, "May I borrow a sheet of paper?" on the "ʃ" and "v." Each child should have several opportunities to say the above as preparation for actually doing it.)

THERAPIST: Now before you have a turn, you will need to practice the answer you may give when it is your turn for someone to ask permission of you. What choice of answers do you have? Which one is more difficult? Why? Yes, the "s" sound in "Yes" is one on which many of you are working. Try it. Listen first.

For some children the responses "O.K.," "All right," "Surely," may be substituted.

CHILDREN: Yes. (*Therapist gives each child an opportunity to say this a number of times. Children with more skill show the others; children with less skill are given directions, encouragement, praise.*)

THERAPIST: Now you are ready to ask permission. Remember, someone may say "No" to you, in which case you will get another turn later, and you will remember that it is often necessary to refuse a request and to accept it without feeling upset. Jimmie, you may ask permission of Bill, first. You can easily choose to ask for the thing which will give you practice on your special sound. Which one was that? Later, if you like, you may ask one of the others.

CHILD: May I write my name on the board?

CHILD: Yes, *or* Yes, you may.

CHILD: Thank you.

THERAPIST: Now, Bill, you may ask permission of someone. What one gives you practice on the sound you are working on?

CHILD: May I borrow a sheet of paper?

Notice that the requests are concerned with actual situations which may arise in class.

CHILD: No. I'm sorry, I don't have any.

CHILD: Thank you, anyway.

THERAPIST: Bill, you didn't get your request, but there was a reason for it, wasn't there? Ann, you may take the next turn. You know that the second one gives you the work you need, doesn't it?

CHILD: May I get . . . one thing . . . from the table?

CHILD: Yes, you may.

CHILD: Thank you.

CHILD: You're welcome.

THERAPIST: I liked the way you responded with "You're welcome" when someone said "Thank you." You are still having difficulty with the "s" sound in "Yes." Before the rest of you have a turn, let's stop and practice it again.

Part of the effectiveness of a lesson like this lies in the therapist guiding it closely, even though the children are carrying on the activity. Her comments and help along the way will serve to keep the exchange of questions and answers centered on use of par-

CHILDREN: "s," Yes, Yes, you may.

THERAPIST: What have you had fun doing today? Yes, you have asked permission. Sometimes you got to do what you asked, and sometimes not. Which would you rather do, ask permission, or be asked? Why? You have to do both many times during a day.

ticular sounds.

What sounds did you work on? In what words? Do you want to do this again?

Supplementary Suggestions

Other requests which may be established carefully, worked on, then used, are suggested here:

May I sit with . . .?

May I sit by both . . . and . . .?

May I have chalk to write my name on the board?

May I go open the door and see who is there?

May I get a book from the shelf?

May I fix the shade?

May I open the door? It's warm in here.

May I close the door? It feels cool to me.

This interchange of asking for and granting permission can be continued until each child has had several turns. This offers opportunity to observe the children interacting with each other — choice of person, choice of request, etc. It will be interesting to note children's reaction to a refusal, their role in the person of authority who can grant permission or not as he chooses.

Unit II · Lesson 6

1. *Interpersonal Situation:* playing a game

2. *Speaking Aspect of Situation:* asking and answering questions; choosing; taking a turn

3. *Particular Speech Patterns:*

"Yes." "No."   "Look at it."
"Hit or miss?"   "Have a look."
"Miss."
"Yes, I ... do, can ...." etc.   "For you."
"I think so."   "May I have ..."
"It's your turn now."
                     "O. K."
"Thank you."   "Can you ... catch it?"
"You're welcome."   "I think I can."

"Reach ..."
"Ready?"
"Right."

4. *Sounds Emphasized:*   s   r   l   f   v   k θ

5. *Equipment:* a target painted on cardboard that may be placed on the floor, or colored paper scotch-taped to the floor to serve as a target, or a target drawn with chalk on the floor; a bean bag

PROCEDURES	NOTES

THERAPIST: You have worked on speech which you use in passing out and collecting articles; inviting someone to a party; making an introduction; asking permission; expressing a like or dislike, etc. You often use speech in playing a game, too. When boys play baseball they choose sides, for example, and yell when it's a home run or an out. In football the players call signals. In jump rope the girls jump to rhymes that they say. Games call for different speech. Today you are going to have fun working on speech in a special game that will be fun

297

for several reasons — both fun to do, and fun to work on special sounds you use.

Most of you here like to play ball. Is that right? What sort of a ball do you use? Yes, you play with a soft ball on the playground, a football, etc. What other kinds of balls do you have fun with?

CHILDREN: (*Individually*) Volley ball, tennis ball, ping pong ball, rubber ball, bowling ball, etc.

THERAPIST: Most of these balls wouldn't be very usable in this room. In addition you'd get so interested in the ball game you'd forget this was speech class. Let's see how well you can use your catching and throwing skill with this bean bag.

THERAPIST: (*Tossing the bean bag to one child*) Can you catch it?

CHILD: Yes, I can (*holds it*), or I think so.

THERAPIST: Can you throw it?

CHILD: Yes, I can.

THERAPIST: When you have a turn, what sound must you watch in "Yes"?

CHILDREN: "s"

THERAPIST: Let's work on it to see if you are getting it better today.

CHILDREN: (*Practice "s" in the phrases* "Yes," "Yes, I can," "I think so," *etc. Teacher gives help as needed.*)

This activity can be done fairly rapidly since the children should have some skill in use of the "s" in "Yes" by now. On occasion the teacher may withhold the bean bag if a child does not produce the "s" as well as he is able at this particular time saying "I'm coming back to you. I think you can do better."

THERAPIST: (*Resumes tossing bean bag after children have worked on "s" in isolation and in the above responses.*) "Can you ᵢatch it?"

The response "I think so" may be used by children able to incorporate an "s" accurately and easily.

CHILD: Yes, I can.

THERAPIST: Can you throw it?

CHILD: Yes, I can. (*Continue until each child has had one turn, or several, depending on the need.*)

(*This exchange of the bean bag can also be adapted for meeting other needs in the way of work on particular sounds. One example is given; others may be utilized.*)

THERAPIST: Jimmie, you have been working on the "r" in the word "R . . . each." Try it by itself. Now in the word. That is so much better than you were doing. I believe you are ready for some practice in putting it in a different response, like this. "R . . . eady?" (*As the teacher says this she indicates that she is about to toss the bean bag. When the child responds "Yes," she does toss it.*) Now, Jimmie, it's your turn to toss it to me, and in order for you to get practice on your sound you ask me the same thing. Listen first. "Ready?"

CHILD: R . . . eady? *or* O.K?

THERAPIST: Yes, I am, *or* Surely. (*Child tosses bean bag.*)

THERAPIST: R . . . eady? *or* O.K?

CHILD: Yes, I am, *or* Surely. (*Teacher tosses bean bag.*)

(This activity should be continued several times between the child and the teacher so that the children hear the entire pattern several times.)

THERAPIST: Now, Jimmie, you may give each person a turn, tossing the bean bag to him, and asking, "R ... eady?" I want you to notice if each child when he answers you is checking himself on this "s." You in turn must watch your "r."

CHILD: R ... eady?

CHILD: Yes, I am. *(First child tosses bean bag.)*

CHILD: *(Who has received bean bag)* Ready?

FIRST CHILD: Yes. *(Continue until each child has had several turns.)*

(Other responses which may be introduced in similar fashion and utilize the same situation are as follows:)

CHILD: Have a look. *(Tosses the bean bag.)*

CHILD: *(Receives the bean bag.)* Thank you.

* * * * *

CHILD: For you. *(Tosses the bean bag.)*

CHILD: Thank you.

* * * * *

CHILD: May I have the bean bag?

CHILD: Yes, you may.

CHILD: Thank you.

CHILD: You're welcome.

*   *   *   *   *

CHILD: Can you catch it?

CHILD: I think I can.

*   *   *   *   *

THERAPIST: Take a look at the target on the floor. Do you see the bull's eye? When the bean bag is all the way on the bull's eye, you call it a "hit." If it is even slightly off the bull's eye, or entirely off, like this, you call it a "miss." I'm going to stand right next to the target, and ask you some questions to be sure you know what is called a "hit" and what is called a "miss." (*Dropping a bean bag on target*) Jean, hit or miss?

CHILD: Hit, *or* Miss. (*Teacher repeats several times, emphasizing at first not phonetic accuracy, but understanding of the target.*)

THERAPIST: You can hear that "miss" has a sound in it like "yes." Try it. Watch that you get the new sound in. Listen to it again. "Miss."

CHILDREN: Miss. (*Each child has several turns saying it, the teacher giving individual help as needed.*)

THERAPIST: Because that is new for you, you will need to practice it more before you have a turn at the target. Let's each ask Ann the question once to see if you are really ready for the game. Listen.

The therapist will need to point out that the name should come first in this speech pattern. This keeps the "s" a truly final one,

I'm going to use Ann's name at the beginning. "Ann, hit or miss?" Listen again. Watch me. Now each of you try it for practice.

and somewhat easier than a medial one in most cases.

CHILDREN: Ann, hit or miss? (*Children each have a turn, teacher giving help.*)

THERAPIST: Now you are ready to have a turn at trying to hit the target, and at using certain speech after you have had a try. Will you each hit the target for sure? Will any of you hit the target for sure? That's right, not for sure. You will try, and you will want to hit it, but you may not. That is the way in games — you don't always win even when you would like being the winner. This game is even fixed so that it is extra hard to make a hit, which means you get lots of practice on the "s" in "miss." I'll do it once more so that you will be sure to hear the speech you will use.

THERAPIST: (*Tosses bean bag toward target*) Billy, hit or miss?

CHILD: Miss.

THERAPIST: Yes. It's your turn now.

(*Note that the "Yes" occurs very naturally here in the speech pattern. The therapist may suggest that the child who is working on "r" reply "Right," to the child's response.*)

THERAPIST: What new speech patterns have you worked on? Why? You use the word "miss" in many different ways. We will talk about it when you come again.

Since this activity is structured so that a hit is not easy, the children usually recognize the challenge and work that much harder to do it. If it becomes too easy so that the children are not having opportunity to use the "miss" response, the target can be placed at a greater distance.

"It's your turn" is introduced here largely for emphasis on use, not phonetic accuracy, although some children may be ready to include the "s" in "It's."

Supplementary Suggestions

Other useful responses:

CHILD: Ready?

CHILD: Sure.

CHILD: Hit or miss?

CHILD: Miss.

CHILD: That's right.

Unit II · Lesson 7

1. *Interpersonal Situation:* guessing
2. *Speaking Aspect of Situation:* asking and answering questions
3. *Particular Speech Patterns:*

"Yes . . . ." "Reach the . . . ." "Just the . . . ."
"What do you miss?" "Right." or "That's
"What else?" right." "Show me . . . ."
"Guess again." "Ready."

"Which one did
"That one?" "Where do you have it?" I touch?"
"These two?" "In the box."
"In my pocket."
"On the shelf."

4. *Sounds Emphasized:* **s** **r**
5. *Equipment:* a group of related articles as desk items, art materials, set of tools, cards with a number series on them, stamps, etc.

PROCEDURES

THERAPIST: Sometimes when your dad comes home from work he says to you, "There is a surprise in the car for you. Guess what it is." Mother may say, "There is a surprise in the oven for you. Can you guess what it is?" Then you have fun guessing. Sometimes one of you comes to me and says, "Guess what today is," or "Guess what I got on my spelling paper today." When else do you guess?

CHILDREN (*Individually*) We try to guess what's in our packages at Christmas or on our birthday, etc.

THERAPIST: You are going to do some guessing today, but it will be easier because you will have some hints. Watch what I have here. (*Therapist takes articles from pocket or box one at a time for children*

NOTES

The therapist will use four items at the outset of this activity. She can increase the number to five or six later depending on the abilities of the group. There

304

to see, lays them on the table, waits until children have examined the article and are looking at her face, then sets the pattern by saying "The paints," "The brush," The water pan," etc. *She can stress a slower rate, pausing between phrases, and including the "ð" sound.)*

THERAPIST: In order for you to know better what is here, let's have several of you name the things just as I did. Listen: "The paints," etc. What sound do you need to watch? Each of you try it first, and then I'll choose one of you to name each thing that is here.

THERAPIST: *(Pointing to an object)* What do you call it?

CHILDREN: The paper.

THERAPIST: Where is it?

CHILDREN: *(Individually)* On the table. *(Continue giving children work on the "ð" sound.)*

THERAPIST: What did you like about Ann's answer?

CHILD: She remembered to use the "ð" sound in both "the" and "on the table."

THERAPIST: Jimmie, you may have a turn naming the things on the table. It will be a chance for you to go slowly, take your time, and talk smoothly. Listen to me. *(Therapist repeats patterns, emphasizing particularly pausing between each phrase.)*

should be enough items so that there is some challenge in checking on the one or two items removed. If there are so many that too much time is consumed in recalling an item then the activity tends to be centered on recall rather than on speech.

The items should be related in function, and large enough to be seen easily, but small enough to be concealed in the hand.

CHILD: The paint cloth, the chalk, the crayons, the charcoal, etc.

THERAPIST: What did you like about Jim's speech?

CHILDREN: (*Individually*) He went slowly enough to be understood easily. He took his time, etc.

THERAPIST: The last time you worked on the "s" sound in "hit or miss." In what different ways do you use "miss"?

CHILDREN: (*Individually*) In a teacher's name, as Miss Smith. When you miss a problem in arithmetic. When you miss a friend who is away. When you miss going swimming in winter.

In this discussion the use of speech is stressed before phonetic accuracy. It helps develop the child's awareness that he is working on speech which he uses often. Therapist should be ready to supply examples.

THERAPIST: That's right, you use the word in many ways. If you think about it, it is an easy word in which to use your new "s." Try it first. Listen: "Miss."

CHILDREN: Miss. (*Therapist gives help where indicated.*)

THERAPIST: Look carefully at the four things I have here. Ann, hide your eyes. (*Therapist removes one object.*) Open your eyes, (*or* Ready). What do you miss?

CHILD: The easel brush?

THERAPIST: Yes, *or* Right.

THERAPIST: Before each of you has a turn, let's see if you can get the "s" in "What do you miss?"

CHILDREN: (*Individually*) What do you

Therapist repeats this activity several times for children to hear the pattern. She may say, "Notice that when you guess correctly what is missing I said, 'Yes.' That is extra practice for those of you who are working on 's.' If you need work on 'r' there are two places for you to use it — saying 'Ready' to the person whose eyes are closed, and 'Right' when he guesses what is missing."

miss? (*Continue practicing, giving help as needed.*)

THERAPIST: Now you are ready to begin. The people working on "r" have two things to watch: "Ready," and "Right." The ones working on "s" need to check "miss" and "Yes."

CHILD: Hide your eyes, Ann. (*Child removes one object.*) Open your eyes, *or* Ready. What do you miss?

CHILD: The . . .?

CHILD: Yes, *or* Right. (*Continue until each child has had a turn removing an object. The therapist may add one or two objects to the original group of four to add interest, or substitute a new group.*)

It is better for the therapist or child leading the sequence to indicate the one child who should close his eyes instead of having the entire group do it. This helps prevent accusations of "peeking" and permits all but one of the children to be in on the process.

THERAPIST: You had fun doing that, didn't you? And you watched your sounds so carefully that I'm going to let you do it again, but make it harder. This time I will take two things away. When I choose you, you will tell me just one thing you miss. Then I'll ask you a question: "What else?" and you'll tell me the second thing you miss. Try it.

Hide your eyes, Jean. (*Therapist removes two objects.*) Open your eyes, *or* Ready. What do you miss?

CHILD: The paints?

THERAPIST: Yes, *or* Right. What else?

CHILD: The brush?

THERAPIST: Yes, *or* Right.

THERAPIST: That was fun, too, wasn't it? Listen to the new pattern: "What else?" Try it, remembering that you use the same sound there which you use in "Yes" and "miss."

CHILDREN: "What else?" (*Therapist gives help where needed. If a child has difficulty with both "l" and "s," only the "s" should be emphasized here.*)

THERAPIST: Mary, you may have the first turn. Name the things first so we can remember everything that is here. Six things are quite a few to keep in mind. You will check your "r," too.

CHILD: The . . . , etc.; Hide your eyes, Jack; Ready; What do you miss?"

CHILD: The . . .?

CHILD: Right. What else?

CHILD: The . . .?

CHILD: Right.

(*This pattern can be followed a number of times. The therapist should help each child anticipate the sounds he will check himself on.*)

THERAPIST: You have had fun guessing today. You do very well at it, and at checking your speech while you do it. Often in speech you may ask "What's missing?" instead of "What do you miss?" That has two "s" sounds in it, and is a little difficult for you now, but you will be ready for it later.

"What's missing?" has been observed to be used more frequently than "What do you miss?" and can be used when children are ready to include two "s" sounds easily.

Supplementary Suggestions

CHILD: Hide your eyes. Open your eyes. What do you miss?

CHILD: The . . .?

CHILD: Yes.

CHILD: Where do you have it?

CHILD: In the box, *or* In my pocket, *or* On the shelf.

*   *   *   *   *

CHILD: Hide your eyes. Open your eyes. Which one do you miss?

CHILD: Just the . . .?

CHILD: That's right.

*   *   *   *   *

CHILD: Hide your eyes. (*Adds two objects*) Open your eyes. Show me the two I put in.

CHILD: (*Pointing them out*) These two?

CHILD: That's right.

*   *   *   *   *

CHILD: Hide your eyes. (*Touches one article.*) Open your eyes. Which one did I touch?

CHILD: That one?

CHILD: No, guess again.

CHILD: That one?

CHILD: Yes.

*   *   *   *   *

CHILD: Hide your eyes. (*Two children leave the group.*) Open your eyes. Who do you miss?

CHILD: Mary?

CHILD: Yes. Who else?

CHILD: Bill?

CHILD: Yes.

Unit II · Lesson 8

1. *Interpersonal Situations:* including a friend; guessing
2. *Speaking Aspect of Situations:* making introductions; asking and answering questions
3. *Particular Speech Patterns:*

"This is . . . ."	"Who else?"
"Miss . . . ."	"Guess again."
"Mrs. . . ."	
"Mister . . . ."	"I'm thinking of . . . ."
"Yes . . . ."	
	"Right."

4. *Sounds Emphasized:*   s   r   θ
5. *Equipment:* none

PROCEDURES

THERAPIST: When you had a party several weeks ago here what did you do after you had welcomed your friend at the door and brought him in? Yes, you introduced him.

Your dad and mother may have introduced you at some time by saying, "George, this is my son, Jim," or "Meet my daughter, Ann." You make an introduction when you want one of your friends to meet another. If you bring a friend home from school to play, you usually introduce him to your mother if she doesn't already know him. If you bring a friend to speech class, you will need to introduce him to me and to the other boys and girls. Ann has a friend here today. She will introduce her to you this way: "Jean, this is Billy." Billy, you will say, "Hi, Jean," and she will say, "Hi, Billy." Ann, you may introduce her to the boys and girls now.

NOTES

The therapist can plan to have a friend of various children in speech class visit frequently, so that such speaking events as greetings and introductions become an integral part of each lesson. Introductions are somewhat difficult, even for those without speech deviations, and need to be experienced many times. They can be utilized when a parent or classroom teacher visits, also.

Permitting the child to bring a friend to speech class has other desirable aspects. He gains recognition in his own class group for choosing a friend to take with him. He is given recognition in speech class from an outsider for a sound or response on which he is working. Since the speech patterns that are being worked on are those every

311

Sometimes you forget someone's name when you are making an introduction. Everyone does that at some time or other. If you do that, then you just ask the person his name.

child has occasion to use, a visitor can fit in easily with the group activities.

CHILD: (*Introducing friend to each member of the class*) Jean, this is Jim.

CHILDREN: Hi . . . .

THERAPIST: When you introduce your teacher you have a chance to use the "s" in the word you have been working on — "miss" — as in my name, "Miss Hale." Listen. "Miss Hale, this is Jean." Try "Miss" by itself.

The therapist may call attention to the "ð" in "this" if she thinks individual children are ready to handle it. As a rule the "s" in "this" is too difficult for many of them at this stage. In particular instances, however, a child may be ready for help here.

CHILDREN: (*Individually*) Miss. (*Each child has additional practice with this pattern.*)

THERAPIST: When you put it with someone's name it is more difficult. Try it. "Miss Hale."

CHILDREN: (*Individually*) Miss Hale.

THERAPIST: Each of you bring a friend to me and introduce him, remembering to watch the "s" sound.

CHILD: Miss Hale, this is Jack.

THERAPIST: Hi, Jack.

CHILD: Hi, Miss Hale.

THERAPIST: Did you notice that Jack got his "s" sound in when he said "Hi" to me, too? I liked that.

(*This should be continued until each child has had an opportunity to introduce one child to the therapist.*)

THERAPIST: Now you will need to work some on your own teacher's name. Five of you have a "Miss" for a teacher, one of you has a "Mister," the rest of you have a "Mrs." "Mrs." is harder but I will give you some help with it; the first part of "Mrs." is like "Miss." It is that way with "Mister" too.

What is your teacher's name?

CHILD: Miss . . . , Mrs. . . . , *or* Mister . . . .

THERAPIST: You have worked on two things today, making an introduction, and using the "s" in "Miss" with someone's name. You will soon be able to surprise your teacher by using the "s" when you say her name.

It should be noted that for children who do not need special work on the sounds mentioned here, the practice in use of speech in performing an introduction is also important.

Supplementary Suggestions

THERAPIST: The other day you worked on saying "What else?" Here is a way to get some more practice on it, and also on the word "thinking" that has a "θ" sound in it.

THERAPIST: I'm thinking of two boys.

CHILDREN: (*Individually*) Harry?

THERAPIST: No, guess again.

CHILD: Jack?

THERAPIST: Yes. Who else?

This activity may be continued for some time, the therapist taking several turns early to set the pattern. If the children reply to her question by saying "Is it Harry?" she may say, "That is one way of asking. An even shorter way is to just use the name like this: 'Harry?'" Many of the children will be ready to include the "s" sound in "guess again." She should point this out, give them special help. Children who are still having difficulty with the "s" should be con-

CHILD: Jim?

THERAPIST: Yes.

cerned with it only in " Yes,"
and "Who else?"

(*The pattern may be varied as follows:*)

CHILD: I'm thinking of two girls here.

CHILD: Ann?

CHILD: Right, *or* Wrong.   Who else?

CHILD: Betty?

CHILD: Right.

Unit II · Lesson 9

1. *Interpersonal Situations:* borrowing and lending; giving and carrying out directions

2. *Speaking Aspect of Situations:* asking and answering questions; making and accepting suggestions

3. *Particular Speech Patterns:*

"A piece of . . . ."	"What do you have?"	"Which one?"
"What do you miss?"	"May I have . . . ?"	"Show me."
		"Put a check . . . ."
"That one."	"Can you . . . ?"	"Will you erase . . . ?"
	"Yes, I can."	"Change . . . ."
"Reach it."	"In my pocket."	
"Write . . . ."		
"Here."	"Get it . . ."	
"Ready?"	"Will you give . . . ?"	
"That's right . . . wrong."		

4. *Sounds Emphasized:*   s   r   v   k   g   tʃ   ʃ

5. *Equipment:* a box containing articles such as a piece of gum, chalk, paper, puzzle, crayon, pencil, newspaper money, candy, string; or a number of pieces of candy wrapped in cellophane; a piece of chalk for each child

---

PROCEDURES	NOTES
THERAPIST: Today I had a "piece of pie" for lunch. Sometimes I have a "piece of cake." When else do you use the word "piece"?	*The objects selected should be real objects, not pictures. Simple things as gum, small note paper, candy wrapped in cellophane, etc., will provide many opportunities for speech patterns.*
CHILDREN: (*Individually*) A piece of watermelon, meat, bread, paper, gum, etc.	

THERAPIST: Watch what I have in the box. As I take each thing out you may be thinking what you would like to have. You may be thinking, too, about the way I use the "s" sound. (*Therapist takes articles from the box one at a time for children to see, lays them on the table, waits until children have examined the article and are*

315

looking at her, and sets the pattern by saying
"a piece of paper," etc. *She may stress a
slower rate, pausing between phrases, and
the "s" sound in "piece.")* You may each
have a piece of something, but first you
will want to be sure you can use the "s"
sound in the new word. Listen. Watch.
"A piece of gum." Try it.

CHILDREN: *(Individually)* A piece of
gum. *(Each child has several turns saying
this. Therapist gives help where needed.
She may call attention to the children who
make it fairly easily, and have them set the
pattern for the others.)*

*Care should be taken that
the "s" in "piece of" is
carefully blended.*

THERAPIST: Saying "A piece of gum"
is somewhat harder. You will need to
practice it carefully. *(Extending a piece
of gum)* What do you call it?

*The "g" in gum need not
be emphasized unless some
child in the group needs
work on "g," not "s." Two
difficult sounds should not
be stressed at the same time.*

CHILDREN: *(Individually)* A piece of
gum. *(Continue, giving children help as
indicated.)*

THERAPIST: You may choose what you
would like now. Before you get it, however, you must show me how well you can
use the "s" when you ask for it. "What
do you want?"

CHILDREN: *(Individually)* A piece of . . . .

THERAPIST: Reach it.

CHILDREN: Thank you.

*(The therapist may choose one child who
needs work on the "r" to lead this activity
so that he can use the "r" in "Reach it" or
"Here.")*

THERAPIST: Mary, listen to the way I'm going to begin collecting the pieces the children have. "What do you have?"

CHILDREN: (*Individually*) A piece of . . . .

THERAPIST: Can you put it on the table?

CHILDREN: (*Individually*) Yes, I can.

THERAPIST: Thank you.

THERAPIST: (*Directing her question to the child who is working on the "k"*) Mary, why am I going to choose you to do what I did? That's right. So you can get practice on saying "can," and the other boys and girls can remember about their "s" in "yes." (*Turning to children*) When the things are back on the table, you will have fun choosing something else.

CHILD: What do you have?

CHILD: A piece of . . . .

CHILD: Can you put it on the table?

CHILD: Yes, I can.

CHILD: Thank you.

THERAPIST: Now all the pieces are back on the table. When you choose something this time, we will give Susan practice on her "g" sound in "get." Listen, Susan, so you will know what to do.

THERAPIST: (*To one child*) What do you want?

CHILD: A piece of . . . .

THERAPIST: Get it from the table.

CHILD: Thank you.

THERAPIST: Try it first, Susan.   Listen: "Get it."

CHILD: Get it.

(*Continue with above pattern as indicated.*)

THERAPIST: You may put what you have in your pocket.   What did you put in your pocket?

CHILDREN: (*Individually*) A piece of . . . .

THERAPIST: Where did you put it?

CHILDREN: In my pocket.

THERAPIST: "In my pocket" uses the "k" sound that Mary and Susan are working on.   Each of you show her how you say it. Now Mary and Susan practice it.

CHILDREN: (*Individually*) In my pocket.

THERAPIST: (*To Mary and Susan*) Where did Jimmie put the piece he had?

CHILDREN: In his pocket.   (*Continue until children working on "k" have several opportunities to use this response.*)

THERAPIST: You may put what you have back in the box now.   What will you put in the box?

It is not expected that all children are using a newly acquired "s" automatically as yet. There will be constant need for the therapist to set the pattern, show the child how to make it, give him special directions.   In such an activity as this she will want to help the child succeed as often as he can.   If this response is too difficult, she may work in several ways of eliciting

CHILDREN: (*Individually*) A piece of . . . .

*   *   *   *   *

THERAPIST: I have "a piece of chalk" for each of you. The chalk is different sizes, but you can write with any piece. You may tell me which piece you'd like by pointing to one and saying, "That one." You do that quite easily now. Try it.

"Yes" from him which will still make it possible for him to take part in the activity. For instance, instead of asking "What do you want?" for obtaining the response "a piece of . . . ," when it is this child's turn she may ask "Do you want a . . . ?" to which he can reply "Yes."

CHILDREN: (*Individually*) That one.

THERAPIST: How do you ask for something?

CHILDREN: May I have a . . .? *or* Will you give me a . . .?

CHILD: May I have a piece of chalk?

THERAPIST: Yes, which one?

CHILD: That one.

THERAPIST: Reach it.

CHILD: Thank you.

THERAPIST: What do you do with chalk?

CHILD: Write with it, *or* Draw.

THERAPIST: The word "write" is one for the people who are working on "r" to practice. Try it. Listen: "wr . . . ite."

CHILDREN: Write. (*Therapist gives individual help where needed.*)

THERAPIST: I have a ladder on the board. Watch, I'm going to begin at the bottom

The ladder serves to keep the written responses fairly

of the ladder and put a number on each step . . . a number between one hundred and two hundred. Listen to what I'm going to do. "Write 121." "Write 178." (*Therapist tells what she is going to do, then does it.*)

THERAPIST: I have erased what I did. Now it is your turn. You may each tell what you will do. "Do you want a turn?"

CHILD: Yes, I do.

THERAPIST: What will you do?

CHILD: Write a . . . .

THERAPIST: What will you use?

CHILD: A piece of chalk.   (*Continue until each child has had a turn.*)

THERAPIST: You began this lesson by working on a word you use often. What was it? Let's see if each of you can say it once before you leave with the very best "s" you can make.

uniform in size.

The therapist may decide what should go on the ladder depending on the abilities of the group.

She should set some limits to the children's choices. Names or initials are also possibilities . . . along with numbers.

Supplementary Suggestions

CHILD: Hide your eyes.   (*Child erases one number.*)

CHILD: Ready?

CHILD: Which one do you miss?

CHILD: Just the . . . ?

CHILD: That's right.

*   *   *   *   *

CHILD: Hide your eyes.   (*Child touches one number.*)

CHILD: Ready?

CHILD: Which one did I touch?

CHILD: That one?

CHILD: That's wrong.   Guess again.

CHILD: That one?

CHILD: That's right.

*   *   *   *   *

CHILD: Show me the number . . . .

CHILD: It's right here.

CHILD: Put a check by it.

*   *   *   *   *

CHILD: Which number will you erase?

CHILD: I think I'll take this one.

*   *   *   *   *

CHILD: (*Erasing one name or number from the ladder*)   Which one do you miss?

CHILD: The . . . .

*   *   *   *   *

CHILD: Change 121 to 123.

CHILD: Is this right?

CHILD: Yes, it is.

Unit II · Lesson 10

1. *Interpersonal Situation:* going on an errand
2. *Speaking Aspect of Situation:* making a request
3. *Particular Speech Patterns:*

"A piece of ..."   "Miss Hale would like ...."
"Miss ...."

                       "Just one piece ...."
"To wrap a package"   "A piece of red chalk."
"Here you are."   "Will you ask ... ?"
"Right here."   "Will you get me ... ?"
                       "Take this piece ...."

4. *Sounds Emphasized:*   s   r   l   dʒ   sk   g

5. *Equipment:* series of related objects, such as paper, string, cardboard, etc.

PROCEDURES

THERAPIST: Sometimes when I come to school I have to borrow some supplies from another teacher. Perhaps I need a piece of chalk, or a piece of brown paper, or a piece of string. I often ask a boy or girl to go on an errand for me to get what I need. When you go on an errand, you need to use speech unless someone writes a note for you to take. But when I'm in a hurry, I do not like to take time to write a note, so you need to ask for the thing, like this: "Miss Hale needs a piece of blue paper," or "Miss Hale needs a piece of string." You may practice borrowing this piece of blue paper for me. When I think you are using the "s" the best you can in my name and in "a piece," I will send each of you on an errand.

CHILDREN: (*Individually*) Miss Hale would like a piece of blue paper. (*Continue until each child has had several opportunities to use this.*)

NOTES

Many children who have speech deviations are reluctant to go on errands which involve speech. The therapist can structure the first experiences very simply as in this lesson. She may then suggest that the classroom teacher see that the children are chosen occasionally for errands. It is also possible for the therapist to gradually increase the difficulty of the errand as to speech involved and situation, and help prepare the child for it, perhaps sending one child each lesson on some errand in the building, such as taking a message to the principal's office, leaving a message for the nurse, etc.

THERAPIST: These are some things I'm going to send you for. Take a look at them: "a piece of . . . string, blue paper, red chalk, yellow chalk, cardboard," etc. I'm going to send Bill over there with these things for you to get. Jean may sit by the door with these things. The rest of you will go on errands, first for me, later on for each other.

THERAPIST: Ann, I need some more string to wrap this package. Will you get a piece for me from Bill?

The children should be held for sounds only in the responses on which they have worked, unless the therapist feels they are ready to include additional ones. For instance, a child who is making a "k" fairly easily may be helped to include it in the word "package," etc.

CHILD: Yes. (*Going to Bill*) Miss Hale would like a piece of string to wrap a package.

BILL: Here you are.

CHILD: Thank you. (*Takes string to teacher.*)

THERAPIST: Thank you, Ann.

THERAPIST: (*Directing question to boys and girls*) What did you like about the way Ann went on that errand for me?

CHILDREN: (*Individually*) She seemed glad she was going. She smiled. She watched her "s" in "yes," "Miss," and "piece." She remembered to say "Thank you."

THERAPIST: (*Continues until each child has gone on one errand. This provides many opportunities for the children to begin evaluating performance in speech. The teacher should call attention to positive assets in each instance, as well as making suggestions for improvement. A comment*

After children have each gone on an errand for the therapist they may prepare to send each other on similar errands.

The children may begin by writing some suggestions on

such as "*What did you like?*" structures the situation for praise.)

the board for errands, practicing the speech to be used, choosing the one which gives them work on their particular sounds, then going ahead with giving the direction and going on the errand.

Supplementary Suggestions

CHILD: Will you ask Bill for a piece of string?

CHILD: Yes, I will. (*Going to Bill*) George would like a piece of string.

CHILD: Take this piece right here.

CHILD: Thank you.

*   *   *   *   *

CHILD: Will you get me a piece of red paper?

CHILD: Yes, I will. Anything else?

CHILD: A piece of blue paper, too.

CHILD: May I have a piece of red and blue paper?

CHILD: Yes, you may.

CHILD: Thank you.

*   *   *   *   *

CHILD: Miss Hale would like just one piece of yellow chalk.

CHILD: Right here.

CHILD: Thank you.

Unit II · Lesson 11

1. *Interpersonal Situations:* requesting and granting permission; giving and carrying out a direction; carrying on a conversation

2. *Speaking Aspect of Situations:* asking and answering a question; making and accepting suggestions; making comments

3. *Particular Speech Patterns:*

    "May I see what you have?"   "Reach in and . . . ."
    "Yes, you may."   "Get me the . . . ."
    "What did you see?"   "Will you give me . . . ?"
    "What else?"   "I got the . . . ."
    "Guess again."   "Go to the window."
    "Guess what I saw?"   "Come back."
                                  "Look out."

4. *Sounds Emphasized:*   s   r   k   g   l

5. *Equipment:* a box with an assortment of small objects

PROCEDURES	NOTES

THERAPIST: After you get to school in the morning you may say to a friend, "Did you see the fire truck go past this morning?" *or* "Guess what I saw last night?" or maybe you will say, "Come see what happened to the fish bowl over the weekend." The words "see" and "saw" you use many times during a day. You can hear the "s" sound, can't you?

I have some things in the box from my desk drawer. You may each see what I have after you have asked permission in this way: "May I see what you have?" Listen again to the way in which you will ask: "May I see what you have?" Each of you practice it first.

CHILDREN: May I see what you have? (*Each child has an opportunity to say this, with the therapist giving special help where needed.*)

She may need to have children work on an "s" in isolation and in "see" but should begin with the whole

THERAPIST: Now you are ready to ask. When someone asks you what you saw, you will only tell one thing, although there are many things in the box, so that other people can have a turn.

CHILD: May I see what you have?

THERAPIST: Yes, you may. (*After child has looked*) What did you see?

CHILD: A pad of paper.

THERAPIST: (*To child who has just looked in the box*) You may choose the next person who will ask permission of you.

CHILD: May I see what you have?

CHILD: Yes, you may.   What did you see?

CHILD: A box of paper clips. (*This activity may be continued until each child has had a turn.*)

THERAPIST: In order for Jimmie to use his "r" today he may tell each of you what to get out of the box in this way: "Reach in and get the scotch tape." (*To Jimmie*) Practice it first to be sure you are using your best "r."

CHILD: Reach in and get the tape. (*Child then directs others to obtain a certain article.*)

THERAPIST: May and Susan, in order for you to work on the "g" sound, one of you may give directions to the other in this way: "Get me the ruler, please." If May tells Susan that, then she will come to

patterns and then work on particular parts.

The children should feel permissiveness to say "no" occasionally. The therapist may set limits in various ways such as suggesting that after a child has refused a request twice, he grant it the next time. She may also point out that "no" is easy, but that since "yes" is more difficult he will need to use it more often.

It should be noted here that the conversational pattern in response to the query "What did you see?" consists of one phrase, usually, as "a pad of paper." The children should not be required to answer in a complete sentence.

you and say, "Will you give me the ruler?" and then take it back to May. You will want to practice it first, watching the "g."

CHILDREN: (*Individually*) Get me the ruler. Will you give me the ruler?

THERAPIST: Now both of you are ready to collect the things the children are holding.

CHILD: (*Directing question to another child*) Susan, get me the blue eraser.

CHILD: (*To the person holding the ruler*) Will you give me the eraser?

CHILD: (*Holding the eraser*) Yes, I will.

CHILD: (*Returning to the one requesting the toy*) I got the ruler.

CHILD: Thank you. (*Continue until articles are collected.*)

THERAPIST: Now let's have some fun looking out the window to see how many different things you can see. It will give you a chance to work on several things you do very easily now in speech. "Go to the window. Look out. Come back. What did you see?" I'll do it first so that you can hear what to say. When you come back you will tell only one thing at first, and then I will ask you, "What else?"

After the therapist has set the pattern several times, the children may continue with this activity until they have explored most of the possibilities of things to see outside that particular window. It may add to the interest if the therapist keeps a list on the board of each thing that is seen.

THERAPIST: Go to the window. Look out. Come back. What did you see?

CHILD: A swing.

THERAPIST: What else?

CHILD: A slide.

(*This pattern sequence may be expanded in
the following way:*)

CHILD: (*After returning from the window*)
Guess what I saw at the window?

CHILD: Did you see a . . .?

CHILD: No, guess again, *or* Yes, I did.

THERAPIST: What have you worked on
today? Yes, you have worked especially
on the "s" in "see" and "saw." You
have also asked permission and given
someone a direction.

Unit II · Lesson 12

1. *Interpersonal Situations:* taking a message; obtaining and giving information

2. *Speaking Aspect of Situations:* relating a message; asking and answering questions

3. *Particular Speech Patterns:*

   "What did Jack say?" "I'm going ...." "You should bring ...."
   "He said ...." "...I can't" "She would like ...."
   "Miss Hale said ...."

   (Additional responses as listed)

4. *Sounds Emphasized:* s k g ʃ r l θ ð

5. *Equipment:* none

PROCEDURES	NOTES

THERAPIST: When you come to speech class you often tell me something your own teacher said to you, or your mother or your dad. You may tell me, "My mother said she was coming to visit next Thursday," or "My dad said he was going to take me fishing." "Said" is a word you use almost as often as you do the ones we worked on last time, "see" and "saw."

Think of one place you will be going sometime this week. We will make a list of several on the board.

CHILDREN: I'm going to the show tonight. I'm going to my grandmother's. I'm going outside after school. I'm going away this weekend.

THERAPIST: From these things you may choose one thing to say to the person next to you. Later on you may choose anything you like to tell, but for practice

This lesson will need to be worked out according to the interests and abilities of the children. If several of them have speech that is difficult to understand, the therapist will need to limit the responses so that the group will understand what is being said. She may also need to limit somewhat the length of what they say, perhaps suggesting that they tell only one thing. The chief emphasis in the lesson is placed on the use of the words "say" and "said." If children hesitate too long in whispering something to the next child it doesn't serve to promote use of these particular patterns. For that reason the therapist may suggest several things at the outset the children can choose to use.

you are to keep to the things on the board.

Jack, suppose you whisper one thing to Jimmie. (*He whispers.*) Jimmie, what did Jack say?

CHILD: He said he was going to the show.

(*This may be continued until each child has had an opportunity to take part. Individual help should be given before the children carry out the activity on the words "say," "said," and others as indicated.*)

The therapist may encourage the children to make a distinction between "real events" and "wished-for events," and to use one group only now, saving the other for a different lesson.

THERAPIST: Often you use "say" and "said" when you take a message for someone. For instance, I may ask one of you to go to the office and tell Mrs. Avery that I need the key to the speech room. I may ask you to tell your teacher I'd like to talk with her. Your message will sound something like this: "Miss Hale said she needed the key to the speech room." "Miss Hale said she would like to talk with you."

I will send a message to each of you, and each of you will also get a chance to take a message. Before you do, let's see if you can use the "s" in "said." Listen. Watch. Try this: "Miss Hale said . . . ."

CHILDREN: Miss Hale said . . . . (*Continue until each child has demonstrated his ability to do this as well as he is able.*)

THERAPIST: Joe, you may take the first message. You will speak slowly, take it easy, and talk loudly enough for us to hear. "Tell Nancy she should bring a pencil and paper with her to speech class."

CHILD: (*Going to another child*) Miss Hale said you should bring a pencil and paper to speech class.

CHILD: Tell Miss Hale I will.

CHILD: (*Returns to therapist*) She said she would.

THERAPIST: (*Directing question to other children*) What did you like about the way Joe took that message?

CHILDREN:(*Individually*) He talked loudly enough for Nancy to hear. He didn't hurry. He waited before he started. He smiled. He used two "s" sounds his new way.

THERAPIST: Kathie, tell Jack that I would like him to help me after school. Before you go, let's hear you use two "s" sounds in "Miss Hale said . . . ."

CHILD: Miss Hale said . . . .

THERAPIST: Listen first. "s" Try that. Now try it in "Miss Hale said . . . ."

CHILD: Miss Hale said she would like you to help her after school.

CHILD: Tell her I can't. I have a music lesson.

CHILD: (*Returning to therapist*) Jack said he couldn't help you tonight. He has a music lesson.

THERAPIST: Thank you.

These messages should be continued until each child has had an experience both taking a message, and sending one. In each instance the message can be planned to give particular children work on sounds other than the "s." Before the child takes the message, he should repeat it, and be given help in areas where it is needed. These first messages should not involve any materials . . . it is easier to keep the messages centered on the speech that is being used.

Supplementary Suggestions

r

Miss Hale would like the rest of the boys and girls to come.
Miss Hale is ready for the children in speech class.
Miss Hale would like some string to wrap a package.

l

Miss Hale would like you to come to speech class.
Miss Hale wants you to look for the new chairs.
Miss Hale wants you to lay this on the office counter.

k

Miss Hale said that you are to come to speech class.
Miss Hale said that she cannot see you today.
Miss Hale said you can go to the movies today.

g

Miss Hale said for you to get the other boys and girls.
Miss Hale said for you to go on the trip with your class.

ð   θ

Miss Hale said "Thank you" for the papers.
Miss Hale said the lights in the room will not turn on.

*   *   *   *   *

THERAPIST: What do you like about taking messages?   What seems
hard to you?   What did you check yourself on?

*Similar situations for messages may be worked out in a succeeding lesson where
each child has some articles for which the therapist sends.*

Unit II · Lesson 13

1. *Interpersonal Situations:* giving and accepting an apology
2. *Speaking Aspect of Situation:* stating the apology
3. *Particular Speech Patterns:*
   "I'm sorry...."   "That's all right."   "You have my chair, I think."
   "I'm late."   (Others as indicated)   "I was just fooling you."
4. *Sounds Emphasized:*   s   l   ð   r   tʃ   dʒ
5. *Equipment:* none

PROCEDURES

THERAPIST: Occasionally when you are late for something you need to apologize for it, such as coming late to class after recess, being late for your music lesson, coming in late to dinner. If you round a corner too quickly and run into someone you didn't see, you apologize. When else do you use apologies?

CHILDREN: When you say something that hurts someone's feelings. When you leave a book at home you were supposed to bring back, etc.

THERAPIST: There are different ways of making an apology. One of the easiest is to say, "I'm sorry I'm late," or "I'm sorry I bumped you. I didn't see you." Practice this much first: "I'm sorry ...." Listen to it. Watch it. Try it.

CHILDREN: I'm sorry .... *(Continue until each child has had several opportunities to say this; give help where needed.)*

THERAPIST: Each of you think of a way of making an apology if you came late to

NOTES

333

speech class. You will need to watch the "s" in "sorry," and some of you will have other sounds to check yourself on.

CHILDREN: (*Individually*) I'm sorry to be late. I forgot to watch the clock. — I'm sorry I'm late. I was on a trip with my class. — I'm sorry I'm late. We had a picture show.

THERAPIST: (*Replies to each apology*) "That's all right for today." I liked the way you gave those apologies. Each of you had a reason for being late. Giving a reason with an apology usually makes the other person feel better.

Let's work on other times when you need to give an apology. Two of you show what happens when you accidentally bump into someone, perhaps make him drop a book or a package.

The value of acting out such situations has the advantage of making it more real to the children. It should be structured somewhat carefully with the emphasis on the speech used. Children will usually have suggestions to make both in regard to the event and the speech.

CHILDREN: (*Acting out this situation*) I'm sorry. I didn't see you there. — That's all right. (*This can be continued until several children have given their version of a situation and the speech used in the apology.*)

THERAPIST: I've noticed that many of you have fun slipping into someone else's chair when that person isn't looking. Usually you do it for fun, but occasionally it starts trouble. When you find someone else in your chair what can you say? How about the person who has your chair? An easy apology frequently makes everything all right. "You have my chair, I think." — "I'm sorry. I was just fooling you." (*Children like to act*

*this out. Carry-over is often observed almost
immediately in this situation.)*

THERAPIST: What have you worked on
today? Why? Are apologies always
easy to make? Why not? What can you
do about it?

Supplementary Suggestions

1. Slamming a door loudly.
2. Knocking over a box, shoving some papers on the floor inad-
   vertently.
3. Interrupting when someone else is talking.
4. Others which the children may suggest.

Unit II · Lesson 14

1. *Interpersonal Situations:* making and accepting a suggestion

2. *Speaking Aspect of Situations:* making and accepting a suggestion

3. *Particular Speech Patterns:*

    "Let's get a toy."   "Put the ... with the rest."
    "That's a good idea."
    "That's mine."   "What did you get?"
    "That's yours."
    "It's a ...."

4. *Sounds Emphasized:*   s   ð   g   r

5. *Equipment:* a series of different readers; comic books

PROCEDURES	NOTES
THERAPIST: Often when you talk you are in a hurry, and use a shorter way of talking instead of a longer one. You may say "It's in here," instead of "It is in here." You may say "That's mine," rather than "That is mine," or "Let's go play," not "Let us go play." Each one of the shorter ways has an "s" in it. Listen. Watch. "It's," "That's," "Let's." Listen again. Try them.	*Because of the frequent use of contractions several lessons can be built around these phrases.*

CHILDREN: It's, That's, Let's.

THERAPIST: I have some comic books here, but you won't come to get one alone, you will choose someone to come with you, and invite him in this way. Listen. "Let's get a funny book." Try it.

CHILDREN: (*Individually*) Let's get a funny book. (*The therapist gives help here as indicated.*)

THERAPIST: The person to whom you say

336

it will answer, "That's a good idea."
Try it.

CHILDREN: (*Individually*) That's a good
idea. (*The therapist gives help as needed.*)

THERAPIST: Let's try that much. You
may each choose the person you would
like to go with you to get a book.

CHILDREN: (*Individually*) Let's get a
funny book.

CHILD: That's a good idea. (*Children
each choose a book from the table, and
return to their chairs. This should be
continued until each child has made and
accepted a suggestion.*)

(*The comic books may be reassembled on
the table by one child working on the "r"
giving the direction, "Put the book with
the rest of them."*)

THERAPIST: You had fun making and accepting a suggestion. You had fun, too,
using the "s" in a new way. This time
we will change it some so that when you
come to the table you will ask and
answer a question about what you have.
I will show you.

THERAPIST: (*Pointing to one book*) That's
the one I want. What's it about? It's
about Roy Rogers.

CHILDREN: (*Work on various parts of
these responses as it is required.*)

CHILD: Let's get a funny book.

*If comic books are used, the
therapist should suggest that
they be kept closed until
everyone has one.*

CHILD: That's a good idea.

CHILD: That's the one I want.

CHILD: What's it about?

CHILD: It's about.... (*This may be continued until each child again has a book.*)

THERAPIST: Gene, you may collect the books now, by asking "Will you give me your book? It's time to go."

Try saying each one of these words that you especially worked on today. They are words you use often. "It's," "Let's," "That's."

Supplementary Suggestions

CHILD 1: Let's go to the table (box, shelf, bookcase) and get a book.

CHILD 2: That's a good idea.

CHILD 1: I think I'll take this one.

CHILD 2: I'll have this one.

CHILD 1: Let's go to our seats and look at them.

CHILD 2: That's all right with me.

Unit II · Lesson 15

1. *Interpersonal Situation:* designating possession
2. *Speaking Aspect of Situation:* asking and answering questions
3. *Particular Speech Patterns:*

"His." and "Hers." or   "She . . . with it."   "What do you want
"A boy's."   "A girl's."   "He . . . with it."   to do?"
"Please."   "I'm thinking of . . . ."
                 "Something of his?"   "Erase one, please."
                                   "Circle one, please."
                                   "Check one, please."
                 "Either one."

4. *Sounds Emphasized:*   z   θ   ð   tʃ
5. *Equipment:* blackboard and chalk

PROCEDURES	NOTES

THERAPIST: Occasionally your caps get mixed in the coat room and the teacher has to help you get them straightened out. She may hold up one cap saying, "Whose is it?" You may answer, "It's mine," or "It's yours," or "It's his." When you play with someone's ball on the playground you have to find out to whom it belongs when recess is over. Sometimes when I come to your room to visit I ask your teacher "Which picture is Ann's?" and she may point to one saying, "That's hers." Some of those answers have a new sound which many of you will begin working on today. Listen to it.

"His," "hers," "yours." Listen to the part at the end. "z" That sound is very similar to the "s" sound. See if you can tell the difference. I will give you two words. Tell me where the "z"

339

sound comes — in the first word or the second.

caps, sweaters	hands, claps
arms, coats	shoes, walks
legs, socks	

Before you try to make it, let's see how well you can make the "s." (*Each child takes a turn at producing the "s" in isolation.*) Notice that it is whispered. The new sound has some voice. "z" Try it in the words "his" and "hers" first.

CHILDREN: His. Hers. (*Where necessary the therapist should give the children individual help on the "z" in isolation. Very often if the child has established an "s" the "z" is relatively simple.*)

THERAPIST: Let's make a list of things on the board that usually belong to a boy, and a list of things that usually belong to a girl. Perhaps some of the things we might put in a list that could belong to either one.

CHILDREN:

marbles	string	purse
bat and ball	pocket knife	sewing kit
hammer	jacks	nail polish
shirt	hair ribbon	ice skates
tie	skip rope	roller skates
wallet	hair clips	bikes

THERAPIST: (*Pointing to one article on the board*) Whose is it?

CHILDREN: His, *or appropriate response.* (*This may be continued until children have had opportunity to use these responses a number of times.*)

The phrase "Whose is it?" is difficult because of the two "z" sounds occurring so closely together. Since some children are just acquiring the "z" sound, the therapist will direct that question herself. She can make a com-

THERAPIST: "Please" also ends with that sound, and is something you use almost as often as "Yes" and "Thank you." Try it.

CHILDREN: Please. (*Children are given individual help as needed.*)

THERAPIST: Jean, check one thing of hers, please.

CHILD: O.K. (*Goes to the board and does it.*)

THERAPIST: Before the rest of you do it, perhaps you should practice parts of it to be sure you get in your sounds. Check one thing of his, please. (*Give individual help on various parts as needed.*)

THERAPIST: What new sound have you worked on today? In what speech responses? "His." "Hers." "Boy's." "Girl's." "Please.", etc.

ment as follows: "You can hear the new sound in the question I'm asking, too. Listen. 'Whose is it?' Later you will work on that also."

A child who has had some work on the "l" may be given some help in including it in this response.

Supplementary Suggestions

What do you want to do?
Erase one, please.
Circle one, please.
Check one, please.

I'm thinking of one.
Something of his? *or* hers?
No. Guess again *or*
Yes *or* Yes, it is.

Tell me what a boy does with it.
He hits with it.
He shoots with it.
He carries money in it.

It is suggested that the response "Yes, it is" be introduced in the following lesson, although there is nothing to prevent its use here if the therapist thinks it advisable.

Unit II · Lesson 16

1. *Interpersonal Situations:* obtaining and giving information; guessing
2. *Speaking Aspect of Situations:* asking and answering questions
3. *Particular Speech Patterns:*

   "What time is it?"   "Yes" or "No"   "That's right."
   "Is it . . . ?"   "It's . . . ."   "Ready."
   "Hide your eyes."   "Guess again."
   "Open your eyes."   "See" or "Look"

4. *Sounds Emphasized:*   z   s   r   l   ð
5. *Equipment:* a clock with hands that turn easily

PROCEDURES

THERAPIST: You often ask your teacher or your mother about the time, don't you? You ask if it's time for recess, time for dinner, time to go home, time to practice your music, etc. How do you ask?

CHILDREN: Is it time for supper? *or* What time is it?

THERAPIST: That's right. Do you notice that the word "is" has the sound in it that you put in "his," "hers," and "please"? Try it by first practicing what you worked on the last time. Listen: "his," "hers."

CHILDREN: His, hers. *(Practice continues with therapist giving individual help where needed.)*

THERAPIST: You will begin using it in "is" today. Try it. Listen. "What time is it?"

CHILDREN: What time is it? *(Therapist gives help as needed. Individual children*

NOTES

It is important here to see that the "z" is blended in the pattern "is it."

342

may need work on the "z" sound alone, then combine it in the response "is it," then incorporate it in the response, "What time is it?"

THERAPIST: You usually have fun guessing. Today you are going to do it with this clock. Look at the board. I am going to set this clock at one of the places shown on the board — at nine, twelve, three, or six o'clock. See if you can guess.

THERAPIST: (*After setting the clock and concealing its face*) What time is it?

CHILDREN: Is it . . .? — No, it isn't. Guess again. — Is it . . .? — That's right. See.

(*The therapist repeats this pattern several times so that the children develop the idea of setting the clock at one of the four times suggested on the board, and making a guess by using the response "Is it . . .?" Before turning the activity over to the children, the therapist may put the clock down, and make sure that various children are ready for using the responses. She may check the following: — "What time is it?" "Is it . . .?" "Yes, it is." "No, it isn't." "Guess again." "That's right." Individual children should understand particular parts on which they are to check themselves.*)

(*The patterns may be varied as follows:*)
Hide your eyes.
Open your eyes.
What time is it?
Is it . . .? (Breakfast time, lunch time, dinner time)

Limiting the children's selection to four different hours makes it possible to keep the emphasis on the speech, not on endless guessing. The children should be shown by the therapist's leading the activity several times that they choose one of the four, and keep their choice to the even hour. Selection may be varied later in the lesson, or on successive days when this activity is used.

Choice of half hours, such as nine-thirty, twelve-thirty, etc., gives opportunity for further emphasis on the " θ."

This series of patterns will supply conversation for considerable time, and with the element of guessing involved offer a number of possibilities for work on the "z" sound

That's wrong. Guess again.
That's right. Have a look.

* * * * *

I'm going to set the clock.
Hide your eyes.
Open your eyes.
Guess what time it is.
Is it . . .?
That's just right.
Now it's your turn.

THERAPIST: Think of some questions you often ask about time. I will make a list of them on the board. Watch the "z" sound as you tell me.

CHILDREN: (*Individually*) Is it time to go home? Is it time for art? Is it time for a story? Is it time for speech class? Is it time to read? Is there time for me to finish? Is it time to go to gym? Is it time to stop work?, etc.

THERAPIST: You see how often you use that in one day and now you can ask it watching especially that you use the "z" sound in "is it?"

and others.

During the guessing one child may be permitted three guesses; if he doesn't get the right answer, the leader may have another turn. As a means of keeping the group better integrated it is suggested that each child be given one turn. The one who guesses correctly may lead then. In the event no one guesses correctly, the leader may then choose the person to follow him.

Unit II · Lesson 17

1. *Interpersonal Situations:* exchanging a greeting; guessing; obtaining information

2. *Speaking Aspect of Situations:* asking and answering questions

3. *Particular Speech Patterns:*

"Hide your eyes."	"Where is the . . . ?"	"Reach in and
"Open your eyes."	"Is it in the . . . ?"	get it."
"Hello . . . ."	"That's right."	"Show me . . . ."
"Who was it?"	"That's wrong."	
"Was it . . . ?"		
	"Who has it?"	
"It's your turn."	"Does . . . ?"	

4. *Sounds Emphasized:*   z   s   r   g   ʃ

5. *Equipment:* box and series of related objects

PROCEDURES	NOTES

THERAPIST: Because speech is part of you, your friends know you by your voice. When they talk to you on the telephone they can usually tell who is talking. Today you will try to guess who is talking by the sound of his voice. Your eyes will be closed. I'll show you.

THERAPIST: Jimmie, hide your eyes. (*Teacher indicates one child who is to come to Jimmie, saying "Hello, Jimmie."*)

CHILD: Hello, Jimmie.

THERAPIST: Open your eyes. Who was it?

JIMMIE: Was it . . .?

THERAPIST: That's right. (*Pattern should be repeated once more. Teacher will need to call attention to the speech that*

345

*is being used, so the children do not become
too absorbed in the guessing.)*

THERAPIST: That will be fun to do, won't
it? Before you each have a turn, let's see
if you know what sounds to watch. When
you tell someone, "Hide your eyes," *or*
"Open your eyes," what must you watch?
Yes, the "z" sound that you practiced
the last time in "is." Try "is" and then
"eyes."

CHILDREN: Is, eyes. *(Each child has
several opportunities to say this. Therapist
gives individual help as needed.)* Open
your eyes. Hide your eyes.

THERAPIST: "Who was it?" will be easy
for you to make. Try it. *(Therapist gives
individual help as needed.)* This guessing
takes three people, one to give the directions, one to hide his eyes, one to give the
greeting. Let's have three people come
and practice it first, so you will know just
how it is done when it is your turn.

CHILD 1: Hide your eyes, Mary.

CHILD 2: Hello, Mary.

CHILD 1: Open your eyes, Mary. Who
         was it?

CHILD 3: (Mary) Was it . . .?

CHILD 1: That's wrong. Guess again.

CHILD 3: Was it . . .?

CHILD 1: That's right. It's your turn.
(This activity provides a number of speaking

*experiences for the children in the roles of
giving a direction, extending a greeting, asking a question, answering a question,
choosing the next person to have a turn.)*

THERAPIST: Ann, I have a penny here.
Hide your eyes. (*Teacher places penny
in one of three boxes.*)   Open your eyes.
Where is the penny?

CHILD: Is it in the red box?

THERAPIST: No, it isn't. Guess again.

CHILD: Is it in the blue box?

THERAPIST: That's right. Reach in and
get it.

THERAPIST: That will be fun to do, too,
won't it? First you will want to work on
some of the sounds there for you to watch.
Let's have Jimmie and Mary try this part.
"That's right." "Reach in and get it."
Try the "r" by itself, the "g" by itself.
Now try "That's r . . . ight"; now "Reach
in and get it." The rest of you try, "Hide
your eyes, open your eyes, is it . . . ,"
watching the "z."

*When the children are work-
ing on their individual
sounds in these responses,
there should be a number of
practice attempts preceding
the actual activity so that the
children experience what is
to be done, and an awareness
of the sounds they are to
watch.*

(*The above activity can be carried on for
some length of time. It has possibilities for
emphasizing the "s," "z," "r," and "tʃ."
The guessing element will serve to interest
the children, both as they have an opportunity to fool someone else, and to be
fooled.*)

Supplementary Suggestions

THERAPIST: "Joe, hide your eyes." While
your eyes are closed I will give the penny

*The therapist may help chil-
dren prepare for this activity*

to someone here, instead of putting it in the box.   Then you have three chances to tell me who you think has it.   "Open your eyes.   Who has the penny?"

as for the above two.   Variations of these groups may extend over several lessons. Other speech responses may also be utilized as indicated.

CHILD: (*Asking person who hid the article*) Does Ann have it?

THERAPIST: That's wrong.   Guess again, *or* That's right.   Reach over and get it. — No, she doesn't.   Guess again, *or* Yes, she does.   Reach over and get it.

ʃ, s, z, ð, r, k

THERAPIST: (*Showing two coins*) Watch: I'm going to put the dime in one hand, the nickel in the other.   See if you can guess where the dime is.   (*Extending two closed fists*) Where is the dime?

CHILD: (*Pointing to one hand*) Is it here?

THERAPIST: Yes, it is.

CHILD: Show me.

THERAPIST: See, here it is.

*   *   *   *   *

THERAPIST: (*Extending two closed fists*) Where is the dime?

CHILD: I think it's here.

THERAPIST: That's right.   Take it, *or* Keep it, *or* Pick it up.

*   *   *   *   *

THERAPIST: (*Giving the dime to one child while another child is blindfolded*) Who has the dime?

CHILD: (*Pointing to one child*) I think she
has it.

THERAPIST: That's wrong. Guess again.

CHILD: I think he has it.

THERAPIST: That's right.   He   does.
It's your turn.

* * * * *

THERAPIST: Let's make a list on the
board of the ways in which you have
used the "z" sound today.   As you
tell me watch that you get a good "z"
in your answer. What other things have
you watched? Let's make a list of them,
too.

Intermediate
Illustrative Lessons

UNIT THREE

INCREASING FACILITY IN THE USE OF SKILLS

Unit Three contains suggestions for conversational patterns which are intended to promote further experience with and wider use of newly acquired sounds along with greater facility in use of speech as a social tool.

These suggestions will serve chiefly as a guide to the therapist in working out suitable patterns for the particular needs of the children as they progress beyond the early stages of the simpler responses contained in Units One and Two. The material is not intended to be inclusive, but merely representative of the kind of work that can be continued.

The therapist may choose parts from several different sequences, make one conversational unit out of them, and build an entire lesson around it. Such a lesson can be developed with two goals in mind: (1) Giving children opportunity to use speech purposefully in a situation closely resembling situations outside class where they are called upon to talk; (2) Giving children experience in using particular sounds on which they have been working.

The procedures employed will be similar to those found in Units

One and Two. The therapist may write several of these conversations on the board, discuss their use, and guide the children in selection of the conversation which gives them the practice they need. Each child may want to demonstrate first his ability to include certain sounds; other children may be encouraged to evaluate as "She used the 's' sound in 'some' and 'ask,' but needs to watch it more in 'store.'" A child may choose the one with whom he would like to talk. Most of the patterns are short and sufficiently simple so that after hearing them once or twice the child can use them fairly easily.

It should be remembered that the following conversational patterns are worked out for the children who have acquired considerable automatic use of newly established sounds. These lessons are designed to give them wider use of such sounds, but under conditions where the use is still somewhat controlled, and where the children have opportunity to check themselves, and be checked. Needless to say, an entire class will not reach this stage at the same time. The therapist will need to adapt some of this material for incorporation in lessons described previously.

A. INTERPERSONAL SITUATIONS WITH THEIR SPEAKING ASPECTS

B. SUMMARY OF ACTIVITIES

C. SPEECH RESPONSES AS INDICATED

D. SUMMARY OF EQUIPMENT. None required for this section except blackboard and chalk.

Unit III · Lesson 1

Interpersonal Situations: obtaining and giving information; exchanging greet-
                                ings
Speaking Aspect of Situation: asking and answering questions
Equipment: none

Particular Speech Patterns	*Sounds Emphasized*	*Activity*
1. "Hi . . . ." "Hi . . . ." "Come in."		*One child knocks at the door, another answers it.*
"May I speak to your mother?"	sp ð	
"Can you come outside and play?"	k s pl	
"Can you go to the store with me?"	k g st ð	
"May I see your spelling list?"	s sp l st	
"Could you go to the schoolyard and play?"	k g sk pl	
"Do you have anything for the paper sale?"	v θ f ð s	
"Can you ride to the store with me?"	k r ð st	
"Sure."	ʃ	
"I think so."	θ s	
"O.K. I'd like to."	k l	
"Yes, if my mother will let me."	s f ð l	

*   *   *   *   *

353

2. "Hi . . . ." *One child knocks at the door,*
"Hi . . . ." *another answers it.*
"Come in."

"Can you spend the **k sp ð**
afternoon with me? **f**

"What kind of a plane
is that?" **k pl z ð**

"Let's get a head start
on the baseball
game." **l s st g**

"That's the first robin
I've seen." **ð s r v**

"Who's keeping score
for the contest at
school?" **z k sk st**

"What other kid can we
get to play ball
with us?" **ð k g pl**

"Is it all right to ride
your bike to the
store?" **z r ð st**

"Sure." **ʃ**
"I guess I don't know." **g s**
"O.K." **k**
"Me, too."

*   *   *   *   *

3. "Hi . . . ." **k θ s**
"Hi . . . ."
"Come in."
"Thank you."
"Won't you sit down?"
"Thank you."

*   *   *   *   *

4. "Hi . . . ."
   "Hello. May I speak
       to your mother?"   **sp ð**
   "Just a minute. I'll
       call her."   **dz st k**
   "Thank you."   **θ**
   "You're welcome."   **k**

      *   *   *   *   *

5. "Hi . . . ."
   "Hello. May I speak
       to your mother?"   **sp ð**
   "I'm sorry. She isn't
       home."   **s ʃ z**
   "Is there a message?"   **z ð s dʒ**
   "No, I guess not.
       Goodbye."   **s g**

      *   *   *   *   *

6. "Hi . . . ."
   "Hi . . . ."
   "Can you come over
       to my house and
       play?"   **k v s pl**
   "When?"
   "After school."   **f sk**
   "I think so."   **θ s**

      *   *   *   *   *

7. "Hi . . . ."
   "Hi . . . ."
   "What room is Jean
       in?"   **r z**
   "That one over there." **ð v**
   "Thanks."   **θ s**

      *   *   *   *   *

8. "Hi . . . ."
   "Hi . . . ."
   "When are you going to
       school?"   **g sk**

"Right now."   r
"Guess I'll go, too."   g s

*   *   *   *   *

9. "Hi . . . ."
"Hi . . . ."
"Where can we play
    ball?"   k pl
"Right here."   r
"That's fine."   ð s f

*   *   *   *   *

10. "Hi . . . ."
"Hi . . . ."
"May I see your spell-
    ing list?"   s sp l st
"Sure."   ʃ
"Should I bring it
    back?"   ʃ br
"No, I'm all through
    with it."   ð

*   *   *   *   *

11. "Hi . . . ."
"Hi . . . ."
"Do you have anything
    to mend this
    page?"   v θ ð dʒ
"Nothing that I know
    of. Wait, I'll ask
    mother."   θ ð v sk
"Thanks a lot."   θ s l

*   *   *   *   *

12. "Hi . . . ."
"Hi . . . ."
"What kind of a bike is
    that?"   k v z
"It's a Colson."   s
"Gee, it's a swell one."   dʒ s
"I think so, too."   θ s

Unit III · Lesson 2

Interpersonal Situations: borrowing and lending
Speaking Aspect of Situation: asking and answering questions
Equipment: blackboard

Particular Speech Patterns	Sounds Emphasized	Activity
1. "Can you lend me some money?"	**k s l**	*Two children face each other, carry on conversation.*
"How much do you need?"	**tʃ j**	*Suggestions may be listed on the board by the teacher, or compiled by the children.*
"Enough to buy	**f**	*Discussion of the various*
a ticket to the show."	**k ð ʃ**	*sounds and some practice*
a ticket to the circus."	**k ð s**	*on them should precede the*
a ticket to the church supper."	**k ð tʃ** **s**	*conversation. Children may choose an answer which gives*
some marbles."	**s z**	*them practice on a sound on*
some jacks."	**s dʒ**	*which they are working.*
some candy."	**s dʒ k**	
some candy."	**s k**	
some funny books."	**s f**	
some cards."	**s k**	
some beebees for my gun."	**s z g**	
some peanuts."	**s**	
some pop."	**s**	
etc.		
"Sure, but don't forget to pay me back."	**ʃ g**	
"I wish I had that much."	**ʃ**	

*　　*　　*　　*　　*

2. "Do you have a . . . I could borrow?"	**k**	
pencil	**s**	
sheet of paper	**ʃ v**	
red crayon	**r kr**	
skate key	**sk k**	

357

pair of scissors	s z
pair of shears	ʃ z
box of paints	ks s
ruler	r l
dictionary	ʃ
spelling list	sp l st

piece of chalk	s tʃ
piece of string	s st
piece of paper	s
piece of crayon	s v kr

some paper	s
some crayons	s kr
some string	s str
some change	s tʃ dʒ
some small sticks	s sm st
some funny books	s f

"Sure. Help yourself."	s ʃ f
"I'm sorry, I'm using it (them) now."	s z ð
"I'm sorry, I don't have one."	s v
"Please help yourself."	pl v s f z

Unit III · Lesson 3

Interpersonal Situations: expressing and accepting appreciation
Speaking Aspect of Situation: giving and receiving compliments
Equipment: blackboard

Particular Speech Patterns	Sounds Emphasized	Activity
1. "I like the way you . . .	l	*Children discuss use of compliments, why they like to give them, why they like to get them. They may be guided to express what's difficult about getting a compliment, about giving one. They may give examples of compliments. The therapist should be ready to add examples as listed here. The phrases may be analyzed then in terms of work on specific sounds. Children should then exchange compliments.*
kick the ball."	k	
toss a ball."	s	
bat a ball."		
ride a bike fast."	r k st	
jump rope."	dʒ r	
skip rope."	sk r	
draw pictures."	dr tʃ z	
do arithmetic."	θ	
get one hundred in spelling."	g sp	
write."	r	
ice skate."	s sk	
roller skate."	r sk	
sew."	s	
play the piano."	pl ð	
keep score."	k sk	
catch a ball."	tʃ	
sing."	s	
dance."	s	
play fair."	pl f	
etc.		
"Thanks for telling me. I like to do it."	s l	
"Thank you. It's just easy for me."	θ s st z dʒ	

    *   *   *   *   *

2. "I like . . . or liked . . .	l	*After working on compliments for each other, they may go on to discuss compliments to be given a teacher,*
the dress you are wearing."	ð dr s	
the way you fixed the	ð ks	

359

door so it won't   **sk**
squeak."

the story you read to   ð **st r**
us."   **s**

the ride into the coun-
try."   ð **r**
the trip to the news-   ð **tr z**
paper office."   **s**
the sandwich you
fixed."   ð **tʃ ks**
the special treat you've ð **sp ʃ**
planned."   **v pl tr**
the plan for a party."   ð **pl**
the nice dinner."   ð **s**
the chocolate cake you
made."   ð **tʃ k**

"Thank you. I like it,
too."   θ **l**
"Thank you. It was fun
to do."   θ **z f**

their mother, an aunt, their
dad, etc.

Unit III · Lesson 4

Interpersonal Situations: including a stranger
Speaking Aspect of Situation: making an introduction and acknowledging it
Equipment: none

Particular Speech Patterns	Sounds Emphasized	Activity
1. "Ann, this is Mary."	s z	*Children discuss use of introductions — when they are important, why. They may be guided then to the use of a question or comment following an introduction so that people aren't left standing awkwardly with nothing to say.*
"Hi, Mary. We're glad you could come to-		
day." or	gl k	
"Hi, Mary. It's warm outside today, isn't		
it?"	s z	
"Hello, Mary. Ann has told me you play the		
piano. Is that	z pl	
right?" or	ð r	
"Hello, Mary. What school do you go		
to?"	sk g	
"Hello, Mary. Whose room are you in?"	z	

    *   *   *   *   *

2. "Jean, I'd like you to meet Ann."	l	*If possible, practice on introductions should be carried on with a visitor there to make the situation real. Or children may work on it, then each bring a friend to introduce during the next class period.*
"Ann, this is Jean."	s z	
"Hi, Ann."		
"Hi, Jean."		
"Where do you live, Ann?"	l v	
"On Fourteenth Street, where do you live?"	f θ l v	
"On Sixth, that's not so		

361

far from here, is it?" s θ z

* * * * *

3. "Miss Hale, this is my
    mother." s z
   "Hello."

   "My mother has wanted
    to come to school z k
    for a long time." or sk l
   "My mother has been
    wanting to meet
    you." or
   "My mother says she
    wants to talk with s z ð
    you." ʃ

* * * * *

4. "Mother, this is a friend ð s z
    of mine, Jim. He's v
    going to play with z g pl
    me this afternoon." ð f s

   "Mother, this is my
    friend, Jack. He's
    going to the show ð s z
    with me today." g ʃ

Unit III · Lesson 5

Impersonal Situations: expressing an opinion
Speaking Aspect of Situation: indicating a preference by asking and answering
questions
Equipment: blackboard

Particular Speech Patterns	Sounds Emphasized	Activity
1. "I'm going to spend some money."	**g sp s**	*Children may discuss some things they'd like to buy if they had some money and a choice. The therapist may make a list on the board. Children will often suggest impossible items, and this gives the therapist an opportunity to encourage use of imagination. The speech utilized here is real; the choices may be highly imaginative.*
"How much?"	**tʃ**	
"Two dollars and thirty-five cents."	**z θ s**	
"What are you going to buy with it?"	**g ð**	
"Some comic books and a tennis racket."	**s k r**	
"A football and helmet."	**f**	
"A sled and a pair of leather gloves."	**sl l gl**	
"Some books and some candy."	**s k**	
"A dollar's worth of peanuts and some pop."	**z θ s v**	
"A bathing suit and an inner tube."	**ð s**	
"A doll house and some furniture."	**s**	
"A new dress."	**dr s**	
"Six tickets to the show" etc.	**s k ʃ**	
"What will you do with that?"	**ð**	

363

(Children make up own
answer.)

*   *   *   *   *

2. "I'm going to the post
office."   **g st s**

"Why?"

"To get some stamps."   **g st s**

"What kind?"   **k**
"One three-cent stamp."   **θ s st**

"Four airmail stamps."   **f st s ps**

"Six special delivery   **s sp ʃ**
stamps."   **st**

"One one-cent stamp."   **s st**
"A hundred special de-   **sp s st**
livery stamps."   **ʃ**
etc.

"That's a good idea. I
need some stamps,
too."   **ð s g st**

*   *   *   *   *

3. "I'm going to take a trip   **g k tr**
someday."   **s**

"Where do you wish you
could go?"   **ʃ k g**
"To California."
"To Texas."
"To China."
"To England."
"To New York.", etc.

"How would you like to
get there?"   **l g ð**

In this situation some of the children will be ready to include sounds in the basic pattern and the answers, some only in the basic pattern.

Note that four of these patterns are set up as basic to the activity. Before the children begin questioning each other they should each practice each part, and be aware of the sounds on which they are to check themselves. This is not to be carried on as a game, but as a discussion with speech foremost.

"By bus."
"By train."
"By plane."
"By car."
"By boat."

"I'd like to go by . . . ."
    etc.   1 g

      *   *   *   *   *

4. "What kind of a sand- **k s tʃ**
    wich do you like?"   1

Some children will be ready to check themselves on sounds in the choices of answers. All should be held for the basic patterns.

I like a . . . best of all. **1 st v**
    barbecue sandwich
    hot dog sandwich
    roast beef
    peanut butter and
      jelly
    butter and sugar
    plain jelly sandwich
    meat loaf
    ham sandwich
    cheese sandwich

"What do you like with
    it?"   1 ð
I like . . . with . . .
    (above)   1 ð
    two glasses of milk."
    ketchup."
    a cup of cocoa."
    some onions."
    a bottle of pop," etc.

Unit III · Lesson 6

Interpersonal Situations: requesting and granting permission
Speaking Aspect of Situation: asking and answering questions
Equipment: blackboard

Particular Speech Patterns	Sounds Emphasized	Activity
1. "May I close the door? It seems noisy in here?"	kl ð z r s	The therapist may discuss with the children the occasions for requesting and granting permission . . . as getting permission from parents to go someplace, from a teacher to do something, from a friend to use a possession of his.
"May I open the door? It seems warm in here."	s z	
"May I move my chair? I can't hear over here."	v tʃ k v	She may then have the children suggest ways in which they need to ask permission of her, and of each other. After they have practiced such speech patterns, the children may go on to practice speech they need in requesting permission of a teacher, parent, etc.
"May I be excused early from class? I am going to the dentist."	ks z ʒ s g ð st	
am going to the doctor."	g ð	
have a music lesson."	v l s	
have some work to finish in my room."	v s ʃ r	
am going on a trip with my class."	g tr ð cl s	
am on an assembly program," etc.	s	
"May I close the window? It feels cool to me."	ð z k	
"May I open the win-		

366

dow? It feels warm
to me."

*   *   *   *   *

2. "Is it all right if I bring
   my dog along on the
   hike?"   z r br

   "Do you mind if I bring
   my little sister with
   me when I come   f br s
   over?"   ð k v

   "Do you care if we play
   ball in your yard?"   k pl

   "Is it all right for me to
   read   your   library
   book?"   z l f r

   "May I come by for you
   early?"   k f r

Unit III · Lesson 7

Interpersonal Situations: going on an errand; taking a message
Speaking Aspect of Situation: making a request; relaying a message
Equipment: blackboard

Particular Speech Patterns	*Sounds Emphasized*	*Activity*
1. "Miss Hale would like the case records of the children when school is out."	s l ð tʃ sk z	*The therapist may guide the children in a discussion of opportunities they have, or wish they might have to go on errands, take messages. She may begin by giving examples of times she needs to send a child for such reasons. They should give examples not only of the occasions, but of possible speech patterns they may be expected to use.*
"Miss Hale would like one boy and girl from your room to visit speech class to-day."	s l r z sp tʃ	
"Miss Hale would like the key to the store-room."	s l k st r	
"Miss Hale would like the assembly room next week at three o'clock, if that's all right."	s l ð st f r	
* * * *	*	
2. "Miss Hale wants to know if there is a picture show to-day."	s ð tʃ ʃ	*As the children make suggestions these may be written on the board, analyzed and worked on as to sounds, then actually used.*
"Miss Hale would like to know when the school nurse comes."	s l sk k z	*The therapist may choose to have the responses mimeographed and included in a notebook for the children, even indicating names of*
"Miss Hale wants to		

know what room is
putting on the as-
sembly."   s r

various children by certain
responses.

"Miss Hale said to tell
you some mothers
are visiting the class
today. She'd like
you to come, too, if   s z ð
you can."   l k

"Miss Hale said she got
your note, and will
stop to see you after   s g st
school."   sk

"Miss Hale said she
liked the new chairs,
and so do we. We   s l ð
want to thank you."   tʃ z θ

Unit III · Lesson 8

Interpersonal Situations: telephoning
Speaking Aspect of Situation: carrying on a conversation
Equipment: two toy or real telephones

Particular Speech Patterns	Sounds Emphasized	Activity
1. "Hello."	1	*Children may discuss with the therapist various uses they make of the telephone, such as inviting someone over to play, finding what time the show begins, finding out an assignment.*
"Hello. This is . . . . May I speak to . . .?"	ð s z sp	
"Yes, I'll call her . . . (him)."	s k	
"Can you come over to my house and play?"	k v s pl	
"I'll ask my mother."	sk ð	*The children may choose one subject about which to make a call. The conversation should be limited. The therapist may write down what the children say, then write it on the board for analysis and practice.*
"Yes, I can. What time?"	s k	
"Right away."	r	
"O.K. Goodbye."	k g	
* * * * *		
2. "Hello."	1	*Various telephone courtesies can be discussed here as announcing oneself, limiting length of talking, etc.*
"Hello. This is . . . . May I speak to . . .?"	ð s z sp	
"This is . . ."	ð s	
"Can you come for a ride with us?"	k r ð s	*While some children need experience in keeping a conversation going on the telephone, it should be remembered that each child should have special goals in mind as to sounds, etc.*
"Yes, I'd like to."	s l	
"We'll stop and get you after lunch."	st g tʃ	
"Thanks a lot."	θ s l	
"Watch for a blue car."	tʃ bl	
"Goodbye."	g	
* * * * *		
3. "Hello."	1	
"Hello. This is . . . . May I speak to . . . .?"	ð s z	

370

"Hi . . . ."

"This is . . . . Will you
    stop in my room
    and get my reading   ð s st
    book?"   r g

"Sure. Anything else?"   ʃ θ s

"No, that's all. Thank
    you."   ð s θ

"Goodbye."   g

"Goodbye."

    *   *   *   *   *

4. "Hello."   1

"Hello."

"Can you tell me how
    much the puppet   k tʃ ð
    show costs?"   st s

"Yes, fifteen cents for
    children,   twenty-
    five for adults."   s f tʃ

"Thank you. I will get
    the tickets tomor-   θ g k
    row."   s

Unit III · Lesson 9

Interpersonal Situations: asking for and giving directions
Speaking Aspect of Situation: asking and answering questions
Equipment: blackboard

Particular Speech Patterns	Sounds Emphasized	Activity
1. "Can you tell me where the principal's office is?"	k s z	The children may discuss times at school when they are asked to give a direction, such as the way to the principal's office, the way to the auditorium, the way to the nurse's office, etc.
"Yes, go to the end of the hall, turn right. It's the first room there."	s g v r st ð	They may then give examples of other times, such as the way to their house, to the baseball diamond, to the bus stop, etc.
"Yes, it's the second room on the left."	s k r l	
"Yes, it's on the first floor, opposite the front door."	s f st fl z ð	The first directions should be simple ones, carefully controlled as to sound production.
* * * * *		Later the children may give a more lengthy direction, such as the way to their house, and tell in advance sounds they are watching. Children like to use the board in giving directions.
2. "Can you tell me where the sixth grade room is?"	k s θ r	
"Yes, it's on the second floor, the first room by the stairs."	s fl f st	
"Yes, it's the room opposite the nurse's office, number 206."	s r z	
* * * * *		
3. "Can you tell me where		

the nurse's office   **k f s**
is?"   **z**

"Yes, go up the stairs at
the end of the hall.
Turn right. It's the
end room on the   **s g st**
right."   **v r ð**

    *   *   *   *   *

4. "How do I get to your
house?"   **g s**

"You turn left in front of   **l v**
the school. Go two   **g s st**
blocks to the stop   **ð st r**
light. Turn right.   **s**
Walk one block.   **ð θ**
Cross the street.
It's the third house
from the corner,
5829 Seville."

Unit III · Lesson 10

Interpersonal Situations: making announcements
Speaking Aspect of Situation: stating certain information
Equipment: blackboard

Particular Speech Patterns	*Sounds Emphasized*	*Activity*
1. "There is going to be a paper sale on Friday. The room that brings in the most will get a prize. Help your room win."	ð g s r br z st g pr z r	*Practice in making announcements should stem from a particular need in speech class: It may be that certain children will have the responsibility of announcing in speech class school activities in progress as a paper sale, a PTA program, a Halloween party, etc. One child may watch the time, announcing when class is over. Various children may prepare announcements to be made in different rooms regarding activities going on in speech class as visitor's day. The principal may often use children from speech class who are ready to make announcements. Safety council, service groups, Boy and Girl Scout meetings afford situations for practice, also. As the children begin to be held responsible for a number of sounds, or for one sound in an increasing number of words, announcements are useful since they are short and specific. The child should plan what he is to say first, the therapist may write it on the board. Together they may check sounds*
* * * * *		
2. "It is time to go. Speech class is over. Walk quietly in the halls."	z g sp tʃ s v k	
* * * * *		
3. "The teachers have a meeting on Friday. There will be no school."	z v ð sk	
* * * * *		
4. "Monday you may bring a friend to speech class. Ask your teacher first."	br fr sp tʃ sk st	
* * * * *		
5. "There will be a short class today. A picture show about		

Spring   begins   at   ð ∫ kl   *to watch, practice them in*
two-thirty."   s t∫ g   *isolation if necessary, then*
                                              in context. Other children
                                              may check various things as
                                              this child practices ... one
may listen for the " s " in " is," another the " z " in Tuesday, etc.
Several entire classes may be centered around the making of announcements. One
announcement may be included and worked on in each daily lesson. This can
provide for the child who is learning rapidly, and give special opportunity
to the less able child.

Unit III · Lesson 11

Interpersonal Situations: short talks
Speaking Aspect of Situation: discussion of particular topics
Equipment: none

Particular Speech Patterns	Sounds Emphasized As indicated.	Activity

HOBBIES

1. "I make model airplanes.
    I have nine of them at
    home.
    I make them with ply-
    wood and glue.
    I like to fly them, too."

    *   *   *

2. "I collect trading cards.
    I have more horses and
    dogs than anything
    else.
    I have eighty packs of
    fifty cards."

    *   *   *

3. "I make puppets out of
    balsa wood.
    I give puppet shows.
    I work the puppets, my
    sister does the talk-
    ing."

    *   *   *

SCHOOL

4. "I am in the fourth
    grade.
    My teacher is Miss
    Jones.

Here the children should have some choice of subject matter, but the therapist should have suggestions ready. Instead of expecting the children to talk just for practice, it may be more real to them if they prepare talks to give for a visitor's day in class, for a parent's visit, or for a part of a school assembly or a class party.

Some discussion about length should precede the work. Perhaps the child can be guided to tell three things about the best trip he ever took, two things about his favorite sport, three things he is doing in his room now. This makes it easier to keep the speech carefully controlled with emphasis on including sounds, an appropriate rate, proper phrasing, blending, etc., rather than on the content alone.

376

She reads us stories."

*   *   *

5. "I am in the fifth grade.
    We are making a
    frieze about trans-
    portation.
    I made a covered
    wagon."

*   *   *

6. "I am in the sixth grade.
    I like to play ball at
    recess.
    Sometimes I can run
    fast."

*   *   *

FAVORITE SPORTS

7. "I like to roller skate.
    Once I fell down.
    I had three stitches
    taken."

*   *   *

8. "I like football.
    My Dad and I go to
    games.
    I want to be a half-
    back."

Summary of Key Responses

RESPONSES	LESSONS		RESPONSES	LESSONS	
	Unit I	Unit II		Unit I	Unit II
k			**v** (cont.)		
Keep it		1, 2	How many		
Can you . . . ?	5	2, 3, 4, 6	do I		
		9	have:	3	9
In my pocket		7, 9	A piece of . . .		9, 10
You're welcome		5, 6	. . . of		
Come in	6	11	one	4, 5	
Take it	4	10	**θ**		
. . . of a car	5				
I can't		12	Thank you.	2, 3, 4	1, 2, 5, 6
O. K.		1, 2, 3, 5		5, 6	
		6, 7, 16	I'm think-		
			ing of a	3, 4, 5	3, 4, 5, 8
g			I think I can		6, 14
Get me	3	9, 10, 11	Both	3	1, 2
May I get . . . ?		5, 14	Both of them		1, 2
Will you			One thing		5
give me			Throw it		6
. . . ?	3, 4	9, 11	Something		15
I got the		11	Anything		10
I'm going		12, 16			
. . . a good idea		14	**ð**		
Let's go		14	The	2, 3, 4, 5	2
f			On the	2, 3, 4	2
			That one	4, 5	2, 3, 4, 7,
For you	6	6			9
Can you find		3	This one	5	14
After		1, 2, 3	This is	6	6, 8
Before		3	One of		
			the	3	
v			One of		
Have a	6		them	3	
Will you			Either one		15
give me			These two		7
the . . . ?	2, 3, 4		With mine	3, 4	
May I			What will you		
have the	2, 3, 4, 6	1, 2, 6, 9	do with it?	2, 15	

378

RESPONSES	LESSONS		RESPONSES	LESSONS	
	Unit I	Unit II		Unit I	Unit II
s			**z**		
Yes	2, 3, 5	1, 2, 3, 5, 6, 7, 16	His	15	15
			Hers	14	15
Sit by me	6		Whose		
Guess	5	3, 7, 8, 11, 15, 16, 17	is it?	15	15
			What time		
			is it?		16
Some	4		Is it . . . ?		16
Hit or miss	6		Hide your		
Miss		6, 8, 10	eyes	7, 9	16, 17
It's your turn	5, 6	6, 16, 17	Open your		
What do you miss?		7, 9	eyes	7, 9	16, 17
What else?		7, 8, 10, 11	Yes, it is		16, 17
			No, it isn't		16, 17
In the box		7	Who was it?		17
A piece of		9, 10	Yours		2
Sometimes		4	Who has it?		17
Can you erase?		3, 4, 9, 11, 15	Does . . . ?		17
I'm sorry		5, 13			
I think so		3, 6			
What's missing?		7			
This is		8			
Mr., Mrs.		8			
May I see?		11			
What did you see?		11, 16			
What did he say?		12	**ʃ**		
He said . . .		12	A sheet of	5	
. . . to set the clock		16	Show me	3, 5	2, 3, 4, 7 9
Will you ask . . .		10			
He wants . . .		12			
. . . the best		1, 2, 4	I wish . . .	3	3
Let's		14	You should		1, 2, 3
That's, It's		14	She would . . .		12, 15
The least		1, 2, 4	Sure, Surely		1, 2, 3, 4 5, 6, 7, 16
More or less		1, 2			
Outside, inside		1, 2			
Sometimes		4			

RESPONSES	LESSONS		RESPONSES	LESSONS	
	UNIT I	UNIT II		UNIT I	UNIT II
tʃ			**r** (cont.)		
Choose one	3	2	Here. There		1, 9
How much	3, 4	2	That's wrong.		9, 17
Change	3	9	With the rest		14
Which one	3, 5	2, 7, 9	Breakfast		16
Touch	7	7	I'll trade	3	
Catch	6	6			
On the shelf		7	**1**		
Put a check		9	Will you let		5
Chalk		10			
Lunch		16	Lay it	3	1, 2
Each		1, 2	Have a look		11, 14, 16
Match		1, 2	May I look	3	1, 2, 6
			I'd like		
dʒ			to	5, 6	4, 5, 6
Join	3		Hello	3	
Just		2, 7, 9, 10, 12	Which would you		
			like . . . ?	5	10, 13
r			I'm late		12
May I write . . . ?		5, 9			
Reach			**GENERAL**		
one	3, 4	1, 2, 6, 7 9, 11, 17	Is your name? What is your		
Wrap a package		10	name?		1
All right	1, 2, 3 5, 6, 7 16	14, 16	Hi.		1
			Numbers		3, etc.
Put it right in	3	3	Street address		3
Put it in here	3	1, 9, 10	Age		3
It's right	4, 5	3, 6, 8, 9 10	Birthdate		3
Is this right?	6	3, 4, 9 16	Telephone number		3
Ready?	6	7, 9, 16	Names of sports		4
Where will you put it?	4	1, 2, 3, 17			

Pre-School
Illustrative Lessons

B. SUMMARY OF ACTIVITIES

C. SUMMARY OF SPEECH PATTERNS

(Many of these responses are introduced with more emphasis on use than on phonetic accuracy. They are designated to promote readiness for speech training.)

Lesson 1. "Hi."   "Up."
          "Bye."   "Down."

          "For you."   "Pull it."
                                "Push it."

          "Thank you."

Lesson 2. "Hi."   "Thank you."
          "Bye."
                                "Pull it."
          "For you."   "Push it."

          "Yes."   "Up."
                                "Down."

Lesson 3. "Hi."   "Up high."
          "Bye."   "Down low."

"For you."

"Thank you."

"Put it in."
"Put it in the drawer."

"Pull it out."
"Push it in."

"Open it."
"Shut it."

Lesson 4. "Hi."
"Bye."

"Yes."

"For you."

"Thank you."

"Put it . . . up high."
"Put it . . . down low."

"Pull it."
"Push it."

"The big one."
"The little one."

"Come."

Lesson 5. "Hi."

"Bye."

"Yes."

"For you."
"One for you."

"In my pocket."

"Have one."

"With mine."

"Keep it."

"Thank you."

Lesson 6. "Hi."
"Bye."

"May I have . . . ?"
"For you."

"Up high."
"Down low."

"The daddy."
"The mama."
"The boy."
"The girl."

"In the house."

"Open the box."
"Shut the box."

Lesson 7. "Hi."
"Bye."

"Open the box."
"Shut the box."

"... For you."

"Up high."
"Down low."

"In the barn."
"Put it in the barn."

"The ...
  dog."
  cat."
  pig."
  cow."
  horse."
  sheep."
  chicken."

Lesson 8. "Hi."
"Bye."

"Come again."

"Yes."

"One for you."

"Have one."

"With mine."

"Thank you."

"In my pocket."
"In my box."

"Open it."
"Shut it."

Lesson 9. "Hi."
"Bye."
"Come again."

"One for you."
"Have one."

"Yes."

"With mine."

"Thank you."

"Keep it."
"Cut it."

"In my pocket."
"In my bag."

"Open it."
"Shut it."

"That one."

Lesson 10. "Hi."
"Bye."

"One for you."
"One for you."

"Thank you."

"Keep it."
"In my pocket."

"Up high."
"Down low."

"On the ladder."

"In the box."
"In the bag."

Lesson 11. "Hi."   "With mine."
"Bye."
"Come again."   "Thank you."

"One for you."   "Keep it."
"Have one."
"May I have one?"   "In my pocketbook."

"Yes."   "To the . . . ."
"Put it . . . ."

"That one."

Lesson 12. "Ring the bell."   "Open the box."
"Blow the whistle."   "Push the car."
"Toot the horn."   "Bounce the ball."
"Wind the clock."

"To the table."
"To the door."

"To the window."

D. EQUIPMENT

Pre-School Suggestions · Lesson 1

Interpersonal Situations: greetings; exchange of toys

Speech Responses:
"Hi."   "For you."   "Thank you."   "Up."   "Down."   "Pull it."
"Bye."   ."Push it."

Sounds Emphasized: f   θ   p

Equipment: wooden train with several detachable cars

PROCEDURES	NOTES

THERAPIST: Hi, Mary. Hi, Jerry. Hi, Ann. Hi, Lloyd. (*Therapist greets each child, smiling pleasantly, going slowly, waiting until each individual child is watching her before she greets him.*) Mary, it's your turn now to say "Hi" to each boy and girl. You stand here by me. I will help you. (*Turning to boys and girls*) When Mary tells you "Hi," you will want to answer her, telling her "Hi," too.

CHILD: Hi.

CHILDREN: Hi. (*Each child is given opportunity to greet others.*)

THERAPIST: I have a big train here. See it. Watch what I can do. "Pull it." (*Therapist pulls train around the small circle of chairs in which the children are sitting.*) Doesn't it go fast? Do you want a turn to pull it, too? Listen again. You will "Pull it." Ann, what do you want to do?

CHILD: Pull it. (*Child draws train around the circle in similar fashion.*)

THERAPIST: Lloyd, what will you do?   *If   some   children   in   the*

388

CHILD: Pull it. (*This may continue until each child has had a turn to pull the train.*)

THERAPIST: The train comes apart, too. Each car can be unhooked. See. There is a car here "for you, Mary," "for you, Lloyd," "for you, Ellen." Ann, you may give a car to each one, saying "for you."

CHILD: For you.

(Therapist *may use the response* "Thank you," *saying it for the children who do not respond, encouraging others to use it in acknowledging the toy.*)

THERAPIST: You each have a car now. Watch what you can do. "Push it." I like the way Jerry pushes his car fast. Each of you do it. (*Children push the car back and forth in front of their chairs.*) Now you may each have a turn to do it by yourself. Jerry, hold your train this way in your lap. Wait your turn. Ellen, what will you do?

CHILD: Push it. (*Continue, giving every child an opportunity to use the response first, then do it. When possible, the pattern "Push it" should be said several times by the therapist in an effort to get each child to respond verbally. When he does not, he should not be penalized, but given a chance to push his car with the therapist saying the response for him, or having some of the other children say it.*)

THERAPIST: You have had fun pushing the long train, and the car. Now you will put the train away. See the three tall boxes here. You will put the train "up."

group are ready, the response "Pull the train" *may be used. A child who makes no verbal response to the question, but indicates a willingness to pull the train should be encouraged to do so.*

Watch me. *(The therapist takes several of the cars, says "up," and places them on top of the boxes. She then returns the cars to the children, asking the question, "Where will you put it?")*

CHILDREN: *(Individually)* Up. *(Place cars on the boxes.)*

THERAPIST: Thank you.

THERAPIST: You are going to another room now. "Bye, Mary." "Bye, David," etc. *(Children are each given an opportunity to say "Bye" to the others. Waving accompanying the response should be encouraged.)*

If the children respond with the response "up high" or "car up" this should be encouraged, since the use of two syllables should be developed as early as possible.

Pre-School Suggestions · Lesson 2

Interpersonal Situations: greetings; exchange of toys

Speech Responses:

"Hi."   "For you."   "Up."   "Pull it."   "Yes."

"Bye."   "Thank you."   "Down."   "Push it."

Sounds Emphasized: f   θ   p

Equipment: Dolly pull (a small wagon with a number of detachable pegs and balls) placed in a large box

---

PROCEDURES

THERAPIST: Hi, Mary. Hi, Jerry, Hi, Ann. Hi, Lloyd. (*Therapist greets each child, smiling pleasantly, going slowly, waiting until each individual child is watching her before she says "Hi."*) Ann, it's your turn now to say "Hi" to each boy and girl. You stand here by me. I will help you. (*Turning to children*) When Ann says "Hi" to you, what will you say?

CHILD: Hi.

CHILDREN: Hi.

THERAPIST: I have something in the box. Listen. Can you guess what it is? (*Therapist shakes the box so that children can hear the contents rattle.*) Do you want a look?

CHILDREN: Yes. (*If children merely indicate by a nod of their head, or rising to come toward the box that they do want a look, the therapist should repeat the pattern "Yes" for them, but permit them to have a look, even though they do not say "Yes."*)

THERAPIST: (*Taking wagon out of box*)

NOTES

As children take turns greeting the others, the therapist may encourage certain children to combine a name with the response "Hi." Some children will be more ready than others for this longer response. A child who is not yet using speech may be taken by the therapist to face each child, who gives the greeting "Hi," while the therapist responds for the child. In this way he is experiencing a greeting even though he is not yet verbalizing.

391

This wagon is empty, but you can "Pull it." (*She pulls wagon around the small circle of chairs in which the children are sitting.*) It goes as fast as the train. Do you want a turn to "Pull it," too? Listen again. You will "Pull it." Ellen, what do you want to do?

CHILDREN: (*Individually*) Pull it. (*After each child has responded to the question, he may draw the wagon around the circle.*)

THERAPIST: (*Pointing to the colored pegs and balls*) Here are some things that go in the wagon. There are two for each of you . . . "for you, Mary," "for you, Ellen," "for you, Lloyd." Lloyd, you may give a ball to each boy and girl, saying "for you."

CHILD: For you.

CHILDREN: (*Individually*) Thank you.

THERAPIST: I liked the way Lloyd smiled, gave each of you a ball. Some of you said "Thank you," too. Watch how I say that. I put my tongue out easily, blow easily, say "θ." Try it. Then I say "Th . . . ank you." Each of you try it. (*Some children will not be ready for this practice on sounds.*) Here are some pegs that will fit the balls you have. Jerry, give one to each boy and girl saying, "for you."

CHILD: (*Distributing pegs*) For you.

CHILDREN: (*Individually*) Thank you.

THERAPIST: Your ball and peg will make a lot of noise. Let's hear them. Loud,

The first concern here is helping the child participate in a satisfying experience, that of pulling the wagon. Secondly, there is concern with developing his use of speech in context with an activity in which he derives some pleasure. For children who take part easily and willingly, using the speech that is required, a third concern is that of phonetic accuracy. Certain children may be given some assistance in using the plosive "p" in isolation, and combining it in the response "Pull it."

loud, loud. Now louder, louder, louder.
Now, softer, softer, softer.

Now you have something to load on the
wagon. The wagon is on top of the big
box, so you will put what you have "up."
Watch me. (*Therapist places several pegs,
one at a time, in the wagon, saying "up"
each time. Turning to children:*) Where
will you put your peg?

CHILD: "Up." (*Places peg in wagon.*)

THERAPIST: Thank you. (*This continues
until children have placed articles in the
wagon.*)

(*This activity may be expanded to the
responses "Put it up." if children are ready
for use of more than one syllable, and emphasis on phonetic accuracy.*)

THERAPIST: When the wagon was empty,
each of you had a turn to "Pull it." Now
it is full. You may "Push it" like this.
Watch. (*Therapist gives wagon a push*)
Listen again to what I will do. "Push
it." Ann, what will you do?

CHILD: Push it. (*This continues until
each child has opportunity to indicate what
he is going to do, and do it.*)

THERAPIST: We are all through now.
Before you leave, I will say "Goodbye"
to you. "Bye, Ann." "Bye, Jean."
"Bye, Lloyd." Now it is your turn to
say "Bye" to everyone.

CHILDREN: (*Individually*) Bye.

CHILD: Bye.

Pre-School Suggestions · Lesson 3

Interpersonal Situations: greetings; giving and following directions

Speech Responses:

"Hi."	"For you."	"Up high."	"Pull it out."
"Bye."	"Thank you."	"Down low."	"Push it in," or
			"Open it."
	"Put it in," or		"Shut it."
	"Put it in the drawer."		

Sounds Emphasized: f   θ   p

Equipment: small cubes or blocks; several drawers that open and close

---

PROCEDURES

THERAPIST: Hi, Mary. Hi, Jerry. Hi, Ann. Hi, Lloyd. (*Therapist greets each child as on previous occasions.*) Who wants to be first to say "Hi" today? All right, Ellen, it is your turn. Let's see if each of you can say "Hi, Ellen" when she talks to you.

CHILD: Hi.

CHILDREN: (*Individually*) Hi, Ellen.

THERAPIST: You may choose the one to say "Hi" next. (*Children continue the greetings, selecting the child to have the next turn.*)

THERAPIST: I have a surprise in the box for you today. Listen. Do you want a look? "Yes?" That's right, if you want a look, you will tell me "Yes." (*Pointing to box that is closed*) Do you want a look?

CHILDREN: (*Individually*) Yes. (*Following the speech response, each child comes to*

NOTES

394

the box, opens it, takes a look, closes it,
sits down. This continues until each child
has a turn.)

THERAPIST: There are many blocks in the
box, aren't there? There is one "for you,
Jerry," "for you, Lloyd," etc. When you
get a block what will you say? "Thank
you." That's right. Mary, you may give
each one a block. Show me first how you
say "for you." You tuck your lip under
your teeth like this: "f" . . ., "for you."
Do it again. Now again. Now give
everyone a block, and I will help you
say it.

CHILD: (*Distributing blocks*) For you.

CHILDREN: (*Accepting blocks*) Thank you.

THERAPIST: Each of you has a block. | *The response, "Shut it,"*
Watch what I'm going to do with my | *has been found to be used fre-*
block. (*Turning to drawer*) "Pull it out." | *quently in a number of*
(*Placing block in drawer*) "Put it in." | *regions, particularly by chil-*
(*Closing drawer*) "Push it back." (*This* | *dren. The therapist may*
group of patterns may be used if a number | *want to select another phrase,*
of children need work on the "p" sound. | *such as "Close it," if it is*
An alternative group of patterns may be | *considered more appropriate.*
used in similar fashion. "Open it." "Put
it in." "Shut it.")

THERAPIST: Ann, what will you do first
to the drawer?

CHILD: Open it.

THERAPIST: What will you do with your
block?

CHILD: Put it in.

THERAPIST: What will you do to the drawer now?

CHILD: Shut it. (*This activity can be set up very carefully, so that the child understands that the speech response precedes the activity. The therapist may hold the drawer closed lightly until the child says "Open it." She should then have the child give the verbal response, "Put it in" before he actually does it. She may then hold the drawer open while she asks, "What will you do to the drawer?" After the child has replied, he may then close the drawer. Here again it should be stressed that while speech is an important aim of the activity, the child who does not use speech can participate, with the therapist or another child repeating appropriate responses for him.*)

(*Another group of blocks may be distributed and placed in the drawers. If two drawers are used — one above the other — as in a desk, the following speech responses may be utilized:*)

THERAPIST: Where will you put it?

CHILD: Up high, *or* Down low.

THERAPIST: Thank you.

THERAPIST: We have put all the blocks away. Before you go, you may say "Bye" to each other. Who wants to do it first?

CHILD: Bye.

CHILDREN: (*Individually*) "Bye." (*Continue until each child has bid the others goodbye.*)

Pre-School Suggestions · Lesson 4

Interpersonal Situations: greetings; designating a particular toy; acknowledging receipt of it

Speech Responses:

"Hi."	"For you."	"Put it . . . up high."	"A big one."
"Bye."	"Thank you."	"Put it . . . down low."	"A little one."
	"Yes."	"Pull it."	"Come."
		"Push it."	

Sounds Emphasized: f   θ   p

Equipment: two airplanes, boats, trains, cars, trucks — one somewhat larger than the other

---

PROCEDURES

THERAPIST: Hi, Mary. Hi, Jerry. Hi, Ann. Hi, Lloyd. (*Therapist greets each child as on previous occasions.*) Who wants to be first to say "Hi" today? Lloyd, now it is your turn. Can each of you say "Hi, Lloyd" when he comes to you?

CHILD: Hi . . . .

CHILDREN: (*Individually*) Hi, Lloyd.

THERAPIST: Lloyd, you may choose the next person to say "Hi." (*Children continue the greetings, selecting the child to have the next turn.*)

THERAPIST: I have a surprise in the box for you today. Listen. (*She shakes box so that children get some idea as to the contents.*) Do you want a look?

CHILDREN: (*Individually*) Yes. (*Following the speech response, each child comes to the box, opens it, takes a look, closes it, sits down. This continues until each child has had a turn. The therapist may begin to call some attention to the "s" in "Yes" if some child seems ready for it, although this is a more difficult sound for children this age, and in many cases will not be stressed at this time.*)

THERAPIST: There are many things in here for you; (*Pointing to the*
397

box) "a big one for you, Jerry"; "a big one for you, Ann"; "a little one for you, Mary."

THERAPIST: Ann, what will you get — a big one or a little one?

CHILD: A big one.

THERAPIST: What will you say when you give it to someone?

CHILD: For you, Mary.

THERAPIST: What will you get now, Ann?

CHILD: A little one.

THERAPIST: What will you say when you give it to someone?

CHILD: For you, Lloyd.

(*This may be continued until one child has distributed each object, or until each child has distributed an article. A slightly more complex pattern, such as "a big one for you," may be used if children are ready for a combination of that many syllables.*)

THERAPIST: What do you have?

CHILDREN: (*Individually*) A big .... (*This is planned to make use of several syllables rather than for purposes of phonetic accuracy.*)

THERAPIST: There are two places you may put your toys. If you put it on the red box, it will be "up high." If you put it on the yellow box, it will be "down low."

Where will you put a big boat?

CHILD: Up high. (*Places object on the box. Continue until each child has placed his toy on either box.*)

(*If the children are ready for a slightly longer response, the following pattern is suggested.*)

THERAPIST: What will you do?

CHILD: Put it up high.

THERAPIST: The toys are here on the two boxes now. You may each have one again. You may tell me what you want: "A big car," or "A little boat," etc. What do you want?

CHILD: A big airplane.

THERAPIST: Where will you get it?

CHILD: Up high. (*Child obtains object.*)

THERAPIST: What will you do with it? Push it? or Pull it?

CHILD: Pull it. (*Continue in this way.*)

THERAPIST: Jerry may choose the people to put their toys in the box by saying, "Come, Mary."

CHILD: (*Designating children to put toys in the box*) Come . . . .

THERAPIST: We will take time for only one of you to say "Bye" today. Who wants a turn?

CHILD: Bye.

CHILDREN: (*Individually*) Bye.

Pre-School Suggestions · Lesson 5

Interpersonal Situations: exchanging articles

Speech responses:

"Hi ...."   "For you."   "Have one."   "In my pocket."

"Bye."   "One for you."   "Keep it."

                            "With mine."

"Yes."

                            'Thank you.'

Sounds Emphasized: f   v   ð   θ

Equipment: small pieces of construction paper cut to resemble tickets; a stapler

---

PROCEDURES

THERAPIST: Hi, Jerry. Hi, Ann. Hi, Lloyd. (*Therapist greets each child as on previous occasions.*) Ann, you haven't been first yet to tell people "Hi." You may take the first turn today.

CHILD: Hi ....

CHILDREN: (*Individually*) Hi, Ann.

THERAPIST: Ann, you may choose the next person to say "Hi." (*Children continue the greetings.*)

THERAPIST: I have a surprise in the box for you today, but it doesn't make any noise. Listen. Do you want a look?

CHILDREN: Yes. (*Following a child's response to the question, he comes to the box, opens it, takes a look, closes it, and sits down. For certain children the therapist may address additional questions as "What will you do?" to which the child replies "Open it," and "Shut it." The therapist may emphasize production of the "s" in "Yes," if certain children show readiness for it. With other children she may still be accepting a non-verbal response, although the majority of children by now will probably be making some sound consistently to indicate "Yes."*)

THERAPIST: There are many tickets in the box, aren't there? You will get some of them, and then you will make a book out of them to take home ... a book of tickets like mine. Let's see ... (*Pulling*

400

out tickets one at a time). Here is "One for you, Ann"; "One for you, Jean," etc.

Mary, what will you say when you give a ticket to each boy and girl? Listen again: "One for you." Try it. Watch the "f" in "for." Try it again. Now give these tickets out. The boys and girls will remember to tell you "Thank you," I'm sure.

CHILD: *(Distributing tickets)* One for you.

CHILDREN: *(Individually)* Thank you.

(Several children may distribute sets of tickets in similar fashion. Another speech response which may be used in the same activity is "Have one." The therapist should use it a number of times for the children to hear, then suggest a child say it when he gives out the tickets.)

THERAPIST: Do you know where I will put this ticket? "With mine." — This one? "With mine." I will give you each a new ticket, asking you, "Where will you put it?" and you'll answer "With mine."

THERAPIST: *(Distributing a new set of tickets)* Where will you put it?

CHILDREN: *(Individually)* With mine.

THERAPIST: Do you know what I will do with this ticket? "Keep it." With this ticket? "Keep it." *(Continue giving the pattern several times.)* Now I will give each of you a new ticket. What will you do with it?

CHILDREN: *(Individually)* Keep it.

THERAPIST: *(Demonstrating how the stapler fastens the tickets together to make a book)* Do you want to make a book?

CHILDREN: *(Individually)* Yes. *(They bring book up for fastening.)* Thank you.

THERAPIST: You're welcome. *(Each child makes a book of tickets.)*

THERAPIST: Now you have your tickets ready to take home. Before

you do, you may put them away so as not to lose them.   Watch me.
I will put mine "in my pocket."   Listen again: "in my pocket."
Where will you put yours?

CHILDREN: (*Individually*)   In my pocket.

THERAPIST: Who wants a turn today to say "Bye" to everyone?
Ann, will you do it?

CHILD: Bye . . . .

CHILDREN: (*Individually*)   Bye.

Pre-School Suggestions · Lesson 6

Interpersonal Situation: manipulating toys

Speech Responses:
 "Hi."   "...for you."   "The daddy."   "In the house."
 "Bye."   "The mama."
          "Up high."   "The boy."   "Open the box."
          "Down low."   "The girl."   "Shut the box."

                             "May I have ...?"

Sounds Emphasized: **f**   **v**   **p**   ð

Equipment: a small doll family and house

PROCEDURES

THERAPIST: Hi, Jerry. Hi, Ann. Hi, Lloyd. (*Therapist greets each child as on previous occasions.*) Kathie, you may be first today to tell the boys and girls "Hi."

CHILD: Hi . . . .

CHILDREN: (*Individually*) Hi, Kathie.

THERAPIST: Kathie, you may choose the next person to say "Hi." (*Children continue the greetings.*)

THERAPIST: I have a surprise in the box for you today. Listen. Do you want a look?

CHILDREN: Yes.

THERAPIST: What will you do?

CHILDREN: (*Individually*) Open the box. (*Child opens the box, looks.*)

THERAPIST: Now what will you do?

CHILDREN: (*Individually*) Shut the box. (*Continue until each child has had a turn.*)

403

THERAPIST: Let's take another look at what is in the box. Watch: "the daddy," "the mama," "the boy," "the girl." Watch again how I say it, with my tongue coming out just a little: "the boy," "the girl," etc. There is "the daddy for you, Jerry," "the mama for you, Ann," etc. Lloyd, you may pass out the dolls, saying it just as I did: "The girl for you . . . ."

CHILD: (*Distributing dolls*) The boy for you.

CHILDREN: (*Individually*) Thank you.

THERAPIST: I'm going to use your dolls for a minute. Watch where I will put "the daddy": "in the house." Watch where I will put "the mama": "in the house." (*Continue with this pattern several times. Return dolls to children.*)

THERAPIST: What do you have?

CHILDREN: (*Individually*) The . . . .

THERAPIST: Where will you put the . . .?

CHILDREN: (*Individually*) In the house. (*Child places dolls in the house.*)

THERAPIST: (*Changing position of the house*) Where is the house now?

CHILDREN: Up high.

THERAPIST: Where is the house now?

CHILDREN: Down low.

THERAPIST: The dollies are all tucked away in the house. If you want one you may ask this way: "May I have the mama?" "May I have the daddy?" "May I have the boy?", etc.

CHILDREN: (*Individually*) May I have the daddy?

CHILD: Yes.

CHILDREN: (*Individually*)   Thank you.   (*Continue until each child has his doll.*)

THERAPIST: It's almost time to go now.   You may put your doll "up high" on the red box or "down low" on the yellow box.

THERAPIST: What do you have?

CHILD: The boy.

THERAPIST: Where will you put the boy?

CHILD: Up high.   (*Continue until each child has returned his doll.*)

THERAPIST: Who wants to say "Bye" to everyone today?   Kathie, would you like to do it?

CHILD: Bye.

CHILDREN: (*Individually*)   Bye . . . .

THERAPIST: Jerry, you come with me to the door, and tell the boys and girls to "Come . . . ."

CHILD: Come, Mary.

Pre-School Suggestions · Lesson 7

Interpersonal Situation: manipulating toys

Speech Responses:

"Hi."	"... for you."	"In the barn."	"The ...
"Bye."		"Put it in the barn."	dog."
	"Up high."		cat."
	"Down low."	"Open the box."	pig."
		"Shut the box."	cow."
			horse."
		"May I have ...?"	sheep."
			chicken."

Sounds Emphasized: f   v   p   ð

Equipment: a collection of familiar farm animals and a barn

PROCEDURES

THERAPIST: "Hi, Jerry. Hi, Ann. Hi, Lloyd." (*Therapist greets each child as on previous occasions.*)   Jerry, you may be first today to tell the boys and girls "Hi."

CHILD: Hi ....

CHILDREN: (*Individually*) Hi, Jerry.

THERAPIST: Jerry, you may choose the next person to say "Hi." (*Children continue the greetings.*)

I have a surprise in the box for you today. Listen. Do you want a look?

CHILDREN: (*Individually*) Yes. (*Therapist may give individual help on the "s" sound as a child shows some readiness for incorporating it in this response.*)

THERAPIST: What will you do with the box?

CHILD: Open it. (*Child opens the box, looks*)

THERAPIST: Now what will you do with the box?

406

CHILD: Shut it.   (*Continue until each child has had a turn.*)

THERAPIST: Let's take another look at what is in the box.   Watch, I will take the things out one at a time.   (*Therapist does so, slowly, placing each object on the table, giving the children an opportunity to look at it, then saying:*) "the cow," "the horse," "the pig," "the chicken," "the dog," "the cat"; "the dog for you, Jerry," "the cat for you, Ann," "the horse for you, Kathie," etc.   Mary, you may pass out the animals to each boy and girl saying, "the cat for you."   Try it first.   I like the way you put your tongue out a little on "the," and made "for" just the way you have been practicing it.

CHILD: (*Distributing animals*)   The dog for you.

CHILDREN: (*Individually*)   Thank you.

THERAPIST: I'm going to use the animals for a minute.   Watch where I will put "the horse."   "In the barn."   Watch where I will put "the pig."   "In the barn."   (*Continue with this pattern several times.   Return animals to children.*)

THERAPIST: What do you have?

CHILD: The . . . .

THERAPIST: Where will you put the . . .?

CHILDREN: (*Individually*)   In the barn.   (*Child then places animal in the barn.*)

THERAPIST: (*Changing position of the barn*)   Where is the barn now?

CHILDREN: Up high.

THERAPIST: Where is the barn now?

CHILDREN: Down low.

THERAPIST: Jerry, where will you put the barn?

CHILDREN: Up high.

THERAPIST: Ann, where will you put the barn?

CHILD: Down low.

THERAPIST: The animals are in the barn. If you want one you may ask this way: "May I have the . . .?" (*For children who are not yet ready for this complex a response, the therapist may ask* "What do you want?" *to which the child replies,* "The . . . .")

CHILDREN: (*Individually*) "May I have the . . .?"

THERAPIST: Yes.

CHILDREN: (*Individually*) Thank you. (*Continue until each child again has an animal.*)

THERAPIST: What do you have?

CHILD: The . . . .

THERAPIST: It's almost time to go now. Where will you put the . . .?

CHILD: In the barn.

THERAPIST: Ann, you may choose someone to say "Bye" to everyone.

CHILD: Bye . . . .

CHILDREN: (*Individually*) Bye . . . .

Pre-School Suggestions · Lesson 8

Interpersonal Situation: exchanging articles

Speech Responses:

"Hi."	"One for you."	"Have one."	"In my pocket."
"Bye."			"In my box."
"Come again."	"Yes."	"With mine."	
			"Open it."
		"Thank you."	"Shut it."
		"Keep it."	

Sounds Emphasized:　f　v　p　ð

Equipment: marbles and small cardboard boxes

PROCEDURES

THERAPIST: "Hi, Jerry, Hi, Ann. Hi, Lloyd." (*Therapist greets each child as on previous occasions.*) Mary, you may tell the boys and girls "Hi" today.

CHILD: Hi . . . .

CHILDREN: (*Individually*) Hi, Mary.

THERAPIST: Mary, you may choose the next person to say "Hi." (*Children continue the greetings.*)

THERAPIST: I have a surprise in the box for you today. It makes a lot of noise. Listen to it. Do you want a look?

CHILDREN: Yes. (*Therapist may give some individual help on the "s" sound.*)

THERAPIST: What will you do with the box?

CHILD: Open it. (*Child opens the box, looks.*)

THERAPIST: Now what will you do with the box?

CHILD: Shut it. (*Continue until each child has had a turn.*)

409

THERAPIST: There are many marbles in the box. "One for you, Ann"; "One for you, Jean"; etc.

THERAPIST: Kathie, what will you say when you give a marble to each boy and girl? Listen again: "One for you." Try it. Watch the "f" in "for." Try it again. Now give these marbles out. Keeping them in your box will make it easy for you to hold them. It is so easy to drop marbles, and they roll away so fast that they are hard to find.

CHILD: (*Distributing one marble to each child*) One for you.

CHILDREN: (*Individually*) Thank you.

(*Several children may distribute marbles in similar fashion. Another speech response which may be used in the same activity is "Have one." The therapist may use it a number of times for the children to hear, then suggest a child say it when he gives out the marbles.*)

THERAPIST: Do you know where I will put this marble? "With mine." This one? "With mine." I will give each of you a new marble, asking you, "Where will you put it?" and you'll answer, "With mine."

(*Distributing more marbles*) Where will you put it?

CHILDREN: (*Individually*) With mine. (*Continue until each child receives another marble. The therapist may wish to emphasize the "ð" sound with certain children.*)

THERAPIST: Do you know what I will do with this new marble? "Keep it." With this marble? "Keep it." With this marble? "Keep it." (*Continue giving the pattern several times.*) You may want to "Keep it" when you get a marble, too.

THERAPIST: (*Distributing marbles*) What will you do with it?

CHILD: Keep it.

THERAPIST: You are getting so many marbles. So am I. Watch where I'm going to put my next marbles: "In my box," "In my box," "In my pocket," "In my pocket."

THERAPIST: (*Distributing marbles*) Where will you put the marble?

CHILDREN: (*Individually*) In my box, *or* In my pocket.

THERAPIST: Jerry, when you say "Bye" to the boys and girls today, tell them to "Come again."

CHILD: Bye . . . . Come again.

CHILDREN: (*Individually*) Bye, I will, *or* Bye, Jerry. Thank you.

Pre-School Suggestions · Lesson 9

Interpersonal Situation: exchanging articles

Speech Responses:

"Hi . . ."	"One for you."	"With mine."	"In my pocket."
"Bye . . ."	"Have one."	"Thank you."	"In my bag."
"Come again."			
	"Yes."	"Keep it."	"Open it."
		"Cut it."	"Shut it."
	"Up high."		
			"That one."

Sounds Emphasized: f   v   p   θ   ð

Equipment: a cellophane string of candy, or small pieces of candy wrapped in cellophane; scissors; small paper bags

---

PROCEDURES

THERAPIST: Hi, Mary.

CHILD: Hi, Miss . . . .

THERAPIST: How are you?

CHILD: Fine.

THERAPIST: Mary, you may be next to tell the boys and girls "Hi." Perhaps you'd like to ask, too, "How are you?" (*Continue with above pattern.*)

I have surprises for you in both boxes today. Listen. (*Therapist shakes boxes.*) You may choose one box in which to look: either "that one" (*Pointing to one box*) or "that one." (*Pointing to the other box.*)

THERAPIST: Which box will you look in?

CHILD: That one.

THERAPIST: What will you do first?

412

CHILD: Open it.   (*Child opens the box, looks.*)

THERAPIST: Now what will you do?

CHILD: Shut it.   (*Continue, each child having turn.*)

THERAPIST: There are many pieces of candy here, but they are all fastened together.   Before you may have a piece you will have to "Cut it" away from the string.   Watch me.   (*Therapist takes scissors and snips off one piece.   If candy is not fastened together, this part may be omitted.*)

THERAPIST: (*Holding string of candy, scissors, and box for candy that is cut.*)   What will you do?

CHILD: Cut it.   (*Some children may be ready for emphasis on the "k" sound.   For most of them the use of the response will be all that is required.*)

THERAPIST: There are many pieces of candy here: "One for you, Ann"; "One for you, Jerry"; etc.   What will you say, Ellen, when you give a piece of candy to each boy and girl?   "One for you."   Try it. Watch the "f" in "for."   Try it again.   Now give everyone a piece of candy.

CHILD: (*Distributing one piece of candy to each child*)   One for you.

CHILDREN: Thank you.

(*Several children may distribute candy in this way.   The speech response "Have one" may also be used.   The children may ask, in addition, "Where will you put it?"   In many instances the therapist will need to ask this question, to which the children may reply, "With mine."*)

THERAPIST: Do you know what I want to do with my candy?   I want to "Keep it."   What would you like to do with yours, Jerry? "Keep it."   If you want to keep it, you will need to put it in a bag so that you can carry it home.

THERAPIST: What will you do with your candy?

CHILD: Keep it.

THERAPIST: (*Extending a paper bag*) Where will you put it?

CHILD: In my bag.

THERAPIST: Where can you put the bag?

CHILD: In my pocket. (*Continue until each child has had a turn.*)

THERAPIST: Now we will put the bags "up high" so that you can take them home later. Where will you put your bag?

CHILD: Up high.

THERAPIST: Who would like to have a turn today saying "Goodbye. Come again"? All right, Ann, you may have the turn today.

CHILD: Goodbye, Mary. Come again.

CHILDREN: (*Individually*) Goodbye, Ann. I will.

Pre-School Suggestions · Lesson 10

Interpersonal Situation: manipulating toys

Speech Responses:

"One for you."	"Keep it."	"On the ladder."
		"In the box."
"Thank you."	"In my pocket."	"In the bag."
		"Up high."
		"Down low."

Sounds Emphasized: f   v   p   θ   ð

Equipment: chalk and blackboard; small bag and box

PROCEDURES

THERAPIST: I have surprises for you in both the bag and the box today. Listen. (*Therapist shakes boxes.*)

THERAPIST: Ann, do you want a look?

CHILD: Yes.

THERAPIST: Where will you look, in the bag, or in the box?

CHILD: In the bag, *or* In the box. (*Continue until each child has had a turn.*)

THERAPIST: There is a piece of chalk for each of you. What could you say, Mary, as you gave each boy and girl a piece? Yes, you could say "Have one." What else? "One for you." That's right. Mary, you may give out the chalk.

CHILD: (*Distributing chalk*) Have one.

CHILDREN: (*Individually*) Thank you.

THERAPIST: In a little while you will write on the blackboard with your chalk. Right now you may put your chalk in your pocket so you won't lose it.

THERAPIST: Where will you put your chalk?

CHILD: In my pocket.

THERAPIST: There is a ladder on the board. You may put a stick on the ladder, this way. Watch me. I put a stick "on the ladder." I will do it again. I put a stick "on the ladder."

THERAPIST: Do you want to use your chalk?

CHILD: Yes.

THERAPIST: Where will you put it?

CHILD: On the ladder.

THERAPIST: Did you put your stick "Up high," or "Down low"?

CHILD: Up high.

THERAPIST: What will you do with your chalk? "Keep it?" or "Give it to me?"

CHILD: Keep it.

THERAPIST: Where will you put it?

CHILD: In my pocket.

(*The ladder may be erased, and a new one made, since children will like doing this activity a number of times. The chalk may even be collected and redistributed to permit more speech responses.*)

THERAPIST: Jerry, you may say "Goodbye, come again," to everyone.

CHILD: Goodbye, come again.

CHILDREN: (*Individually*) Goodbye.

Pre-School Suggestions · Lesson 11

Interpersonal Situation: manipulating toys

Speech Responses:
"Hi . . . ."   "One for you."   "With mine."   "To the . . . ."
"Bye . . . ."   "Have one."
"Come again."   "Yes."   "Thank you."   "Put it . . . ."

                                "Keep it."
            "May I have one?"   "In my pocketbook."

                                 "That one."

Sounds Emphasized: f   v θ ð   t

Equipment: coins and small pocketbooks

PROCEDURES

THERAPIST: "Hi, Mary. Hi, Jerry. Hi, Ann. Hi, Lloyd." (*Therapist greets each child as on previous occasions. Children choose each other to lead activities.*)

I have some pennies in my pocketbook. Do you like to get pennies? What do you do with them? I have a pocketbook for each of you to keep the pennies that you get.

THERAPIST: Do you want a pocketbook?

CHILD: Yes.

THERAPIST: What will you do with it?

CHILD: Keep it.

THERAPIST: Ann, you may give each one a penny, saying, "Have one, Mary."

CHILD: Have one, Mary.

CHILDREN: (*Individually*) Thank you.

417

THERAPIST: Jerry, you may give each one a penny, saying "One for you, Ann." Try it first.

CHILD: One for you, Ann.

CHILDREN: (*Individually*)   Thank you.

THERAPIST: This time you may ask me for a penny, this way: "May I have a penny?"

CHILDREN: (*Individually*)   May I have a penny?

THERAPIST: Yes.

CHILDREN: (*Individually*)   Thank you.

THERAPIST: Watch what I do with this penny. I put it "with mine." Listen again: "With mine."

THERAPIST: Where will you put the penny?

CHILDREN: With mine.

THERAPIST: Now watch what I do. "Put it in my pocketbook." Listen again. "Put it in my pocketbook." (*Giving children another penny*) What will you do with it?

CHILD: Put it in my pocketbook. (*This response may be too complex for some of the children, in which case the therapist may ask*, "Where will you put it?" *to which the child will reply*, "in my pocketbook," *or merely* "pocketbook.")

THERAPIST: Let's put your little pocketbooks in the big pocketbook. Where will you put your little pocketbook?

CHILDREN: In the big pocketbook.

THERAPIST: I will say goodbye to you today. Goodbye, Ann. Come again.

CHILD: Goodbye, Miss . . . .

Pre-School Suggestions . Lesson 12

Interpersonal Situation: manipulating toys

Speech Responses:

"Ring the bell."	"Open the box."	"To the table."
"Blow the whistle."	"Push the car."	"To the door."
"Toot the horn."	"Bounce the ball."	"To the window."
"Wind the clock."		

Sounds Emphasized: those indicated by needs of the group

Equipment: a bell, whistle, horn, clock, box, car, ball

PROCEDURES	NOTES

THERAPIST: I have some things in the box. Watch what I do with them.
"Ring the bell." *or* "Ring it."
"Blow the whistle." *or* "Blow it."
"Toot the horn." *or* "Toot it, etc."
"Wind the clock."
"Open the box."
"Push the car."
"Bounce the ball."

Two syllables may be substituted for three where the child's speech development is considerably delayed.

Other patterns may include "Hit it." "Pinch it." "Snap it." "Roll it." "Throw it." "Bang it." "Brush it." "Pat it." "Make it big." "Make it little."

THERAPIST: (*Extending objects one at a time to children*) What will you do?

CHILDREN: (*Respond with above patterns depending on the article extended to them. Therapist may want to set the pattern, if child does not respond when he first sees article.*)

THERAPIST: Watch what I'm going to do. I will take "the clock" "to the window," "the box" "to the door," "the horn" "to the table."

THERAPIST: What do you have?

CHILD: The boat.

THERAPIST: Where will you take it?

CHILD: To the window. (*Continue until each child has placed his object in one of the three places designated.*)

THERAPIST: What do you want now?

CHILD: The car.

THERAPIST: Where will you go to get it?

CHILD: To the table. (*Continue in this pattern.*)

THERAPIST: It is time to go now. You will put what you have back "in the box."

THERAPIST: Where will you put the horn?

CHILD: In the box.

CHILDREN: (*End period by telling each other* "Good-bye.")

It should be noted here again that phonetic accuracy does not represent a primary goal in use of any of these speech patterns. They have been selected to provide children with pleasurable experiences, of which speech is only one part.

Chapter 10

Adapting Group Lessons to Individual Work

Procedures described in the previous illustrative lessons have had as their basis situations in which a therapist works with a number of children. The therapist who works with one child will find that the same activities, speech patterns, and materials can be adapted readily for individual teaching. While certain basic procedures are similar in bringing about changes clinically whether the teaching involves one, two, or ten children, the differences in working with a child individually need to be taken into account. There are certain advantages, such as a greater amount of time per child, a greater opportunity for concentration on needs, and situations involving less complex interaction for the child; full use should be made of them. But there are also certain limitations which need to be minimized, such as fatigue in the child during a period, a tendency to focus on the child's liabilities rather than to enlarge his assets, the lack of opportunity for a child to relate to his peers, and less chance for varied speaking events.

Some consideration will be given here to adaptations of group procedures as a guide to individual teaching.

1. The therapist can maintain the framework of a social experience which utilizes conversational speech in individual teaching although obviously there are fewer opportunities for interaction between thera-

pist and child than among members in a group class. For some children this more simple interpersonal situation will have positive values early in training. For others the therapist will want to provide a variety of activities in speech to promote the child's relating to him and to others. For instance, the child can borrow a series of objects from the therapist, acknowledge receipt of them saying "May I have a . . . ?" and "Thank you." The therapist in turn can borrow the same series from the child. Or the child may ask permission of the therapist to perform certain activities as "May I write on the board?" "May I write on the book?" "May I write on the paper?", etc. and later grant permission to the therapist for similar activities. Again the child may work on speech to be used in purchasing ice cream at a store, then be taken on a trip to do it.

2. The therapist can work out a systematic progression within a lesson planned with a balance of easier — more-difficult tasks. Although this is essential in group lessons, it has particular importance in working with one child, since he cannot work at the same level of concentration for an entire period, and since each activity has somewhat less variation when one child alone is participating. A lesson may be divided into three parts, reviewing some responses which are fairly easy first, introducing a new pattern next, then making different use of the same pattern in conclusion.

Just as the children in the group classes need to develop an awareness of the class activity in relation to their specific part in it, so one child in an individual class needs to view the work for a period in relation to the various tasks to be accomplished. If he drones at one thing the entire period he will gain little sense of accomplishment, but if he understands that in the first part of the lesson he will be reviewing a pattern he does easily and well, that he will then go on to something new that will be fun, and conclude with a different activity using the new speech pattern, interest will be heightened and fatigue level reduced. Some tangible evidence of progression is especially valuable in an individual class. For a younger child an illustrated device such as a clock marked off in three sections, a ladder with three steps on it, or three blocks may represent the divisions in the lessons. As the child completes one part he may color it in rapidly, or check it off, or mark it in some way to indicate to him completion of part of his job. An older child may keep a small notebook in which the therapist writes at the beginning of the lesson the three activities for that period, including the speech patterns to be emphasized. The child may keep an account of the number of times he uses each response, or the different ways in which he uses them.

3. The therapist will need to make certain in individual class just as in group class that the responses used are limited in number and centered around only one particular sound for a given period of time. It will be confusing to the child if he is held responsible for too many responses involving one sound, and it will lessen the possibility of his using them outside the clinical situation. Likewise use of one response with several difficult sounds in it may result in discouragement. Consequently there need to be rather sharply defined areas of concentration at first, some balance of easier — more-difficult work, definite variation within a period.

To illustrate, a child who is just beginning to acquire facility in the use of the "θ" sound and "s" should not be expected to include both in one activity early in training. The therapist may first give him a series of blocks saying, "I have a block for you," to which the child responds each time with "Thank you," paying attention to his production of the "θ" sound. In a second activity with the series of blocks the therapist may ask "Do you want a block?" to which the child may respond with "Yes," including as acceptable an "s" sound as he is capable of making at this particular time. Later on he may use both responses, "Yes" and "Thank you" in reply to the latter question. As he acquires more skill in both sounds the complexity of the response may be increased to include such replies as "Yes, I think so," or "Yes, I guess I'd like the green one. Thank you."

These speech responses should also be included in a number of different activities within a lesson so that the same "part" becomes embedded in a variety of "wholes." While one activity in a group class may provide each child with different ways of using the same response, variety is not as easily achieved in one activity with one child. The therapist will want to structure the activities so that, for instance, a child may use the response "down" in placing blocks, then marbles, then coins in a box. Or the child may place separate cars in a train "down" on the floor, pegs "down" in a wagon, discs "down" on a color cone. Another child may use an "s" in "some."

as he borrows materials: "May I have some ink, some paper, some blocks?"; as he orders at a drug store: "I'd like some ice cream, some candy, some gum"; as he makes an announcement: "I have some news for you"; as he passes out materials: "Have some paper, some paint, some clay."

4. The therapist should provide opportunity for the child to engage in experiences offering motor activity as an integral part of the work on speech. While learning by doing is a basic postulate in group as well as individual teaching, a child working alone has special needs to be active, either through manipulating toys or through moving about the room in a number of purposeful acts associated with the speech he is using. He may collect items such as toy animals, coins, dolls, pieces of a puzzle from the therapist one by one by requesting and acknowledging them. Reaching out to get them and placing them in a designated place requires a "doing" process associated with the speech he is using. He may go on to place the animals singly in the barn, the coins in a purse, the dolls in a house, the parts in the puzzle as a part of the speech response he makes in reply to the therapist's question "Can you put the horse in the barn?" or "Where will you put the horse?" or "What will you put in the barn?"

The activity involved in talking on the telephone, going on various errands about the room, carrying out directions of the therapist and then giving them as "Come to the door," "Come to the window," "Write a ten on the board," and "Write a one on the board," and similar directions provide some freedom of motor response.

Such provisions serve to reduce fatigue, heighten interest, increase interaction as well. The individual situation allows the therapist greater freedom in this phase of teaching, makes it possible to meet the child's need for activity in a variety of ways.

5. The therapist should see that the activities in which the child engages in the individual as in the group lesson are sufficiently simple and of such a nature as to make speech the *chief core* of interest. Materials such as crayons, paints and mechanical toys may absorb or distract the child to such an extent that speech becomes secondary. This is true of complicated games where manipulating the spinner or winning takes on more importance than the speech involved. Each of these mediums can be utilized for speaking purposes, but the

material and the situation must be kept as the *instrument* for speech, not the end product.

Let us explore, for example, the ways in which a box of crayons may be employed. As a child gains some facility in use of the "s" sound the therapist may work on several responses with the child to promote wider use of the sound. The therapist may hold the crayons first, asking "Do you want a crayon?" to which the child may respond with "Yes" or "No." As the child indicates interest in a particular color, the therapist gives it to him. Or the child may begin by requesting the crayons, saying, "Pass me the red crayon." After he has the crayons the child may draw a round face and the therapist ask "Where will you put the eye?" When the child replies with an adequate "s" in "On the face," he may draw the eye on the face, then respond to a similar series of questions until the face is completed. Throughout the activity the speech the child uses is kept primary, the coloring secondary. The therapist may then request the crayons one by one, perhaps asking "What will you do?" to which the child replies "Pass you a green crayon." Then the therapist may draw a face, saying "I'm going to put on an eye." The child may answer each time "What else?" This simple set of materials can be used and reused, but the speech involved in the successive activities is kept the center of focus.

6. The therapist will want to investigate the personal as well as the speech needs of the individual child with whom he is working, pattern these needs, and provide for them in the therapeutic situation. While seeing the child alone rather than in group classes gives the therapist less information about the child's functioning in his interpersonal relations with his peers, and fewer situations for helping the child relate to other children, there are numerous opportunities for changing the child's behavior in the interaction occurring between therapist and child.

If the child needs to develop a sense of personal adequacy the therapist can rely on the child to get the room ready, arrange the equipment, replace materials when the lesson is over. The child may be given responsibility for selecting some of the toys to be used, choosing one activity in each lesson. He may be helped to succeed in specific ways meriting praise, gradually come to develop some awareness of his assets.

If the child has been held to rigid standards of behavior at home and at school the therapist can structure the speech work in a somewhat more permissive atmosphere. He may offer wider choices to the child, accept expressions of hostility, attempt to reduce tensions in the child.

The child may be guided to develop greater flexibility in role-taking, directing the therapist part of the time as well as being directed, initiating as well as following an activity, making suggestions as well as accepting them.

The child who has tended to withdraw from other children may be encouraged to bring a brother, sister, or friend to class in order to demonstrate the improvement he is making, begin using his speech as a social tool with his peers.

The following lesson designed for a child in the early elementary age range who is beginning to include an acceptable "s" sound in a limited number of responses is adapted for individual teaching from the group suggestions in Lesson 4 of Unit II. It makes use of some of the material contained in Lessons 5, 8 and 11 as well. It illustrates the considerations discussed in this section, namely, use of a social experience which utilizes conversational speech, systematic progression, limited number of speech responses centered around one particular sound, motor activity, speech as the center of interest, and provisions for personal needs of the child.

(Colored strips of construction paper cut to resemble tickets are used as materials.)

Part I

THERAPIST: I have some tickets for you. There are lots of them. You will make them into books of six to take home, like this. Would you like that? In order for you to get and keep these tickets you are going to work on saying "Yes" with that "s" sound you are making so much better now. "Do you want the ticket?"

CHILD: Yes. (*Therapist gives child a ticket.*)

THERAPIST: I liked the way you said that.   Watch and listen to me as I say it once for you.   "Yes."   You have to remember to keep your tongue back a little further.   Try it alone once.   "s"

CHILD: "s"

THERAPIST: Now watch it as you answer me.   Do you want a ticket?

CHILD: Yes.

THERAPIST: I liked that.   Here is the ticket.   Let's see if you can get six tickets now, each time watching the "s" you use in "Yes." "Do you want the ticket?"

CHILD: Yes.   (*Continue until the child has six tickets.   Occasionally if the child's production of the "Yes" is not acceptable the teacher may put that ticket away, help the child and guide him in obtaining the next ticket.   The child should not be penalized for making an error, but helped to do better the next time.*)

THERAPIST: That is getting easier for you.   Let's see if you can make another book of six tickets very quickly, too.   (*Proceed as above.*)

THERAPIST: Keep those two books of tickets now.   I'm going to mark on one book each time you watch your "s" in your answers to the next questions.   You remember last time you worked on the "s" in "on the face" and "in the house."   Listen to my question.   Watch your "s" sound as you reply.   "Where is the eye?"

CHILD: On the face.

THERAPIST: Where is the chimney?

CHILD: On the house.

THERAPIST: Where is the nose?   Watch the "s" as you answer.

CHILD: On the face.   (*Therapist marks the child's book with a check indicating he included the sound adequately, then continues with questions to which the child makes one of the above replies.*)

Part II

THERAPIST: You are doing better at that, too. I know you want some more tickets now. Here are three. Listen to the way I ask you for them. You will do it the same way. "Pass me a ticket." *(Repeat three times, the child giving her a ticket each time.)* Now you try it. This is a new way of getting work on your "s."

CHILD: Pass me a ticket.

THERAPIST: Let me help you with that. Try "Pass." Now "s." Now "Pass me a ticket." Now you are ready.

CHILD: Pass me a ticket. ⎮ *(Therapist gives child a ticket. This may continue until the child has acquired six more tickets.)*

Part III

THERAPIST: It is almost time to go. You have three books of tickets now, and some marks on two of the books. You have worked on your "s" in four ways. What are they? The rest of the tickets I have in my hand. You don't know yet what other colors I have for you. For instance I have a red one. Are you wondering, "What else?"

CHILD: Yes. What else?

THERAPIST: I have a green one. *(Gives it to the child.)*

CHILD: What else?

THERAPIST: Before you go on getting all the rest of my tickets, practice "What else?" Now you are ready. I have a blue one.

CHILD: What else?

THERAPIST: What have you worked on today? What is getting easier for you to say?

Bibliography

Philosophy of Science

Barnett, L., *The Universe and Dr. Einstein*. New York: Harper & Brothers, 1948.

Brown, J. F., *Psychology and the Social Order*. Chapters 1, 2, and 3. New York: McGraw-Hill Book Company, Inc., 1936.

Cohen, M. R., and Nagel, E., *An Introduction to Logic and Scientific Method*. New York: Harcourt, Brace & Company, Inc., 1934.

Fromm, Erich, *Man for Himself*. New York: Rinehart & Company, Inc., 1947.

Hartmann, G., "The Field Theory of Learning and Its Educational Consequences," Chapter 5 in *The Psychology of Learning*. National Society for the Study of Education, Yearbook XLI, Part II, 1942.

Hayakawa, S. I., *Language in Thought and Action*, Revised Edition. New York: Harcourt, Brace & Company, Inc., 1948.

Johnson, Wendell, *People in Quandaries*. New York: Harper & Brothers, 1946.

Korzybski, Alfred, *Science and Sanity*. The International Non-Aristotelian Library Publishing Company. Lancaster, Pa.: The Science Press Printing Company, Distributors, 1933.

Lecorbeiller, Philippe, "Stars, Proteins, and Nations," *The Atlantic Monthly*, December, 1946.

Lee, Irving, *Language Habits in Human Affairs*. New York: Harper & Brothers, 1941.

Lewin, Kurt, *Dynamic Theory of Personality*. New York: McGraw-Hill Book Company, Inc., 1935.

———, *Principles of Topological Psychology*. New York: McGraw-Hill Book Company, Inc., 1936.

———, "Field Theory of Learning," Chapter 6 in *The Psychology of Learning*. National Society for the Study of Education, Yearbook XLI, Part II, 1942.

———, "Behavior and Development as a Function of the Total Situation," Chapter 16 in *Manual of Child Psychology*. Carmichael, L., Ed. New York: John Wiley & Sons, Inc., 1946.

Lieber, L. R., *The Education of T. C. Mits*. New York: W. W. Norton & Company, Inc., 1944.

Rapoport, Anatol, *Science and the Goals of Man.* New York: Harper & Brothers, 1950.

Sullivan, J. W. N., *The Limitations of Science.* Mentor Books M35, New York: The New American Library, 1949.

Whyte, Lancelot, "Scientific Thought in the Coming Decades," *Harper's,* November, 1948.

Dynamics of Behavior

Alexander, F., and French, T. M., *Psychoanalytic Therapy.* New York: The Ronald Press Company, 1946.

Allen, F., *Psychotherapy with Children.* New York: W. W. Norton & Company, Inc., 1942.

American Council on Education, *Helping Teachers Understand Children.* Washington, D.C.: 1945.

Axline, V. M., *Play Therapy.* Boston: Houghton Mifflin Company, 1947.

Cameron, Norman, *The Psychology of Behavior Disorders.* Boston: Houghton Mifflin Company, 1947.

Fromm, Erich, *Escape from Freedom.* New York: Rinehart & Company, 1941.

Gesell, Arnold, and Ilg, F., *The Child from Five to Ten.* New York: Harper & Brothers, 1941.

Horney, Karen, *Neurosis and Human Growth.* New York: W. W. Norton & Company, Inc., 1950.

————, *Neurotic Personality of Our Time.* New York: W. W. Norton & Company, Inc., 1937.

————, *New Ways in Psychoanalysis.* New York: W. W. Norton & Company, Inc., 1939.

————, *Our Inner Conflicts.* New York: W. W. Norton & Company, Inc., 1945.

————, *Self-Analysis.* New York: W. W. Norton & Company, Inc., 1942.

Hunt, J. McV., Ed., *Personality and the Behavior Disorders,* 2 volumes. New York: The Ronald Press Company, 1944.

Kluckhohn, Clyde, *Mirror for Man.* New York: McGraw-Hill Book Company, Inc. (Whittlesey House), 1949.

Korner, A. F., *Hostility in Young Children.* New York: Grune and Stratton, 1949.

Levy, J., and Munroe, R., *The Happy Family.* New York: Alfred A. Knopf, Inc., 1938.

Lewis, D. C., and Pacella, B. L., *Modern Trends in Child Psychiatry.* New York: International Universities Press, 1945.

Mead, Margaret, *Male and Female.* New York: William Morrow & Company, 1949.

Meyers, Russell, M.D., "The Nervous System and General Semantics: III. Perceptual Response and the Neurology of Abstraction," etc.; *A Review of General Semantics,* Vol. VI, No. 3, p. 169.

Mullahy, P., *A Study of Interpersonal Relations.* New York: Hermitage Press, 1949.

Newcomb, T., Hartley, E. T., *et al., Readings in Social Psychology.* New York: Henry Holt & Company, Inc., 1947.

Overstreet, H. H., *The Mature Mind.* New York: W. W. Norton & Company, Inc., 1949.

Porter, E. H., *An Introduction to Therapeutic Counseling.* Boston: Houghton Mifflin Company, 1950.

Rogers, Carl R., *Counseling and Psychotherapy.* Boston: Houghton Mifflin Company, 1942.

————, *Client-Centered Therapy.* Boston: Houghton Mifflin Company, 1950.

Slavson, S. R., *Practice of Group Psychotherapy.* New York: International Universities Press, 1947.

Sullivan, Harry Stack, *Conceptions of Modern Psychiatry.* Washington, D.C.: William Alanson White Psychiatric Foundation, 1947.

Strauss, A., *Psychopathology of the Brain Injured Child.* New York: Grune and Stratton, 1948.

Symonds, P., *The Dynamics of Parent-Child Relationships.* New York: Bureau of Publications, Teachers College, Columbia University, 1949.

Speech

Ainsworth, Stanley, *Speech Correction Methods.* New York: Prentice-Hall, Inc., 1948.

Backus, Ollie, *Speech in Education: A Guide for the Classroom Teacher.* New York: Longmans, Green & Company, 1943.

Backus, O., and Dunn, H., "Use of Conversational Speech Patterns to Promote Speed and Retention of Learning," *Journal of Speech and Hearing Disorders,* June, 1947, p. 135.

Backus, O., and Dunn, H., "Intensive Group Therapy in Speech Rehabilitation," *Journal of Speech and Hearing Disorders,* March, 1947, p. 39.

Backus, Ollie, "Letter to the Editor," *Journal of Speech and Hearing Disorders*, September, 1949, p. 265.

Backus, Ollie, "Personality Structure in Relation to Speech Therapy," *Quarterly Journal of Speech*, February, 1950, p. 51.

Backus, Ollie, "Collaboration Among Psychiatrists, Pediatricians, Clinical Psychologists, and Speech Therapists," *The Nervous Child*. (To be published.)

Beasley, Jane E., "Group Therapy in the Field of Speech Correction," *Journal of Exceptional Children*, January, 1951.

——, "Techniques of Therapy for Pre-School Children," *Journal of Speech and Hearing Disorders*, December, 1949, p. 307.

Berry, M., and Eisenson, J., *The Defective in Speech*. New York: Appleton-Century-Crofts, Inc., 1945.

Dunn, Harriet, "A Speech and Hearing Program for Children in a Rural Area," *Journal of Speech and Hearing Disorders*, June, 1949, p. 166.

Johnson, W., Brown, S. F., Curtis, J. F., Edney, C. W., and Keaster, J., *Speech Handicapped School Children*. New York: Harper & Brothers, 1948.

Johnson, W., Editor, *Speech Problems of Children*. New York: Grune and Stratton, 1950.

Kantner, Claude, and West, Robert, *Phonetics*. New York: Harper & Brothers, 1941.

Sondel, Bess, *Are You Telling Them?* New York: Prentice-Hall, Inc., 1947.

VanRiper, C., *Speech Correction, Principles and Methods*. New York: Prentice-Hall, Inc., 1947.

West, R., Kennedy, L., and Carr, A., *The Rehabilitation of Speech*, Revised Edition. New York: Harper & Brothers, 1947.

Index